How to Understand the History of Christian Mission

Jean Comby

How to Understand the History of Christian Mission

SCM PRESS LTD

Translated by John Bowden from the French
Deux Mille ans d'évangelisation,
published 1992 by Desclée, Paris

© Gedit S A Tournai and Begedis, Paris 1992

Maps by John Flower

0 334 026156

First British edition published 1996
by SCM Press Ltd,
9–17 St Albans Place, London N1 0N X

Typeset at The Spartan Press Ltd,
Lymington, Hants
and printed in Great Britain by
Redwood Books, Trowbridge, Wiltshire

Contents

Preface

First, the aim and limits of this book. Evangelization is an essential dimension of Christianity: 'For if I preach the gospel, that gives me no ground for boasting. For necessity is laid upon me. Woe to me if I do not preach the gospel!' (I Corinthians 9.16). These words of Paul are echoed by all Christians of all centuries who have lived out their faith. In a way a history of evangelization amounts to a history of the church or Christianity.

However, it is not my plan to write a history of the church here. Those who wish to read such a history can refer to the two volumes of my *How to Read Church History* in this series. The content of the present work is rather different. It is more like one of the numerous 'histories of mission' which have appeared in the past. Still, the term 'mission' does have its disadvantages. It does not quite express every aspect of an evangelization which began at Pentecost of the year 30. Where 'mission' was used in early theology, it was applied to the 'divine missions': the sending of the Son by the Father, the Spirit by the Father and the Son. In turn Christ sends his disciples into the world. It goes without saying that this aspect is connected with the aim of the present volume. But from the sixteenth and above all the seventeenth centuries 'mission' and 'missionary' took on a special technical meaning. Men and women, mandated by a community, were sent to propagate the faith and set up church institutions. Usually they set out from Europe for countries overseas. However, from the seventeenth century until quite recently there have also been home missions, consisting in an exceptional and more intensive preaching in a region or a parish to revive Christians who were lukewarm or had received little instruction. These home and foreign missions were connected: many societies of priests provided missionaries for both forms of mission.

Today, the words 'mission', 'missionary' and 'evangelization' are often difficult and uncertain. On the one hand they conjure up the image of a colourful figure, bearded, dressed in a white or khaki cassock, wearing a colonial helmet, and the missions associated with colonialism and cultural imperialism have been discredited. However, at the same time the whole church is said to be in a state of mission.

As for evangelization, it relates to people who are ignorant not only of Jesus Christ but also of many of the basic features of our day: culture, technology, leisure, etc. Furthermore, for several years there has been talk of the need for a 'new' or 'second' evangelization of the old Christian countries which are stamped by secularization and religious indifference, and especially those countries which were formerly under Communist rule.

This book seeks to provide a history of Christian expansion from the beginnings to our day. We shall see how men and women have become Christians over the centuries, how the message of the gospel, proclaimed for the first time in Palestine, a remote corner of the Roman empire at the time of the emperor Tiberius, has been carried all over the world. This history of evangelization is not limited to the listing of territories won over to Christianity or the development of baptism statistics. It tries to bring out the passage of the gospel from one culture to another, its 'adaptation' or, as people now say, its 'inculturation'. It tries to understand the reasons for the welcoming and the rejection of Christianity throughout the world. In fact evangelization cannot be dissociated from a confrontation of peoples and cultures which often takes place in a context of violence. Finally, this history has to take into account the shock caused to the old Christians of Europe by their knowledge of the new peoples who were evangelized.

I want to bring out the different ways in which the gospel has been proclaimed; the missions of recent centuries must not be thought to be the only model. In the course of the first twelve centuries evangelization came about at close quarters, by contagion or by osmosis. Christianity has been preached in many ways, by people who have not necessarily been clergy or professional missionaries. They have gone to a neighbouring territory and drawn resources from their place of origin. St Paul is a good example of this, and he was to be followed by many others. Christianity slowly penetrated the cultures, the ancient religious traditions and the political world. From the thirteenth century in a limited way and to a great extent in the sixteenth century, a new period began which could be called the period of mission. Europe developed an original civilization based on Christianity. Christianity spread out and conquered the world. Convinced of the universality of the gospel and its culture, at the same time it sought to transmit the faith to different countries and to draw economic and political advantage from it. There is no common geographical or cultural factor shared by Europe and the countries which were evangelized overseas. Evangelization became 'mission', with its specialists, its 'missionaries' sent by superiors of congregations and mandated orders. Mission necessitated support from political powers and financial aid from the states and ancient churches of Europe. With decolonization in the second half of the twentieth century we shall see the beginning of a new stage of evangelization, very different from those which preceded it.

This work is not a treatise on missiology or a theology of evangelization, though it takes account of these disciplines to understand the events reported. It is not for specialists. It simply seeks to provide for the widest possible readership a panorama of the history of the development of Christianity.

I have had to begin from a particular standpoint: I am a French Catholic. But as far as possible I have tried to find a place for all Christian confessions, though I accept that members of some of these confessions will feel that my treatment has been inadequate. And because of the limits of the book, I have not been able to give a detailed account of the mission field, particularly in the nineteenth and twentieth centuries.

1

The Evangelization of the Ancient World

A history of evangelization has its roots in the message of Jesus, and is based on the words of the prophet Isaiah: 'The spirit of the Lord is upon me, because he has anointed me to preach good news to the poor. He has sent me to proclaim release to the captives and recovering of sight to the blind, to set at liberty those who are oppressed, to proclaim the acceptable year of the Lord' (Luke 4.18–19). By this 'good news', the gospel, those who hear it are invited to see in him the messiah announced for centuries in the people of Israel. But the mission of this messiah was understood in very different ways in Jewish milieux: the triumphant messiah who was going to restore its splendour to Israel among the nations, or the messiah who would convert the heart; the messiah for Israel alone or the messiah for the world. Everyone who preaches the gospel will refer to this sending of Christ in which the sending of the messengers has its roots: 'As the Father has sent me, even so I send you' (John 20.21). Then there is the final scene in the Gospel of Matthew with a clearly universalistic sense, 'Go therefore and make disciples of all nations, baptizing them in the name of the Father and of the Son and of the Holy Spirit' (Matt.28.19), though the same Gospel reports the words of Jesus: 'Go nowhere among the Gentiles, and enter no town of the Samaritans, but go rather to the lost sheep of the house of Israel' (Matt.19.5–6). This indicates that among the first Christian generation there were differences over

the potential recipients of the good news: some could refer to one saying of Jesus and others to another. We cannot investigate here the discussions of scholars about the intentions of Jesus, but we know that half a century after his death the gospel had been proclaimed in the greatest cities of the Roman empire and that in three centuries it supplanted all the ancient religions of the Mediterranean world.

The apostolic church

Jesus the Messiah proclaimed to the Jews of Jerusalem

One Pentecost, around 30 CE, Peter, the foremost of the twelve closest companions of Jesus, proclaimed to a number of Jews who had made a pilgrimage to Jerusalem for the festival: 'Jesus of Nazareth, a man attested to you by God with mighty works and wonders and signs which God did through him in your midst . . . you crucified and killed by the hands of lawless men. But God raised him up . . . and of that we are all witnesses. Being therefore exalted at the right hand of God, and having received from the Father the promise of the Holy Spirit, he has poured out this which you see and hear . . . Let all the house of Israel therefore know assuredly that God has made him both Lord and Christ, this Jesus whom you crucified' (Acts 2.22ff.).

Jesus sends his disciples to proclaim the good news

'And this gospel of the kingdom will be preached throughout the whole world, as a testimony to all nations; and then the end will come' (Matthew 24.14).

'Go therefore and make disciples of all nations, baptizing them in the name of the Father and of the Son and of the Holy Spirit, teaching them to observe all that I have commanded you; and lo, I am with you always, to the end of the age' (Matthew 28.19-20).

'You will stand before governors and kings for my sake, to bear testimony before them. And the gospel must first be preached to all nations' (Mark 13.9).

'Go into all the world and preach the Gospel to the whole creation' (Mark 16.15).

'Thus it is written, that the Christ should suffer and on the third day rise from the dead, and that repentance and forgiveness of sins should be preached in his name to all nations, beginning from Jerusalem' (Luke 24.46).

'As the Father has sent me, even so I send you' (John 20.21).

Peter called on his audience to be converted and to receive baptism in the name of Jesus in order to obtain the remission of sins and the gift of the Spirit. A new group, we might call it a sect, was formed in this Jewish world where there were already many other sects: the 'Nazarenes', who saw the risen Jesus as the awaited Messiah, joined the Pharisees, the Sadducees, the Zealots, the Essenes, and yet others. Baptism in the name of Jesus, the breaking of the bread which unites them as a community of brothers and sisters, did not prevent the disciples of the 'Nazarene' from belonging to Judaism: they went to the temple, observed the dietary laws and were circumcised. At the very start there was nothing very missionary about all this, but the church was born.

The gospel message in Greek culture

Jerusalem was also the meeting place for the Jews of the Dispersion (the Diaspora). Having spread all over the Roman empire, they had adopted the language of the time, Greek. They had their own Greek translation of the Bible, 'the Septuagint': in it the very marked particularisms of the Hebrew Bible are disguised, and divine revelation appears in a more universalistic light. These Jews, who were called 'Hellenists', also welcomed the message of Pentecost and formed their own community around the Seven (Acts 6.3), since there were tensions between the 'Hebrews' and the 'Hellenists': the latter read the history of Israel in a different way. They relativized the role of the temple and the Jewish law. They discovered a more universal dimension in the gospel than the first disciples of Jesus saw there. The traditional Jews reacted: Stephen, the leader of the Twelve, was stoned and the persecuted Hellenists had to leave Jerusalem (Acts 6–8). Thanks to this departure, the proclamation of the gospel was extended beyond the walls of Jerusalem.

The first missionaries

'Now those who were scattered went about preaching the word' (Acts 8.4).

The gospel was proclaimed in Judaea, in Samaria, in Phoenicia, in Cyprus and as far as Antioch (Acts 8; 11.19). It was welcomed by people who came from afar, like the eunuch of the queen of Ethiopia (Acts 8). On the basis of a revelation and a vision sent by the Spirit, Peter baptized a non-Jew, the centurion Cornelius (Acts 10). And Saul (Paul), who was present at the stoning of Stephen and took part in the persecution of the 'Hellenists', was seized by Christ on the Damascus road (Acts 9). Paul was to become the greatest preacher of the gospel.

Antioch, the starting point for a universal evangelization

The 'Hellenists' preached the gospel to the Jews of the Diaspora, but non-Jews, Greeks, Gentiles – they would later be called 'pagans' – were also interested in the good news. The Jerusalem community, both happy and disturbed at this interest, sent Barnabas to discover what was going on. He looked for Saul (Paul) and took him to Antioch. The two of them 'taught a large company of people; and in Antioch the disciples were for the first time called "Christians".' From now on they were distinguished from other religious groups; they were no longer defined in terms of race or rite but by their attachment to a person, Jesus.

The community in Antioch felt impelled by the Spirit to proclaim the gospel everywhere. Antioch was the third city in the Roman empire, a crossroads of communications and cultures in the eastern Mediterranean. Even more than in Jerusalem, it was in Antioch that the gospel was to become a universal religion, making use of the means offered it by the unified Mediterranean world created by Rome. There were no frontiers to be obstacles to the exchange of merchandise or

---

The progress of the gospel in the Acts of the Apostles

'But you shall receive power when the Holy Spirit has come upon you; and you shall be my witnesses in Jerusalem and in all Judaea and Samaria and to the end of the earth' (1.8).

'Each one heard them speaking in his own language. And they were amazed, saying . . . "How is it that we hear, each of us in his own native language, Parthians and Medes and Elamites and residents of Mesopotamia, Judaea and Cappadocia, Pontus and Asia, Phrygia and Pamphylia, Egypt and the parts of Libya belonging to Cyrene, and visitors from Rome, both Jews and proselytes, Cretans and Arabians, we hear them telling in our own tongues the mighty works of God"' (2.6–11)

'(*After the stoning of Stephen*) A great persecution arose against the church in Jerusalem; and they were all scattered throughout the region of Judaea and Samaria . . . Now those who were scattered went about preaching the word. Philip went down to a city of Samaria, and proclaimed to them the Christ' (8.1, 4–5).

'Now those who were scattered because of the persecution that arose over Stephen travelled as far as Phoenicia and Cyprus and Antioch, speaking the word to none except Jews. But there were some of them, men of Cyprus and Cyrene, who on coming to Antioch spoke to the Greeks also, preaching the Lord Jesus . . . And in Antioch the disciples were for the first time called Christians' (11.19–20, 26).

'In Antioch, the Holy Spirit said, "Set apart for me Barnabas and Saul for the work to which I have called them." Then after fasting and praying they laid their hands on them and sent them out. So, being sent out by the Holy Spirit, they went down to Seleucia; and from there they sailed to Cyprus . . . And from Paphos, Paul and his company set sail and came to Perga in Pamphylia' (13.2–5, 13).

'And after some days Paul said to Barnabas, "Come, let us return and visit the brethren in every city where we proclaim the world of the Lord, and see how they are"' (15.36).

'At Troas a vision appeared to Paul in the night; a man of Macedonia was standing beseeching him and saying, "Come over to Macedonia and help us." And when he had seen the vision, immediately we sought to go into Macedonia, concluding that God had called us to preach the gospel to them. Setting sail therefore from Troas, we made a direct voyage to Samothrace, and the following day to Neapolis, and from there to Philippi, which is the leading city of the district of Macedonia' (16.9–12).

'At Athens, Paul argued in the synagogues with the Jews and the devout persons, and in the market place every day with those who chanced to be there. Some also of the Epicurean and Stoic philosophers met him' (17.17–18).

ideas, to people moving around. With Greek one could make oneself understood anywhere. At this time, when a number of the inhabitants of the empire were displaced persons – officials, soldiers, slaves who had lost their roots – the religion of the ancient cities declined and religious disquiet increased. Many people readily welcomed Eastern religions, which promised them salvation through a personal encounter with the deity. Christianity was to benefit from this passion. Because of this context, at a very early stage many people saw the Roman empire as a 'preparation for the gospel'.

Rather than people with a particular authority, it was the Spirit which chose Barnabas and Paul to send them on a mission as 'apostles' (the word means 'sent', and is not reserved to the twelve companions of Jesus, cf. Acts 14.4–14). The first missionary journey of Paul and Barnabas led them along the roads of Cyprus and Asia Minor. First they addressed the Jews in the synagogues, then non-Jews, but without imposing Jewish practices on them. Miraculous healings confirmed their preaching: the risen Jesus was the awaited Messiah, the one who had conquered evil and sin; he gave eternal life to those who believed in him. The two apostles returned to Antioch full of enthusiasm (Acts 13; 14).

However, in Jerusalem some disquiet was shown: Paul and Barnabas did not impose Jewish practices like circumcision and dietary prohibitions on pagans who became Christians. The authorities in the mother community thought that all Christians had to have been Jews first. Now to those pagans who had become Christians, circumcision was repugnant. At Antioch, where two Christian communities existed in parallel, the dietary regulations prevented Christians of different origins from eating together. Peter gave way to the Jerusalem people and refused to eat with the uncircumcised. Paul firmly rebuked him for this (Galatians 2). A way was found out of the impasse by the compromise which has been called the 'Council of Jerusalem' (Acts 14). Paul secured a ruling that Jewish regulations would no longer be imposed on converts coming from paganism. James, the head of the Jerusalem community, obtained some concessions from the other camp: Christians who came from paganism would abstain from consuming blood, and in marriage would accept the prohibition against certain degrees of affinity observed by Christians who had come from Judaism. This important decision has been handed down by a solemn letter: 'It has seemed good to the Holy Spirit and to us . . .' (Acts 15.28). Christian faith was no longer bound up with Judaism. There was no need of any cultural transplantation in order to accept the gospel. Christianity had become a universal religion.

Paul, apostle to the Gentiles

The first fifteen chapters of the Acts of the Apostles present a host of active preachers of the gospel. From chapter 16 on, there is only one main figure, Paul, whom we also know from his letters. Certainly, through Paul's own letters we can see that there were other preachers, most of whom remain anonymous. Eusebius of Caesarea cites a tradition according to which the evangelization of the world was shared between the apostles. With Paul, the gospel takes the road west after a dream in which a Macedonian is said to have begged him, 'Come over to Macedonia and help us' (Acts 16.9). Paul was not only an exceptional evangelist but also the first theologian of Christianity; some even say that he was its 'co-founder'. There can be no question of presenting Paul's theology here. I shall simply outline the major features of his missionary activity which were to serve as a point of reference for all who preached the gospel. 'Seized by Christ' (Phil.3.12) on the Damascus road, by the same token Paul felt himself to be 'called to be an apostle, set apart for the gospel of God among the Gentiles' (Rom.1.1–15). This theme of the call of God and of mission recur constantly in Paul's writings (Rom.10.14–15). Paul is primarily the servant of the Word. Baptizing is not his first preoccupation (I Cor.1.10). He founds churches, but leaves it to others to administer them. In this first church, in which itinerant missionary ministers are clearly distinguished from local sedentary ministers (I Cor.12.18; I Tim.3; Titus 1), the proclamation of the gospel is urgent, since Christians believe that the parousia (the return of Christ) and judgment are imminent (I Thess.1.9–10; 4.15).

While Paul affirms that his vocation is to proclaim the mystery of Christ to the Gentiles, he feels himself completely in solidarity with the Jerusalem community, and he gives this solidarity tangible form by means of the collection which he organizes for the community (I Cor.16.1–4). Paul adapts the initial message, the kerygma, to his hearers: to Jews, he shows how Jesus is the heir of the promises given to Israel (Acts 13). When he addresses the Greeks, his preaching focusses on the one God and on the parousia. He refers to the order of the world, to which the Greeks were sensitive; the parousia will be the day of judgment, the triumph of justice through the action of Christ (Acts 17.22–34).

When Paul writes to the Romans at the end of his third journey (in 57), he is aware of having partly fulfilled his mission: 'In Christ Jesus, then, I have reason to be proud of my work for God . . . From Jerusalem and as far round as Illyricum I have fully preached the gospel of Christ' (Rom.15.17–19). He then thinks of visiting the community in Rome in order to go on from there to Spain and fulfil his task. Paul certainly reached Rome, but as a prisoner (62–63); we do not know how he died.

The Johannine communities

The Apocalypse of John begins by presenting itself as a message to the seven churches of Asia. Thus we can identify a context for John's influence. However, many exegetes emphasize that unlike Paul, John does not seem to have any missionary preoccupations. There is no reference in the Johannine writings to the universal character of the Christian mission. With time, expectation of the parousia has been blunted. John opts for a realized

---

Paul, messenger of the Good News, from Jerusalem to Spain

Today, most historians think that Paul never realized his desire to go to Spain

'But how are men to call upon him in whom they have not believed? And how are they to believe in him of whom they have never heard? And how are they to hear without a preacher? And how can men preach unless they are sent? As it is written, "How beautiful are the feet of those who preach good news." . . . So faith comes from what is heard, and what is heard comes by the preaching of Christ' (Romans 10.14–17).

'From Jerusalem and as far around as Illyricum I have fully preached the gospel of Christ, thus making it my ambition to preach the gospel, not where Christ has already been named, lest I build on another man's foundations . . . This is the reason why I have so often been hindered from coming to you. But now, since I no longer have any room for work in these regions, and since I have longed for many years to come to you, I hope to see you in passing as I go to Spain, and to be sped on my journey there by you, once I have enjoyed your company for a while' (Romans 15.19–24).

---

eschatology; in other words, Christians are called to bear witness, to 'martyrdom', to a certain way of being in the world, particularly in times of persecution; this is a form of witness which is not opposed to proclamation but is another form of it.

The apostolic age: a summary

At the end of the first century, the gospel had been preached in all the great cities of the eastern Mediterranean as far as Rome: Jerusalem, Damascus, Antioch, Ephesus, Sardis, Troas, Philippi, Thessalonica, Athens, Corinth, Rome, probably Alexandria and perhaps Spain, if Paul really was able to achieve his aim. Before the end of the

The apostles and their disciples share the task of evangelizing the world

Eusebius, Bishop of Caesarea in Palestine (c.263–c.340), is regarded as the 'father of church history'. In his History of the Church *he has handed down to us a host of documents from the first centuries. In the following passage, Eusebius mixes information from the New Testament with unverifiable traditions or legends. Eusebius was profoundly convinced of the universalism of the Christian faith, which he traced back to the apostles.*

So truly, by the power and co-operation of heaven, the word of salvation like a ray of the sun flashed its light in a moment upon the whole world; and straightway, in accordance with the divine scriptures, the sound of its inspired evangelists and prophets went forth through all the earth, and their words to the end of the world. And truly throughout every city and village, as on a well-filled threshing floor, churches thronged with multitudes sprang up all at once . . .

When the holy apostles and disciples of our Saviour were dispersed over the whole world, Parthia was allotted to Thomas, according to tradition, Ethiopia to Matthew, India to Bartholomew, Scythia to Andrew, and Asia to John, where he lived, dying at Ephesus. Peter, it seems, preached in Pontus and Galatia and Bithynia, in Cappadocia and Asia, to those Jews who were of the dispersion. He also at the last came to Rome, and was crucified head downwards; for he requested that he might suffer thus. What need is there to speak of Paul, who from Jerusalem to Illyricum fully preached the gospel of Christ, and afterwards was martyred at Rome under Nero?

(Eusebius of Caesarea, *History of the Church* II, 3, 1–2; III, 1, 1–3)

century, two decisive events marked the life of the church. The persecution of Nero in 64, which was probably the cause of the deaths of Peter and Paul, shows that the imperial authorities distinguished the Christians from the Jews. The destruction of Jerusalem in 70 definitively detached the Christians from Judaism, which had lost its point of reference in the temple and thus seemed doomed. The universalism of Christianity was reinforced.

From the end of the first century to the peace of the church (313)

While we have the impression of following the preachers of the gospel step by step through the New Testament, particularly in Acts and in the letters of Paul, it is difficult for us to construct a continuous narrative of the progress of Christianity in the two subsequent centuries. However, its expansion was exceptional. We can grasp this indirectly from literary allusions and epitaphs, but it is rarely described as such. That explains why later attempts were made to fill the gap by more or less legendary accounts, like that of Gregory of Tours.

The disappearance of the missionary ministers

We have already seen how the apostles, the prophets and the doctors were itinerant ministers; they were missionary rather than sedentary. We again find a mention of them in the Didache, a work which is difficult to date precisely: it probably comes from the end of the first or beginning of the second century. After that, however, they disappear. The successors of the apostles are identified with the *episkopoi* (bishops), and the title 'apostles' is given only to the Twelve, who are referred to as the authority for doctrine. It is quite difficult to find really kerygmatic texts addressed to non-Christians in this period. Apparently a concern for the conversion of the pagans appears rarely in prayer, with the exception of a prayer of Clement of Rome: 'May all nations know that you are God alone, that Jesus Christ is your child, and that we are your people and the sheep of your pasture' (I Clement 59.4).

Evangelization by example or osmosis

Certainly the testimony of Eusebius and Origen indicates that a certain number of Christians, 'evangelists', were devoting themselves wholly to the task of evangelization. However, if we leave aside a few great names like Gregory the Wonder Worker and Gregory the Illuminator, whom we shall be discussing later, they remain anonymous. Strictly speaking, these Christians did not have any mandate, a notion which would be anachronistic for that time; they acted on their own initiative under the inspiration of the Spirit. When Eusebius tells us that Pantaenus 'was sent', he does not say by whom: it is Christ or the Spirit who sends him. This explains how a large number of Christians, merchants, soldiers, officials and slaves evangelized because their work forced them to move around. The first Christian community of Lyons was made up of men and women of Greek origin who are said to have included slaves, a doctor, a lawyer and perhaps merchants (cf. Eusebius, *History of the Church*, V). We can also understand how marginal groups described as heretics or regarded as sects were just as much missionaries as Christians deemed to be orthodox.

To use present-day terminology, it could be said that all Christians felt themselves to be more or less in a 'state of mission'. Here are three examples. The first is the indirect testimony of a pagan, Celsus, who around 170 wrote a work against the Christians, the *True Discourse*. Christians seemed to him to be a danger to the state. They were poor people who let themselves be hoodwinked by just about anyone. Celsus gives a colourful description of Christian propaganda in families and on the streets. The second example is that of the Apologists, who in response to the attacks and persecutions of which Christians were victims, addressed those

---

The enthusiasm of the evangelists

Eusebius presents the evangelists of the post-apostolic generation as though they belonged to the past. Origen mentions Christians who in his day (the first part of the third century) devote the whole of their lives to preaching the gospel.

Many of the disciples of that day felt their souls struck by the divine word with a more ardent passion for philosophy (an ascetic Christian life-style). So they at first obeyed the Saviour's command, by distributing their goods to the needy. Afterwards they set out on journeys from their homeland, performing the work of evangelists, making it their aim to preach to such as had not yet heard the word of the faith at all, and to give them the books of the divine Gospels. But they were content to lay the foundations only of the faith in some foreign places, appointing others as pastors to whom they entrusted the care of those lately brought in; then they would depart to other lands and nations, with the grace and co-operation of God. For the divine Spirit still to that day worked mightily through them in many miraculous powers, insomuch that at the first hearing whole multitudes in a body embraced in their souls piety towards the Creator of the universe.

(Eusebius of Caesarea, *History of the Church* III, 27, 2–3)

Christians leave no stone unturned to spread the faith in all parts of the world. Some, in fact, have done the work of going round not only cities but even villages and country cottages to make others also pious towards God. One could not say that they did this for the sake of wealth, since sometimes they do not even accept money for the necessities of life.

(Origen, *Against Celsus* III, 9)

Christian propaganda in the second century, according to Celsus

We know Celsus' True Discourse Against the Christians, written around 170, by the extracts from it given by Origen in his refutation composed around 250, the Contra Celsum. Through the malevolence of Celsus we can see that Christianity is being propagated by word of mouth among the most ordinary people, which an intellectual like Celsus will not admit.

Here is one of the maxims of the Christians: 'Let no one educated, no one wise, no one sensible draw near.' In saying that such men are worthy of their God, they are showing that they want to convince only the foolish, dishonourable, and stupid, and only slaves, women and little children.

Moreover, we see that those who display their secret lore in the market-places and go about begging would never enter a gathering of intelligent men, nor would they dare to reveal their noble beliefs in their presence; but whenever they see adolescent boys and a crowd of slaves and a company of fools they push themselves in and show off. In private houses also we see wool-workers, cobblers, laundry-workers, and the most illiterate and bucolic yokels, who would not dare to say anything at all in front of their elders and more intelligent masters. But whenever they get hold of children in private and some stupid women with them, they let out some astounding statements as, for example, that they must not pay any attention to their father and school-teachers, but must obey them; they say that these talk nonsense and have no understanding, and that in reality they neither know nor are able to do anything good, but are taken up with mere empty chatter. But they alone, they say, know the right way to live, and if the children would believe them, they would become happy and make their home happy as well.

And if just as they are speaking they see one of the school-teachers coming, or some intelligent person, or even the father himself, the more cautious of them flee in all directions; but the more reckless urge the children on to rebel. They whisper to them that in the presence of their father and their schoolmaster they do not feel able to explain anything to the children, since they do not want to have anything to do with the silly and obtuse teachers who are totally corrupted and far gone in wickedness and who inflict punishment on the children. But, if they like, they should leave father and their schoolmasters, and go along with the women and little children who are their playfellows to the wooldresser's shop, or to the cobbler's and the washerwoman's shop, that they may learn perfection. And by saying this they persuade them.

Let us hear what folk these Christians call. Whosoever is a sinner, they say, whosoever is unwise, whosoever is a child, and, in a word, whosoever is a wretch, the kingdom of God will receive him. Do you not say that a sinner is he who is dishonest, a thief, a burglar, a poisoner, a sacrilegious fellow, and a grave-robber? What others would a robber invite and call?

(Origen, *Against Celsus* III, 49–59)

who did not share their faith – the authorities, intellectuals, public opinion. Justin, the best known of them, who lived in the middle of the second century, tried to use a language which his audience would understand. He presented Christianity as a philosophy which bore comparison with the classical philosophy of the Greeks. Furthermore, he said, in this philosophy all that is good and true had been established by the Word, which is invisibly present in creation and in every human being. A third example is the witness of the martyrs before the tribunals which condemned them to death; this was often a form of missionary preaching. Tertullian's words have become famous: 'The blood of the martyrs is a seed.'

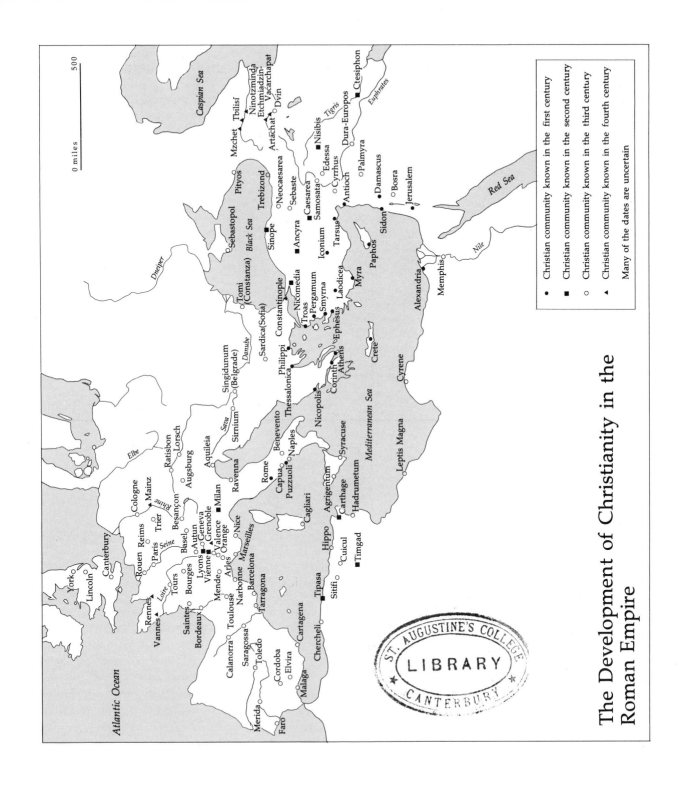

The Development of Christianity in the Roman Empire

Legend:
- • Christian community known in the first century
- ■ Christian community known in the second century
- ■ Christian community known in the third century
- ○ Christian community known in the fourth century
- ▲ Many of the dates are uncertain

The word has been proclaimed all over the world

It is possible to explain the relative absence of a call to mission by the impression Christians had that the gospel had been proclaimed everywhere and that they were present in all the regions of the world, which for them was the Roman empire. For Eusebius, as we have seen, the evangelization of the world had been shared among the apostles, and around 150 Justin says: 'Twelve men set out from Jerusalem to cover the world. They were simple men with no gifts of oratory, but in the name of God they proclaimed to all men that they had been sent by Christ to proclaim the word of God to all' (*Apology* I, 39, 3). Shortly afterwards, Irenaeus

affirmed this universal presence of the church with a calm assurance. A century later, Origen made the same affirmation. And in the third century Tertullian proudly presents the increase in the number of Christians: 'We are men of yesterday, and already we have filled the earth and all that is yours: the cities, the islands, the strongholds, the towns, the villages, the very camps, the decuries, the palaces, the senate, the forum; we have left you only the temples' (*Apologeticum* 37.4). In the same period, in his epitaph, the Phrygian bishop Abercius, who had travelled from Nisibis in Mesopotamia to Rome, marvelled: 'I met Christians everywhere. The faith guided me everywhere.'

In short, Christianity spread because Christians proved attractive by their courage, their customs, their common life. The opposition which they encountered, the persecution which they suffered, did not dissuade them; quite the contrary. That led Adolf von Harnack, the great church historian from the beginning of this century, to say, 'The church's mission was fulfilled through its existence, its resources and its sacred institutions rather than through professional missionaries.'

Stages in a process

There can be no question here of following the progress of Christianity city by city, province by province, through literary sources or inscriptions. Such accounts are to be found in more specialist works. Here we can note only some significant stages. In the second century, Christianity continued to spread from Antioch into Syria, Asia Minor, Greece and Macedonia. In Egypt, Alexandria became one of the greatest Christian centres. However, we have more traces of Gnostic, marginal and heretical groups than of Christians of the mainstream church. Eusebius has preserved for us the name of an Alexandrian, Pantaenus, who is said to have evangelized as far as India, where he found Christians already existing. A new field of evangelization opened west of Rome, in Gaul and in Africa. In Gaul, a letter preserved by Eusebius in which the

The whole earth has been evangelized

From Justin and Irenaeus (middle and end of the second century) onwards, Christians thought that the gospel had been proclaimed all over the world. The argument, which has an apologetic aspect, was taken up in the third century by Origen. These authors more or less identified the world with the Roman empire.

Having received this preaching and this faith, the Church, although scattered through the whole world, yet, as if occupying but one house, carefully preserves it. For although the languages of the world are dissimilar, yet the import of the tradition is one and the same. For the churches which have been planted in Germany do not believe or hand down anything different, nor do those in Spain, nor those in Gaul, nor those in the East, nor those in Libya, nor those which have been established in the central regions of the world (Rome). But as the sun, that creature of God, is one and the same throughout the whole world, so also the preaching of the truth shines everywhere, and enlightens all men who are willing to come to a knowledge of the truth.

(Irenaeus of Lyons, *Against the Heresies* I, 10, 2–3)

If we consider the immense progress of the gospel in a few years despite persecution and torture, death and confiscation, despite the small number of preachers, the word has been proclaimed throughout the earth. Greeks and barbarians, wise and foolish, have adhered to the religion of Jesus. We cannot doubt that this goes beyond human strength, since Jesus taught with all the authority and persuasion necessary for the word to establish itself.

(Origen, *On the First Principles* IV, 1, 2)

The Christians are everywhere

The presence of Christians in all the regions of the empire and among all social classes is an argument which Christian apologists used against pagans who wanted to regard Christians only as an obscure and contemptible sect. The brief work To Diognetus *dates from the 200s.*

The distinction between Christians and other men is neither in country nor language nor customs. For they do not dwell in cities in some place of their own, nor do they use any strange variety of dialect, nor practise an extraordinary kind of life ... Yet while living in Greek and barbarian cities, according as each obtained his lot, and following the local customs, both in clothing and food and in the rest of life, they show forth the wonderful and confessedly strange character of the constitution of their own citizenship. They dwell in their own fatherlands, but as if sojourners in them; they share all things as citizens, and suffer all things as strangers.

(*To Diognetus* 5, 1–4)

Christians of Vienne and Lyons describe the martyrdom of about fifty of their brothers in 177, attests a Christian presence in the valley of the Rhone which could go back to around 140–150. Most of these Christians had Greek names, and several of them came from Asia Minor. They spoke Greek, even if the text indicates that some of them knew Latin. We do not know where Pothinus, the first bishop, came from, but Irenaeus, the second, tells us of his childhood in Smyrna. In his work, Irenaeus indicates that there were churches in Germania and on the Iberian peninsula. Also in the second half of the second century there is evidence of a church of Africa (the Roman province of this name, present-day Tunisia and eastern Algeria) in the Acts of the Scillitan Martyrs (180). The Christians of Africa were the first to use Latin regularly in the liturgy, whereas in Rome Greek was to hold its own for a long time as a rival to Latin.

Right at the beginning of the third century, a king of Edessa, Abgar IX, was converted; he was to be the first Christian ruler. From Edessa the gospel

Pantaenus, herald of the Gospel as far as India (c. 180–200)

Pantaenus, with a thorough philosophical training and experience of preaching the gospel in foreign parts, founded a school of theology in Alexandria. This school, which was directed subsequently by Clement and then by Origen, had benefited from his teachings. Clement of Alexandria called for reflection on the world religions. He is the first Greek writer to speak of Buddha, probably referring to Pantaenus' teaching.

Now at that time there was a man of great renown for learning named Pantaenus, who had charge of the school of the faithful at Alexandria, where it has been a custom from the earliest days that a school for sacred studies should exist . . . It is recorded that Pantaenus was especially distinguished at that time, inasmuch as he had come from that sect of philosophers who are called the Stoics. Now it is said that he displayed such ardent love and zeal for the divine word that he was appointed as a herald of the Gospel of Christ to the nations of the East, and that he journeyed even as far as the land of the Indians. For there were, yes, even still at that time, many evangelists of the word, desirous to contribute an inspired zeal, after the manner of the apostles, for the increase and building up of the divine word.

Pantaenus also was one of these, and is mentioned as having gone to India; and the story goes that there he found, in the hands of some persons who had come to know Christ in that land, the Gospel of Matthew, which had anticipated his arrival; for that Bartholomew, one of the apostles, had preached to them and left behind the writing of Matthew in the actual Hebrew characters, and that it was preserved up to the said time. After many good deeds Pantaenus ended by becoming head of the school of Alexandria, where he expounded the treasures of the divine doctrine both orally and by means of treatises.

(Eusebius of Caesarea, *History of the Church* V, 10, 2–3)

reached Mesopotamia, which was part of the Persian empire. The earliest known Christian church has been discovered at Dura-Europos (middle of the third century). With the nationalistic Persian reaction by the Sassanid dynasty (224), Christianity was persecuted because it came from the hostile Roman empire. It was also in the Persian empire that Mani (216–277) developed a dualistic Gnosticism which claimed to be Christian: Manichaeism was an amazing missionary force in every direction, and was constantly persecuted. This eastern area on the frontier of the Roman empire has preserved the recollection of two missionaries by the name of Gregory. The first, a disciple of Origen, became bishop of Neocaesarea (northern Cappadocia) around 243. His preaching, confirmed by numerous miracles, brought him the name Gregory Thaumaturgus (Wonder Worker). At the end of the century, between 280 and 290, another Gregory,

from Armenia, who had been baptized and instructed in Christianity at Caesarea in Cappadocia, returned to Armenia, and converted king Tiridatis. That immediately made Christianity the religion of the kingdom. All the Armenians had to convert, the pagan clergy moving over to the new religion and retaining their ancient privileges. Gregory, who thus proved the Illuminator of the nation, became head of the Armenian church as 'Catholicos', a role which he handed down to his descendants. Later, at the beginning of the fifth century, the wise monk Mesrop created an Armenian alphabet which was thus to become a national language of Christian culture.

Christianity also made progress in the West, but more slowly than in the East. The legends handed down by Gregory of Tours indicate that from then on Gallic Christianity was Latin. By the end of the third century there were about thirty episcopal sees

Gregory the Wonder Worker, a prophet inspired by the Spirit

Against some who denied that the Holy Spirit was equal with the Father and the Son, Basil appeals to witnesses who support his view. Gregory the Wonder Worker, who evangelized Pontus (north of Cappadocia), is one of them. His miracles merely serve to confirm his witness.

The power over demons which Gregory had was tremendous, and so gifted was he with the grace of the word for obedience of faith among the nations that, although only seventeen Christians were handed over to him, he brought the whole people alike in town and country through knowledge to God. He too by Christ's mighty name commanded even rivers to change their course, and caused a lake, which afforded a ground of quarrel to some covetous brethren, to dry up. Moreover his predictions of things to come were such as in no wise to fall short of those of the great prophets. To recount all his wonderful works in detail would be too long a task. By the superabundance of gifts, wrought in him by the Spirit in all power and in signs and in marvels, he was style a second Moses by the very enemies of the church.

(Basil of Caesarea, *On The Holy Spirit*, 29)

The foundation of the seven churches in Gaul in the Third Century

This text, from Gregory of Tours in the sixth century, seeks to fill gaps in our historical knowledge. It is based on a pious legend, but at least introduces us to the traditional founders of the several churches in France.

At the time of the emperor Decius, seven men consecrated bishop were sent to Gaul to preach there . . . Under the consulate of Decius and Gratus, as the memory of the faithful has preserved the recollection, for the first time the city of Toulouse had a priest, the great saint Saturninus. Here are those who were sent: Bishop Gatian to Tours, Bishop Trophimus to Arles, Bishop Paul to Narbonne, Bishop Saturninus to Toulouse, Bishop Denys to Paris, Bishop Austremoine to Clermont, Bishop Martial to Limoges. Of these, the blessed Denys, bishop of the Parisians, after suffering many torments for the name of Christ, had his earthly life ended with the sword. Saturninus was tied to a savage bull and hurled from the top of the Capitol. Gatian, Trophimus, Austremoine, Paul and Martial, after lives of the utmost holiness, in which they won over peoples to the church and spread the faith everywhere, happily left this life, confessing their faith.

(Gregory of Tours, *History of the Franks* I, 30–31)

in Gaul. In Spain the Council of Elvira (around 300) shows us that there were thirty-three episcopal sees there. In 256 Pope Cornelius brought together sixty Italian bishops, and the same year Cyprian of Carthage brought together eighty-seven.

Diocletian's persecution and the peace of the church

So there were Christians in all the regions of the empire. Historians estimate that around 300 they represented 15% of the population of the empire, but their distribution was uneven. In several regions in the East Christians made up more than half the population. Feeling that Christianity was going to submerge traditional society, Diocletian unleashed a terrible persecution aimed at destroying the church. It was harshest and longest in the East, where Christians were the most numerous (303–313). In the West, particularly in Gaul, it was far more limited. At the end of a desperate struggle for power against half a dozen claimants to the throne, Constantine, the victorious emperor, who sympathized with the Christians, granted religious freedom to all (313, 'Edict' of Milan). A new era for Christian expansion began.

From the peace of the church to the end of the Western Roman Empire (fifth century)

The 'Edict of Milan' was meant to put all the religions of the empire on an equal footing. In reality, Constantine and his successors, regarding themselves as Christian emperors, were soon to favour Christianity at the expense of the ancient religions. The fourth century saw a slow elimination of paganism by increasingly restrictive, if not persecuting, legislation, with the result that, on the decision of Theodotius, in 380 Roman Christianity became a state religion. The mental structures of the time of paganism had not changed. From now on it was through the Christian faith that the emperors aimed at securing the religious and political unity of the empire. For many centuries the church joined forces with the powers, and motivations for conversion to Christianity reflected this.

The progress of evangelization within the empire

The ancient pagan religions still kept their devotees at both ends of the social scale. The senators and the intellectuals were attached to the Graeco-Roman cultural heritage, of which religion was a major component. They were to resist the triumph of Christianity for some time. The return of the emperor Julian (361–363) to the traditional religion and his efforts to restore it are the most visible aspect of this resistance. But paganism was gradually brought under control, first through women, who were admirers of Rufinus and St Jerome. Among the men, the orator Marius Victorinus was converted around 355 and put his art at the service of theology. We might also recall the conversion of the orator Augustine in Milan, though he had never really been attached to paganism.

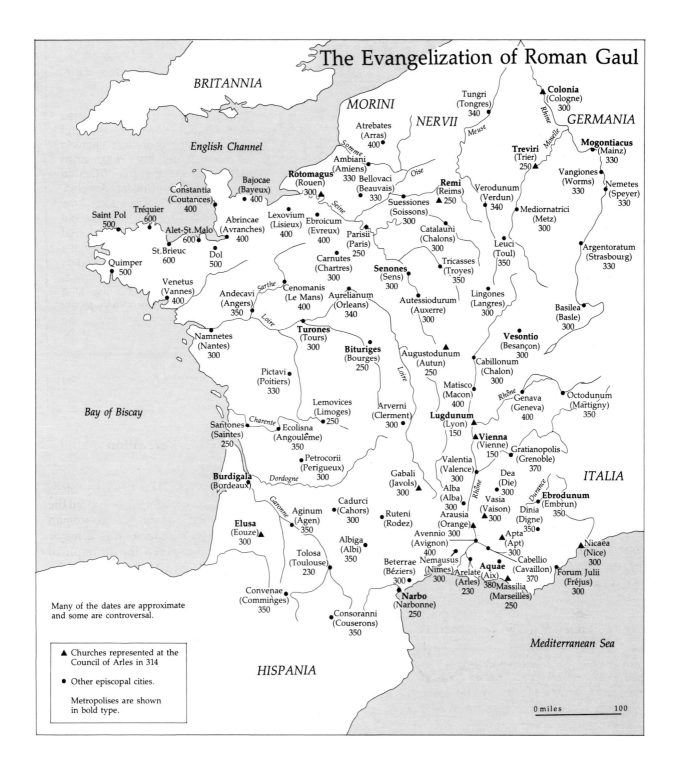

The Evangelization of Roman Gaul

BRITANNIA

MORINI

NERVII

Tungri
(Tongres)
340

Colonia
(Cologne)
300

GERMANIA

English Channel

Atrebates
(Arras)
400

Treviri
(Trier)
250 ▲

Mogontiacus
(Mainz)
330

Ambiani
(Amiens)
330

Vangiones
(Worms)
330

Nemetes
(Speyer)
330

Rotomagus
(Rouen)
300

Bellovaci
(Beauvais)
330

Remi
(Reims)
250 ▲

Verodunum
(Verdun)
340

Mediornatrici
(Metz)
300

Bajocae
(Bayeux)
400

Constantia
(Coutances)
400

Suessiones
(Soissons)
300

Argentoratum
(Strasbourg)
330

Tréquier
600

Lexovium
(Lisieux)
400

Ebroicum
(Evreux)
400

Catalauni
(Chalons)
300

Leuci
(Toul)
350

Saint Pol
500

Abrincae
(Avranches)
400

Parisii
(Paris)
250

Alet-St.Malo
600

Tricasses
(Troyes)
350

St.Brieuc
600

Dol
500

Carnutes
(Chartres)
300

Senones
(Sens)
300

Lingones
(Langres)
300

Basilea
(Basle)
300

Quimper
500

Venetus
(Vannes)
400

Sarthe

Cenomanis
(Le Mans)
400

Autessiodurum
(Auxerre)
300

Andecavi
(Angers)
350

Aurelianum
(Orleans)
340

Vesontio
(Besançon)
300

Loire

Turones
(Tours)
300

Augustodunum
(Autun)
250 ▲

Cabillonum
(Chalon)
300

Namnetes
(Nantes)
300

Bituriges
(Bourges)
250

Bay of Biscay

Pictavi
(Poitiers)
330

Loire

Matisco
(Macon)
400

Genava
(Geneva)
400

Octodunum
(Martigny)
350

Lemovices
(Limoges)
250

Arverni
(Clermont)
300

Lugdunum
(Lyon)
150 ▲

Charente

Ecolisna
(Angoulême)
350

Vienna
(Vienne)
150 ▲

Gratianopolis
(Grenoble)
370

Santones
(Saintes)
250

Petrocorii
(Perigueux)
300

ITALIA

Burdigala
(Bordeaux)

Dordogne

Gabali
(Javols)
300

Valentia
(Valence)
300

Dea
(Die)
300

Elusa
(Eouze)
300 ▲

Aginum
(Agen)
350

Cadurci
(Cahors)
300

Alba
(Alba)
300

Vasia
(Vaison)
300 ▲

Dinia
(Digne)
350

Ebrodunum
(Embrun)
350

Ruteni
(Rodez)

Arausia
(Orange)
300 ▲

Apta
(Apt)
300 ▲

Nicaea
(Nice)
300

Tolosa
(Toulouse)
230

Albiga
(Albi)
350

Avennio
(Avignon)
400

300

Cabellio
(Cavaillon)
370

Forum Julii
(Fréjus)
300

Beterrae
(Béziers)
300

Nemausus
(Nîmes)
300

Aquae
(Aix)
380

Convenae
(Comminges)
350

Arelate
(Arles)
230

Massilia
(Marseilles)
250

Consoranni
(Couserons)
350

Narbo
(Narbonne)
250

Mediterranean Sea

HISPANIA

Many of the dates are approximate
and some are controversial.

▲ Churches represented at the
Council of Arles in 314

● Other episcopal cities.

Metropolises are shown
in bold type.

0 miles   100

Preaching supported by miracles

The destruction of pagan temples and holy places is commonplace in accounts of the evangelization of the countryside. Here are two examples, involving St Martin of Tours and the monk Jonas in Thrace.

This is what happened in the country of the Eduens. When Martin was destroying a temple, a crowd of pagans rushed on him in fury. One of them, bolder than the rest, drew a sword and tried to strike him; throwing off his cloak, Martin offered his bare neck to the assailant. The pagan did not hesitate to strike, but lifted his right hand too high and fell over backwards. Immediately smitten with holy terror, he asked Martin's pardon . . . However, most of the time, when peasants opposed the destruction of their temples, he calmed the spirit of these pagans by the holiness of his preaching, explaining the light of the truth to them so well that they demolished their temples with their own hands.

(Sulpicius Severus, *Life of St Martin*, 15)

Hardly had Jonas learned that the people worshipped trees or similar objects than he arrived there with his monks, cut down the tree and consumed it with fire. In this way from now on the people gradually became Christians. In fact the lord Jonas, who had been the spiritual father of Hypatius, had civilized Thrace in this way and made its inhabitants Christians.

(*Life of St Hypatius of Rufinianae*)

At the other extreme, the isolated country populations maintained the agricultural fertility rites. These *pagani*, inhabitants of the countryside, gave their name to the terms 'pagan' and 'paganism'. More significant than the evangelization of the city is the evangelization of the countryside illustrated by numerous missionaries, the best known of whom is Martin of Tours (316–397). However, many other figures could be mentioned, like St Victricius of Rouen, St Simplicius of Autun, St Vigilius of Trent and, at the other end of the empire, the monk Jonas of Halmyrissos, the evangelist of Thrace. In general, their action was twofold, particularly in the West. After performing miracles, they destroyed the places of pagan worship, or had them destroyed, in order to discredit traditional religion completely. Then they established parishes, territories entrusted to priests detached from the cities which were the seats of the bishops. Churches were often built on the sites of ancient temples.

So the fourth century marks an acceleration of evangelization within the empire. The multiplication of episcopal sees in Gaul and northern Italy is

evidence of this. Christianization did not necessarily change habits. Pastors worked hard to purify the motives of those who rushed to the churches in order to adopt the emperor's religion.

Christian expansion outside the empire

We should not imagine this expansion as the fruit of a concerted and organized programme by a Roman or episcopal religious authority. It has often been remarked that St Augustine, bishop of Hippo, perhaps too absorbed by the internal problems of the church in Africa, never thought of sending 'missions' to the Berbers, pagans who were very close. No one thought of sending missionaries over the Rhine to the barbarian Germans who threatened the empire. After Constantine, Western Christians readily identified the church with the empire. It was hard to think that barbarians outside the empire could be Christians.

In the East, things looked rather different. Several peoples were converted to the Christian faith as a result of fortuitous circumstances which had many features in common. Christians from the empire who were taken prisoners of war and carried off outside it would often come to be valued for their wisdom or their miracles. The local ruler would become interested and convert, taking his people with him, and call for a bishop from a church of the empire. Moreover conversion was often the occasion to develop a national language from oral to written form, since it was necessary to hand on the Christian scriptures and develop a liturgy. So the reception of Christianity contributed to an affirmation of national, political and cultural identity. We have already seen the example of Armenia. Saint Nino, a slave carried off by the Romans, converted Georgia in the Caucasus after a miracle (around 330). King Minian then asked the emperor Constantine for priests. Georgian became a written language. Frumentius, a young intellectual taken prisoner in Ethiopia, proclaimed the gospel there, and his wisdom attracted the attention of the king. He was sent to Alexandria to ask for a bishop and was himself chosen by Athanasius to govern the new church of Ethiopia (middle of the fourth century). The national language, Ge'ez, acquired an alphabet. And a last example: Ulfilas was the grandson of Christians from Cappadocia whom the Goths had taken captive in the north of the Danube at the end of the third century. He came to Constantinople for instruction and received ordination from an Arian bishop (341). On his return to his country, he evangelized the Goths. Through them Aryan Christianity spread among a number of German peoples. Ulfilas developed a Germanic alphabet for transcribing the holy scriptures.

The evangelization of Ethiopia by Frumentius

In the course of a study visit, two young pupils of a philosopher were taken prisoner in Ethiopia after the killing of their master. Their wisdom was appreciated, and soon they held high office in the kingdom, especially Frumentius.

While Frumentius was holding the reigns of power in his hands, God guiding his spirit, he enquired carefully whether there were Christians among the Roman merchants who frequented the country; he advised them, and made it easier for them to establish in each of their trading posts little oratories where they could meet to pray according to the Roman rite. Indeed he did even more: he invited all the others, granting them favours and privileges, to install churches wherever it seemed opportune to them; he provided all that was necessary for Christianity to bear fruit in this land.

Frumentius returned to Alexandria, saying that it was not right not to make known the work of the Lord. He explained everything that had happened to the bishop and asked him to choose a worthy man and send him as bishop, since a number of Christians had been gathered and several churches had already been built in the country of these barbarians. Then Athanasius, who had recently been made bishop (328), paying great heed to the report and action of Frumentius, declared in the course of a synod of his priests: 'Can we find anyone else who will be as full of the spirit of God as you, to fulfil such a mission?' He bestowed the priesthood on him and ordered him to return whence he had come, with the grace of God. So Frumentius returned to India [Ethiopia], and it is said that he received so many graces and virtues from God that the predictions of the apostles were realized in his work and he converted a large number of barbarians to Christ.

(Rufinus, *History of the Church* I, 9)

National churches and separated churches

I have no intention of recounting here the history of the dogmatic controversies of the fourth and fifth centuries as presented in the first four ecumenical councils. We simply need to note the influence that they had on evangelization. The definitions of the Council of Chalcedon (451) were meant to put an end to the disputes over the person of Christ. The Chalcedonian Definition, which said that in Christ the human nature and the divine nature are united in a single person, was to be accepted as the sole orthodoxy throughout the empire, and the emperor in Constantinople took pains to impose it. There was a good deal of resistance both inside and outside the empire. The opposition often appeared as a way in which the populations of different cultures could show their independence from the Greek imperialism of Constantinople. Within the frontiers of the empire, Monophysitism, the belief that there is only one 'nature' in Christ, became the national religion of Coptic Egypt, as also of the Syriac-speaking Christians in the hinterland of Antioch. More subtly, beyond the frontiers, politics influenced dogmatic choices. The Christians in the Persian empire, still suspected of treacherously supporting the Romans, opted for Nestorianism (the view that there are two persons in Christ, divine and human) in opposition to imperial Christianity. The Armenians rejected Chalcedon and were regarded as Monophysites. However, for them it was a way of marking themselves off from their powerful neighbours, the Roman empire, which imposed the Chalcedonian faith, and the Persian empire, where the Christians had chosen Nestorianism. All these peoples evangelized in their turn, putting forward their dogmatic option. In particular, the Nestorians of the Persian empire were prodigious missionaries throughout Asia as far as India and China.

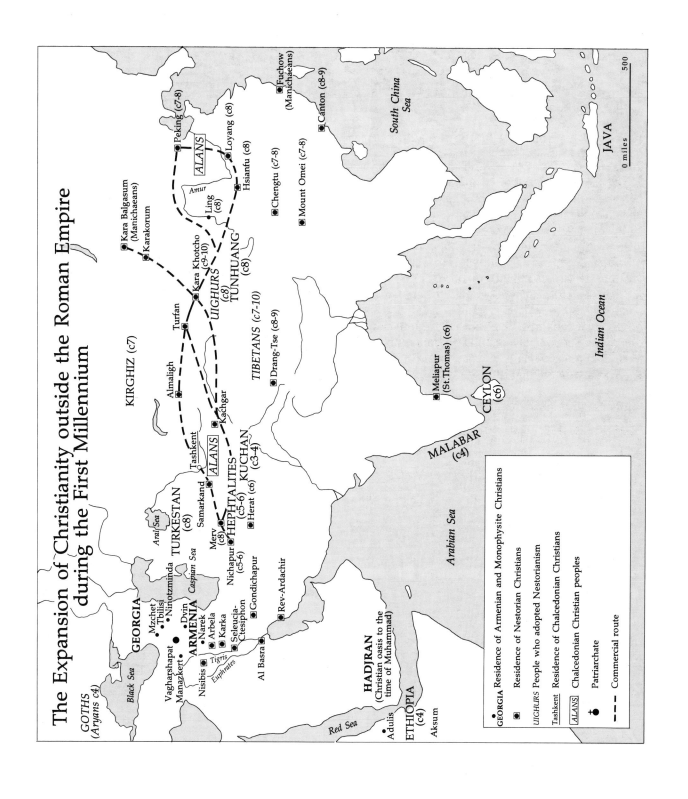

The Expansion of Christianity outside the Roman Empire during the First Millennium

GOTHS (Aryans c4)

Black Sea

GEORGIA
Mzchet Tbilisi
Vagharshapat Ninotzminda
Manazkert Dvin
ARMENIA Narek
Arbela
Karka
Seleucia-Ctesiphon
Nisibis
Tigris
Euphrates

HADJRAN
(Christian oasis to the time of Muhammad)

ETHIOPIA (c4)
Aduiis
Aksum

Red Sea

Al Basra

Gondichapur

Rev-Ardachir

Nichapur (c5-6)

Merv (c8)

HEPHTALITES (c5-6)
KUCHAN (c3-4)
Herat (c6)

Samarkand

TURKESTAN (c8)

ALANS

Tashkent

Aral Sea

Caspian Sea

Almaligh

KIRGHIZ (c7)

Kachgar

Turfan

Kara Khotcho (c9-10)

Kara Balgasum (Manichaeans)
Karakorum

ALANS

Peking (c7-8)

Ling (c8)

Loyang (c8)

Amur

UIGHURS (c8)

TUNHUANG (c8)

Hsianfu (c8)

TIBETANS (c7-10)

Drang-Tse (c8-9)

Chengtu (c7-8)

Mount Omei (c7-8)

Fuchow (Manichaeans)

Canton (c8-9)

South China Sea

Arabian Sea

MALABAR (c4)

Meliapur (St.Thomas) (c6)

CEYLON (c6)

Indian Ocean

JAVA

0 miles   500

Residence of Armenian and Monophysite Christians

Residence of Nestorian Christians

People who adopted Nestorianism

Residence of Chalcedonian Christians

Chalcedonian Christian peoples

Patriarchate

Commercial route

GEORGIA
UIGHURS
Tashkent
ALANS

2

The Birth of a Christian Europe (Fifth to Eleventh Centuries)

A century after the peace of the church in 313, Christians were closely associating the church with the empire and did not think that the church could exist without the empire. However, during the fourth century this fine imperial edifice began to collapse. On the death of Emperor Theodosius in 395, the division of the empire into West and East was complete. During the fifth century, in the West, the empire succumbed to the onslaught of the barbarians; in the East it still continued for ten centuries, but with increasingly limited territory. Through many ups and downs, the church preserved the imperial heritage, but saw its geography change profoundly. It lost a great part of the Mediterranean basin and shifted northwards; six centuries of a chaotic history saw as many reverses as successes.

From the Germanic invasions to the Arab invasions

The Germans in the empire

From the end of the second century, the Germans pressed in on the frontiers of the empire. For a long time they were contained – some of them had been conscripted into the Roman army – but from 406, impelled by the Huns, an Asian people, they crossed the Rhine and the Danube *en masse* and spread through the empire. The sack of Rome by the Visigoth Alaric in 410 profoundly disturbed believers. Wasn't this the end of the world and the church? Why hadn't the bodies of the apostles Peter and Paul protected Rome? Why hadn't so many innocent victims, children, dedicated virgins, monks, brought it security? Jerome shed tears, and Augustine tried to make sense of events in *The City of God*. The advance of the barbarians continued inexorably. Ostrogoths, Visigoths, Burgundians, Franks and many others carved out kingdoms for themselves in the ancient Western empire. The Vandals continued their march as far as Africa, and Augustine died in a Hippo under siege (430). The Angles and the Saxons launched an attack on Romanized Great Britain.

Many bishops made up for the lack of an imperial administration which had completely disintegrated. Augustine welcomed refugees in Hippo. Bishops inspired resistance in their city, organized food supplies and negotiated with the invaders. Pope Leo the Great negotiated the departure of Attila (452). And nuns, too, like St Geneviève in Paris, and monks like St Severinus in the Danube valley, helped and consoled their Christian brothers and sisters.

The consequences of the invasions for the church varied, depending on the region. At least for the moment, the church disappeared from a number of frontier regions where there were fewer Christians and where the fighting was rougher: the Danube

Valley, the North Sea near the Rhine delta, the whole of the eastern part of Great Britain from which the Celts had fled. While the Franks and some others like the Angles and the Saxons had remained pagan, the majority of Germans had chosen the Arian Christianity preached to them by Ulfilas; in Gaul and in Italy the Burgundians and the Goths proved tolerant, but in Africa the Vandals persecuted the Catholics violently. In many regions once Romanized and Christianized, little by little a *modus vivendi* came into being between the old populations and the new arrivals, who usually had a great admiration for Roman civilization and employed the old imperial officials.

The conversion of the barbarians within the old empire

The first stupor passed. The church went on. 'Must we not welcome the Germans in our churches?' Orosius asked, doubtless under the illusion that these barbarians would come together within the church framework which made up the empire. Relations between these Arians and the old Christians were inevitably tense. So the conversion to Roman Christianity of Clovis, king of the Franks, who had remained pagan, was of considerable importance for the future of the church and of Europe (around 500). This conversion was the fruit of the joint efforts of Clotilde, his Catholic wife, and Remy, bishop of Rheims. Though not the first example, the baptism of the king of the Franks illustrates the main method of evangelization for centuries: the conversion of leaders which entailed the conversion of their people. Such Christianization did not change customs much, but in this way Clovis reconciled the Gallo-Romans, appearing as a new Constantine. The bishops rallied to him rather than to other barbarian rulers who had been conquered in battle. Furthermore, little by little, under the pressure of Catholic wives, bishops or populations, all the Arian princes came over to the Roman church. Leovigild, king of the Visigoths in Spain, killed his son Hermenegild because he had become

---

The barbarians in the churches

Orosius, a priest in Braga (the north of present-day Portugal), had fled from the Vandals and taken refuge in Hippo, with St Augustine. In his History Against the Pagans *he attempts a Christian reading of history, from the creation of the world to his own time.*

Who knows? Perhaps the Barbarians have been able to penetrate the Roman empire so that everywhere, in East and West, the churches of Christ might be full of Huns, Suevi, Vandals and Burgundians, and other innumerable peoples as believers. Should we not praise and celebrate the divine mercy since, thanks to our ruin, so many nations have come to the knowledge of the truth with which they would not otherwise have had contact?

(Orosius, *History against the Pagans* VII, 41)

---

a Catholic (585). However, his second son, Reccared, joined the Roman faith after acceding to the throne (587).

Ireland, evangelized and evangelizing

In Romanized Britain, the Angles and the Saxons had driven Christianity from the east of the island. The Celtic Christians took refuge in the western extremities, Wales and Cornwall. Others crossed over to the continent, to what is now Brittany. This Celtic church, which was predominantly monastic, continued to be concerned with evangelization. Patrick, who was born around 390, in an old Christian family in Great Britain, had in his youth been captured by pirates, who took him off to Ireland, where he remained for six years as a slave. When he returned to Great Britain, he engaged in some religious study, became a priest and perhaps a monk, and made several journeys to Gaul. He dreamed that the Irish asked him to come to them. Ordained bishop, he then left to evangelize the

The baptism of Clovis and the religious future of the West

In a letter to Clovis, Avitus, Bishop of Vienne, congratulates him warmly on his conversion (c.500). In the eyes of the Gallo-Roman Christians, the king of the Franks occupies a special place among the barbarians. The emperor of Constantinople is no longer able to set himself alone at the head of the Catholic faith.

Divine Providence has discovered the arbiter of our time. The choice that you have made for yourself applies to all. Your faith is our victory. When the pontiffs or those around them call on others to adhere to the true doctrine, many of them suddenly appeal to the traditions of their race and respect for the cult of their ancestors ... Despite your ancient genealogy, you have wanted to retain only your nobility, and you have desired your descendants to make all the glories which adorn a lofty birth begin with you. You follow in the footsteps of your ancestors in governing here below; you open the way to your descendants by wanting to reign in heaven. Greece can rejoice at having chosen one of ours as emperor; in the future it will no longer be alone in enjoying such a favour. Thanks to you, your fortune shines with due splendour, and the West sees one of its sovereigns resplendent in a new light ... Your splendour is affirmed at this festival of the birth of our Redeemer, when the water of regeneration has brought you to birth for your salvation, on this day when the world received the Lord, born for its redemption. So from now on let us be among those who together celebrate the birth of our Lord: at the very moment when Christ appeared to the world, you appeared to Christ. By this act you have consecrated your soul to God, your life to your contemporaries and your glory to your descendants.

island, on which Palladius had perhaps already made some Christians. Patrick's apostolate probably falls between 430 and 460.

Patrick transported Celtic Christianity to Ireland, and its particular characteristics were further emphasized there. In fact Ireland had never been Romanized. The heart of the church was not the city and its bishop, but the monastery and the abbot. Either the abbot or perhaps one of his monks often received episcopal ordination. Christianity gave birth to a distinctive culture in Ireland. The monks had to learn Latin for their training and for reading the Bible. The Latin alphabet equally served to transcribe Gaelic and to fix a national literature in writing. Ireland became a stronghold of civilization as compared to the decadence of the continent. It fed the Carolingian renaissance. The universal church owes to the church of Ireland a new form of penitence, the penitential tariff, private and repeatable. Another ascetic practice of the Irish monks was *peregrinatio* for Christ; this led them to multiply monastic establishments in Great Britain and on the continent. By *peregrinatio*, in their holy restlessness, they became evangelizers.

St Columban is the most famous of these travellers. He left his monastery in Bangor with twelve companions in 590, and crossed to Gaul to travel eastwards. He founded three monasteries in Burgundy – Annegray, Luxeuil and Fontaine – but came into conflict with the royal court, as a result of which he was banished. He then returned to the Rhine valley, evangelized some pagans in Alsace and Switzerland, founded a monastery at Bregenz on Lake Constance, continued through northern Italy, and died in Bobbio in the last monastery which he had founded. His disciple St Gall created the monastery which bears his name. The action of the Irish was often turbulent. In addition to clashing with rulers, they encountered the opposition of the local clergy, who did not take to their particular customs over liturgy, tonsure, and so on.

The evangelization of the Anglo-Saxons

It was difficult to ask the Celts, monks though they were, to evangelize the Angles and Saxons who had driven them from their country and forced them to take refuge in the mountains of the West. However, Pope Gregory the Great was aware of the desire of these barbarians to know Christianity. To make up for the ill-will of the neighbouring bishops, the Pope decided to send Augustine, prior of St Andrew's monastery in Rome, along with forty monks, to England (June 596). Queen Bertha, who was already a Christian, and her husband Ethelbert, king of Kent, gave the monks a solemn welcome. At Pentecost 597, the king and his officers received baptism. The following Christmas, 10,000 of his subjects were baptized. Augustine, who was ordained bishop while travelling through Gaul, became Archbishop of Canterbury and was responsible for establishing a number of dioceses. In a letter, the Pope gave wise advice to Augustine about how to evangelize. His concern to understand ancient customs contrasts with the violence of the monks who destroyed idols, like Columban or Gall.

This evangelization of England might seem to be a 'mission' in which the Pope took the initiative. Subsequently it was often to be a point of reference, suggesting that all evangelization should be the responsibility of Rome. In reality, Gregory's intervention was fortuitous. It arose out of the negligence of the bishops. For a long time still, in the majority of cases, it would be monks, princes and bishops who took the initiative in evangelization. But they liked to have papal recognition after the event.

Thus in the first part of the seventh century, Christian and Roman faith had almost regained its ancient domains in the regions of the empire which had been overrun by the barbarians: Great Britain, Gaul, Spain. We must remember that a large number of preachers of the gospel had no precise mandate; several of them gave their names to cities. One of the most famous is St Amand (586–679), an itinerant bishop who began from the Vendée, preached at Bourges, evangelized Belgium, and made apostolic forays into the countries by the Danube. In fact this was a somewhat revised Christianity. The cities had perished. Country parishes had multiplied on the great estates. The religion of the cities was succeeded by a peasant religion, marked by a taste for miracles and the cult of saints and relics. It inherited many features of pagan religion.

The missionary vocation of Patrick (c.410)

Dreams were very frequent in antiquity, not least in the Bible and the writings of the church fathers. Several calls to mission, beginning with the call of the Macedonians to Paul (Acts 16.9), arose out of dreams. That was the case with Patrick. (Before recalling the call of the Irish in a dream he related his slavery among the Irish who had captured him.)

And after a few years I was in Britain with my people, who received me as their son, and sincerely besought me that now at last, having suffered so many hardships, I should not leave them and go elsewhere. And there I saw in the night the vision of a man, whose name was Victoricus, coming as it were from Ireland, with countless letters. And he gave me one of them, and I read the opening words of the letter, which were, 'The voice of the Irish'; and as I read the beginning of the letter I thought that at the same moment I heard their voice — they were those beside the Wood of Voclut, which is near the Western Sea — and thus did they cry out as with one mouth: 'We ask you, boy, come and walk among us once more.' And I was quite broken in heart, and could read no further, and so I woke up. Thanks be to God, after many years the Lord gave to them according to their cry.

(St Patrick, *Confession*, 23)

Not a very evangelical evangelization (610)

Preachers did not hesitate to use force: they destroyed temples, idols and sacred trees. Their method was nearer to the Old Testament than the New. Walafrid Strabo (died 849), abbot of Reichenau on Lake Constance, one of the architects of the 'Carolingian renaissance', describes these radical methods.

Having been granted by the king permission to choose a place where they might settle, after crossing several countries Columbanus and his disciples arrived in the country of the Alemanns, on the banks of the river called the Limmat. Going up from there they arrived at the lake of Zurich, and reached its head by following the shore, at a place called Tuggen. The beauty of the place and its convenient setting pleased them. Alas, however, the population which occupied it was cruel and wicked: it was devoted to the cult of false gods whom it honoured by sacrifices, and was given over to the practice of auguries, oracles and numerous other superstitions incompatible with the worship of the true God. The holy men had begun to live in the midst of this population and was teaching them the religion of the Father, the Son and the Holy Spirit and the prescriptions of the true faith. However, one day St Gall, a disciple of the holy man, armed with a pious zeal, set fire to the temple in which they were offering sacrifices to the demons and threw into the lake all the idols which he could find there.

This fine act inflamed the pagans with anger and hatred: they descended upon the holy monks, wanting to kill Gall and drive Columban from their midst, after scourging him with rods and showering blows upon him. The blessed father, having recognized their aim, intoxicated with a sense of justice, hurled at them the following anathema: 'O God, whose providence maintains and governs the universe, make the outrages that these people have inflicted on your servants rebound on their head. May their children die young, and may they be struck with sudden madness before they grow old; may they and their land be oppressed by harsh servitude; may their ignominy fall upon them all for eternity, as it is written: "May the sorrow that they have sown rebound on their heads, and may the iniquity which they have committed press heavy on their necks!"'

(Walafrid Strabo, *Life of St Gall*)

The Arab invasions

During this period the Arab invasions turned the political and religious map of the East and the southern Mediterranean upside down. Muhammad, the prophet of the one God, had united the tribes of the Arabian peninsula between 622 (the Hijra, the beginning of the Muslim era) and 632 (when he died in Mecca). With the enthusiasm of new believers, the Arabs launched an attack on the two worn-out empires of Rome (Byzantium) and Persia. The Christian populations of Egypt, Palestine and Syria, which had been in permanent conflict with Constantinople for cultural and dogmatic reasons, did not put up much resistance to an invader whom they sometimes regarded as a liberator. Jerusalem was captured in 638, Alexandria in 642, Persia in 651. Then the Arabs turned westwards. In 670 they founded Kairouan, in 698 they took Carthage, and in 711 they began the conquest of Spain. This lightning advance was stopped only in 718, under the walls of Constantinople, and in 732, at Poitiers, with the victory of Charles Martel.

The places where Christianity had been born, the earliest churches, fell under Arab domination. With a few exceptions, the Arabs were relatively tolerant, but for them Christians and Jews were second-class believers. Slowly Christianity weakened in the conquered countries. Certainly communities with strong structures have continued in the East to our day: the Copts of Egypt, the Maronites of the Lebanon, and so on. However, in North Africa the extinction was progressive and final: at the time of the Arab conquest there were around forty bishops; there were five in 1053 and only two in 1076. The last Christians disappeared at the beginning of the twelfth century. The Christians of Spain undertook the reconquest of their country from Islam; this *reconquista* was not completed until 1492.

A new geography of the Christian world

At the end of the sixth century and the beginning of the seventh, other invaders from the north and east had established themselves in Central Europe: the Avars, the Bulgars and the Slavs. These last had crossed the Danube and come down the Balkan peninsula as far as the Peloponnese. All these movements of peoples considerably transformed the Christian geography of the ancient Roman empire. The Mediterranean, the eastern and southern shores of which had fallen into the hands of Islam, was no longer the uniting factor of the Christian world. Rome, formerly at the heart of the church, was now at its southern extremity. On the continent, the Slav invasions set up a barrier between the Latin Roman church and the Greek Byzantine church. The two cultural spheres became increasingly isolated from each other, and misunderstandings increased. The future of evangelization presented itself in a new way. In the West, with the conversion of the Germanic peoples, the church's centre of gravity moved northwards, between the Loire and the Rhine. The Byzantine empire, encircled by Islam, could not have any great plans for evangelization eastwards. At the same time, the new pagan arrivals, the Slavs, Avars and Bulgars, became the prize in an apostolic competition between Rome and Constantinople.

The completion of the conversion of the Germanic peoples

The Germanic people belonged to two major group-

'Inculturation' in England

The invitation of Pope Gregory to take account of the peoples being evangelized would often be referred to in the future.

I have long reflected on the affairs of the English; this is my reply. The temples of the idols in that nation ought not to be destroyed; but let the idols that are in them be destroyed; let holy water be made and sprinkled in the said temples, let altars be erected, and relics placed. For if those temples are well built, it is requisite that they be converted from the worship of devils to the service of the true God; that the nation, seeing that their temples are not destroyed, may remove error from their heart, and, knowing and adoring the true God, may the more familiarly resort to the places to which they have been accustomed. And because they have been used to slaughter many oxen in the sacrifices to devils, some solemnity must be exchanged for them on this account, that on the day of the dedication, or the nativities of the holy martyrs, whose relics are there deposited, they may build themselves huts of the boughs of trees, about those churches which have been turned to that use from temples, and celebrate the solemnity with religious feasting, and no more offer beasts to the Devil, but kill cattle to the praise of God in their eating, and return thanks to the Giver of all things for their sustenance; to the end that, whilst some gratifications are outwardly permitted them, they may the more easily consent to the inward consolations of the grace of God. For there is no doubt that it is impossible to efface everything at once from their obdurate minds; because he who endeavours to ascend to the highest place, rises by degrees or steps, and not by leaps.

(quoted in Bede, *Ecclesiastical History of the English Nation* I, 30)

---

ings, and evangelization took different forms in each of them. The more northerly Scandinavian group sowed terror throughout Europe in the ninth and tenth centuries, which explains why it was only converted later, in a process which did not end until the eleventh century. The continental group, which can be taken to include the Anglo-Saxons of Great Britain, extended from the Elbe to the Atlantic. However, several spheres need to be distinguished in this second grouping. The larger part was under the Frankish empire, which had been broadly Christianized, apart from sectors in the Eastern regions which remained pagan: Hessen, Thuringia, part of Alemannia and Bavaria. In the north, between the Rhine and the Elbe, two peoples escaped Frankish authority and remained savagely pagan, the Frisians and the Saxons.

Methods of evangelization

Here we find aspects we already glimpsed at the beginning of this chapter. Until the advent of the Carolingians, there was hardly any pre-established plan. Among those involved in evangelization, several acted on their own initiative in a somewhat anarchical way: some of these figures had received episcopal ordination, though we do not know in what conditions. The monks were the most serious apostolic workers. In this connection, emphasis must be placed on the role of the Anglo-Saxon monks, who had profited from the Celtic experience in Northumbria, the religious differences between Celts and Saxons having been settled at the Synod of Whitby (663). Many of these Anglo-Saxons migrated to the continent, founding monasteries and evangelizing.

The preachers aimed at the conversion of princes or chieftains, so that they would bring their people over with them, as had been the case with Clovis or Ethelbert. However, this did not always work out. Once the princes had been converted, the political factor reared its head in another way: the Carolingian sovereigns associated political conquest with conversion. The conquered country was divided into sectors entrusted to preachers; baptism was a pledge of allegiance to the conqueror. However, there was often resistance, and the temptation to the power was then to use force: the destruction of pagan holy places, and physical violence against the people. Missionaries themselves could threaten to call on the ruler when the pagans became too recalcitrant. However, when a Scandinavian king knew that his power came from his ancestral religion, he was afraid of losing it if he became a Christian. We find both missionaries who tolerated a considerable degree of syncretism – scenes from the passion are mixed with Scandinavian mythology on crosses – and others who proved the ineffectiveness of the ancient gods by destroying temples and sacred trees. As to the form taken by their preaching, we have some traces of basic missionary addresses, like the programme which Alcuin proposed to Charlemagne.

The Germans on the continent

The evangelization of the Germans took on new vigour with the Anglo-Saxon monks. Wilfrid of the abbey of Ripon in Northumbria, Bishop of York, passed through pagan Friesland (at the mouth of the Rhine) on a journey to Rome and converted several chieftains there (678). On his return to York he suggested to the monks of Ripon that they should make a *peregrinatio* to the continent to convert the people related to the Saxons of England. At the head of a dozen companions, Willibrord thereupon left for Friesland, which had just been conquered by the Franks (690), and the region of Utrecht became Christian. In the course of a journey which Willibrord made to Rome in 695, Pope Sergius consecrated him Archbishop of Friesland; however, limited in his action by the pagan king of northern Friesland, he sought other mission fields in Denmark and Thuringia and founded the monastery of Echternach in Luxembourg, where he died in 739.

The greatest missionary on the continent was

Baptism or death

Charlemagne's Capitulary on Saxony (785) transformed baptism into an act of political submission. There will be other examples later in the history of the church.

Anyone who enters a church violently and, by force or theft, removes any object from it, will be put to death.

Anyone who, out of contempt for Christianity, refuses to respect the holy fast of Lent and eats meat, will be put to death.

Anyone who kills a bishop, priest or deacon will be put to death.

Anyone who delivers the body of a dead person to the flames, following the pagan rite, will be put to death.

Any unbaptized Saxon who seeks to hide among his compatriots and refuses to have baptism administered to him will be put to death.

(Capitulatio de partibus Saxoniae)

Wynfrith, whom we know better under the name of Boniface (c.675–754). In charge of studies at his abbey of Nursling in southern England, at the age of forty he left to evangelize the Frisians (716). After a setback, he went to Rome to call for the support of Pope Gregory II. This appeal to Rome was to be a constant during his evangelizing activity. The Pope confirmed his mission among the Frisians and for three years Boniface accompanied Willibrord. In 721 he reached Hessen, where he founded the monastery of Amöneburg. In 722, the Pope consecrated him bishop in Rome and required him to put himself at the service of Charles Martel, the Majordomo of the Frankish kingdom. From then on Boniface devoted himself more to the organization of the church in Germany than to direct evangelization; he marked out the dioceses of Bavaria, Hessen and Thuringia, and chose Anglo-Saxon monks as bishops. He founded abbeys for men (Fritzlar, Fulda) and women. In 732 he was nominated archbishop of Germany, with his see at Mainz, and

A short treatise on missiology

Charlemagne's methods of evangelization in Saxony had been somewhat peremptory: baptism or death. When he had defeated the Avars of the Danube plain (795), the king of the Franks also wanted to Christianize them. His 'minister', the monk Alcuin, counsels moderation.

May your Excellency take care to provide for this young people preachers who are honest in their customs, wise in theology and steeped in the precepts of the gospel. When they preach the word of God, let them take the holy apostles as their models. These first distributed milk to their new hearers; that is, they first taught the precepts which were easiest to follow.

That having been considered, let your Holiness mediate on this question. Is it good to impose the burden of tithes immediately on uncultivated peoples who have been recently converted, in such a way as to make them weigh equally on each domain? There is a need to ask whether the apostles, who had received the divine teaching from the very mouth of Christ and who had been sent by him to preach the gospel to the whole world, received tithes or claimed them anywhere they preached. We know that the collection of tithes is a good thing for our way of living, but it is better not to collect them if progress in faith suffers as a result.

There is also a need most attentively to take into account that the work of preaching and baptism must be carried out methodically and that people must receive the water of holy baptism not only on their bodies but also in their souls in a rational way; in no case must it precede knowledge of the Catholic religion.

I also think that it is necessary to preserve for those who have reached adulthood the order of teaching that St Augustine advised in his treatise on catechizing the ignorant: first people must be taught about the immortality of the soul, the future life, the judgment on actions good or bad and the eternity of this judgment. Then they must be taught that they will suffer eternal punishment in company with the devil for their crimes and sins, but by their good actions they will enjoy eternal glory in the company of Christ. Then with great care they must be taught belief in the Holy Trinity and the coming of our Lord Jesus Christ, Son of God, for the salvation of all humankind. This could be taught in this way: the mystery of his passion, the truth of his resurrection, the glory of his ascension into heaven, his future coming to judge all the nations, the resurrection of our hearts, eternal punishment for the evil and reward for the good. In this way, as I have already said, the soul of the neophytes could be assured. In this way the person who has thus been fortified will be ready to receive baptism.

(Alcuin, *Letters* 110)

then received from the Pope the title of 'legate' for the reform of the church in Gaul. In his old age he was again seized with a desire to proclaim the gospel to the pagans, and he left for Friesland, where he was killed (754). By his action, Boniface gave the church in Germany a solid organization based on a close link with Rome.

With the advent of Charlemagne, the evangelization of Germany took another turn. It was seen as the conclusion of military conquest. The ruler of the Saxons, Widukind, led a revolt in 778. The Franks had to retreat and Charlemagne resorted to terror, the famous Capitulary on Saxony of 785: baptism or death. Baptism constituted the seal of political submission. After a second revolt was put down, dioceses were established: Münster, Paderborn and Hamburg (804). All the Germans on the continent received baptism, and Christianity reached the Elbe and the forests of Bohemia. When Charlemagne defeated the Avars in the Danube plain in 796, Alcuin, his minister, called on them to be converted, but in a more evangelical fashion than that practised for the Saxons!

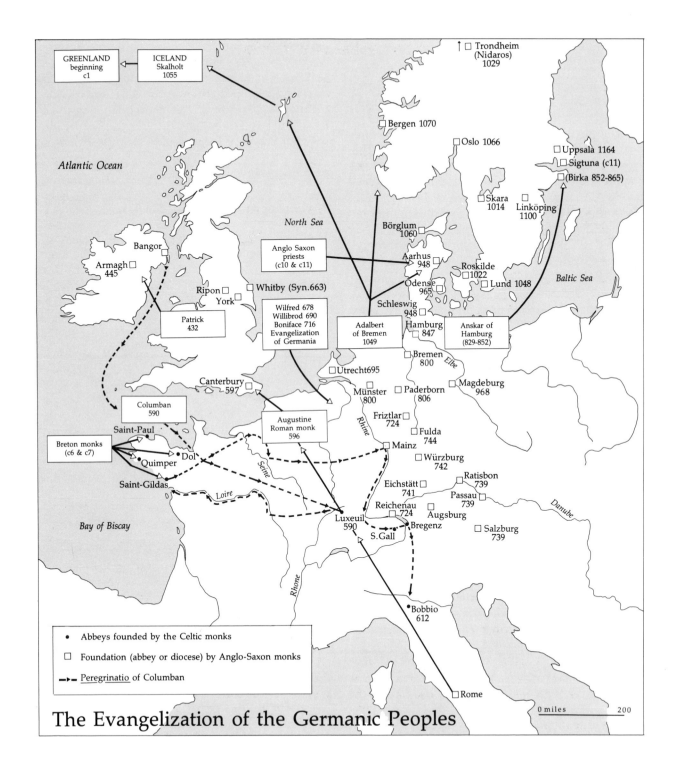

GREENLAND
beginning
c1

ICELAND
Skalholt
1055

Trondheim
(Nidaros)
1029

Atlantic Ocean

Bergen 1070

Oslo 1066

Uppsala 1164
Sigtuna (c11)
(Birka 852-865)

Skara
1014

Linköping
1100

North Sea

Börglum
1060

Bangor

Armagh
445

Ripon
York

Whitby (Syn.663)

Anglo Saxon
priests
(c10 & c11)

Aarhus
948

Roskilde
1022

Lund 1048

Odense
965

Baltic Sea

Patrick
432

Wilfred 678
Willibrod 690
Boniface 716
Evangelization
of Germania

Schleswig
948

Adalbert
of Bremen
1049

Hamburg
847

Anskar of
Hamburg
(829-852)

Bremen
800

Columban
590

Utrecht 695

Canterbury
597

Münster
800

Paderborn
806

Magdeburg
968

Saint-Paul

Breton monks
(c6 & c7)

Dol

Quimper

Saint-Gildas

Augustine
Roman monk
596

Seine

Rhine

Elbe

Friztlar
724

Mainz

Fulda
744

Würzburg
742

Ratisbon
739

Eichstätt
741

Passau
739

Reichenau
724

Augsburg

Loire

Luxeuil
590

S.Gall

Bregenz

Salzburg
739

Bay of Biscay

Rhone

Danube

Bobbio
612

• Abbeys founded by the Celtic monks

□ Foundation (abbey or diocese) by Anglo-Saxon monks

▪-►- <u>Peregrinatio</u> of Columban

Rome

0 miles   200

The Evangelization of the Germanic Peoples

The Scandinavian peoples

The history of the evangelization of the Scandinavian countries is somewhat confused. In Denmark, the conversion of the Saxons arose out of a pagan reaction: the military defences against the Carolingian empire were strengthened. In the ninth century, Anskar (801–865), monk of Corbie (on the Weser), then archbishop of Hamburg–Bremen, made a number of unsuccessful attempts to convert the Swedes. This was the time when the Scandinavians, the Vikings, were making many expeditions to plunder Western Europe. Evangelization resumed only in the next century. First to be converted were the Scandinavian leaders who had established themselves in England or in France (Rollo in Normandy in 911). An archbishop of Hamburg, Unni (936), entered into relations with the Danes and the Swedes. Shortly before 950, the king of Denmark, Harald Blue Tooth, was converted. Some years later it was the turn of Norway. King Olaf the Great (1014–1030), who died fighting against rebellious pagan nobles, became the martyr St Olaf. Iceland became Christian in 1000; Sweden at the beginning of the eleventh century (King Olaf, 1026) and in the course of the twelfth century (the saintly King Erik, 1160); Greenland at the beginning of the twelfth century. The evangelization was above all the work of missionaries from England, which for a while was ruled by a Danish dynasty. The establishment of dioceses was very slow and the abandonment of past customs even more so; for a long time new-born children were exposed; cultic libations were made at great religious festivals, births and marriages; and divorce, concubinage and piracy were tolerated. Roman legates brought normality in the course of the twelfth century.

The conversion of the Slavs, the Bulgars and the Magyars

The plains of northern Europe and the Danube valley had always been corridors by which invaders from the steppes of Asia penetrated Europe. Between the sixth and the tenth centuries, Slavs, Avars, Bulgars and Magyars succeeded one another. Once they became sedentary, these different peoples gradually mixed their cultures. After overcoming their fears, their Christian neighbours tried to convert them. Situated geographically midway between the Latin church and the Byzantine church, the new arrivals hesitated, since conversion always involved political allegiance.

The first evangelization of the Slavs

The first Slavs to become Christians were those closest to the Frankish empire: Croats, Slovenes, Slovaks in the eighth century and the beginning of the ninth. The Franks hoped from there to win over the Bulgars, an Asiatic group which had become Slav, to the Latin faith. Rastislav, prince of Moravia, already a Christian, fearing the invasive policy of the Franks, proposed a military alliance to Constantinople and called for missionaries who could speak in the Slavonic dialect (862); he wanted cultural autonomy along with political independence. The Byzantine emperor looked favourably on this approach, which then allowed him to put pressure on the Bulgars. He chose two brothers, Constantine (Cyril), a deacon, and Methodius, a priest, who came from Thessalonica. Highly educated, they had a thorough knowledge of Slavonic and had taken part in embassies to distant countries. With a view to their mission, Constantine (Cyril) created an alphabet which made it possible to transcribe Slavonic; this was the Glagolitic alphabet (the Cyrillic alphabet is a later transformation of this first script). In this way Slavonic as a written language came into being; the first translations into it were passages from the Gospels. The two brothers and their entourage arrived in Moravia in the spring of 863. Their linguistic work was well received. The two brothers translated both Latin and Greek liturgical texts into Slavonic. However, while the use of local languages (Coptic, Syriac, Armenian, etc.) was accepted in the East, this was not the case in the West. The Frankish missionaries thought that a barbaric language could not be used in official prayer; God could be addressed only in the languages inscribed on the cross of Jesus: Hebrew, Latin and Greek. This was the starting point for a conflict which had many political connotations.

The two brothers left for the south to secure the ordination of priests. There they aroused the enthusiasm of other Slavs in Pannonia and on the way received an invitation to Rome from the Pope, who at that time was practising an overall policy of attaching the Slavs and Bulgars to the Roman church. The Czar of the Bulgars, Boris, who had received baptism in Constantinople in 856, annoyed that the Byzantines were refusing to let him have a patriarch for the Bulgar church, was at that time inclined towards Rome. The Czar also called on the Pope to recognize a certain number of Bulgar customs. The Pope was quite prepared to accept different modes of dress, but not polygamy! And in default of a patriarch, he proposed an archbishop. The welcome of Constantine and Methodius to Rome was part of the Pope's policy towards the Slavs and Bulgars. The two brothers received an even warmer welcome, since they brought with them the relics of St Clement of Rome, which had been recovered in the Chersonnese. Approving the work of the two brothers, Pope Adrian II had their disciples ordained and the mass was celebrated in Slavonic in four Roman churches. Constantine, who became the monk Cyril, died in Rome in February 869.

Later, however, Boris turned back towards Constantinople. Aiming to compensate this loss, Adrian II designated Methodius archbishop of Sirmium, where he had jurisdiction over the territory of greater Moravia. Here he could use the Slavonic language. However, Methodius encountered the opposition of the Frankish clergy, who felt dispossessed, and the Archbishop of Salzburg had him imprisoned. Pope John VIII secured his release and, after many hesitations, officially recognized the Slavonic liturgy (880). Popes succeed one another, but do not always resemble one another! On the death of Methodius in 885, the German

The mission of Constantine (Cyril) and Methodius

When the Slavs were baptized along with their prince Rastislav, Sviatopolk and Kotsel (of the royal family) addressed the emperor Michael [of Constantinople, 842–67], saying: 'Our country has been baptized and we have no master to preach to us, teach us and explain the holy books to us. We understand neither Greek nor Latin: some teach us in one way and some in another; nor do we understand the meaning of the holy books and their energy. So send us masters who will be capable of explaining to us the letter of the holy books and their spirit.'

On hearing this, the emperor Michael gathered together all his philosophers and repeated to them what had been said by the Slav princes. The philosophers said: 'In Thessalonica there is a man called Leo: he has sons who know the Slavonic language well, two sons versed in science and philosophy . . .'

On their arrival Constantine (Cyril) and Methodius established the letters of the Slavonic alphabet, and they translated the Acts of the Apostles and the Gospel. The Slavs rejoiced to hear the mighty acts of God in their language. Then some began to censure the Slavonic books, saying, 'No people has the right to have its alphabet except the Hebrews, the Greeks and the Latins, as is proved by what Pilate wrote on the Saviour's cross.'

(*Nestorian Chronicle* – eleventh century)

bishop Wiching hastened to Rome and obtained from Pope Stephen V a ban on the Slavonic liturgy. The disciples of Methodius, driven out of Moravia, took refuge in Bulgaria, where the heritage of Cyril and Methodius was thus saved. From Bulgaria, the Slavonic language and Slavonic usages were to pass on to Russia and Serbia.

Successive Popes differ completely from each other

The following two texts are completely contradictory.

*Approval of the Slavonic liturgy by
Pope John VIII (880)*

We totally approve of what the philosopher Constantine (Cyril) has written in Slavonic to the praise of God and we ordain that the actions and words of Our Lord Jesus Christ shall be enunciated in this language; for it is not in three languages but in all the languages that the sacred authority calls on us to praise the Lord, since it is written: 'Let all nations and peoples praise the Lord'. The apostles, filled with the Holy Spirit, spoke in tongues by a divine miracle and St Paul blew on the celestial trumpet 'let every tongue confess that Jesus Christ is Lord to the glory of God the Father'. So there is nothing against the use of the Slavonic languages for singing the mass, reading the divine scriptures of the Old and New Testament, carefully translated, and saying the hours and other offices.

(John VIII, *Letters* 255)

*Prohibition of the same liturgy by
Pope Stephen V (885)*

Methodius brought to those who listened to him not edification but superstition, not peace but polemic . . . The celebration of the divine offices, the holy mysteries and the solemn masses that Methodius claimed to perform in the Slavonic language were not authorized by anyone . . . In the name of God and our apostolic authority we therefore forbid, on pain of anathema, except for simple souls who would not otherwise understand, the Gospels and the texts of the Apostles to be read out in this Slavonic language by educated people.

(Stephen V, *Letters*)

The Christianization of the Magyars and Poles

At the end of the ninth century, there was a new upheaval in Central Europe as a result of the invasion of a people from the steppes. These were the Magyars, who sowed devastation as far as Burgundy. Some of the work of evangelization was destroyed. After their defeat in 955 by the Germanic emperor Otto the Great on the banks of the Lech in Bavaria, the Magyars or Hungarians settled in the Danube plain. Evangelization of the Poles and the Magyars resumed under the stimulus of Adalbert, bishop of Prague (died 997), and of Czech princes. On his marriage to Dobrawa, the daughter of the Czech duke Boleslav, the Polish prince Mieszka was baptized; in this way the Polish church and the Polish state came into being (966). Around twenty years later, Geisa Duke of Hungary and his son

Vajk (Stephen) received baptism from Adalbert (985). Stephen married Gisela, the daughter of the Duke of Bavaria; succeeding his father in 997, he organized the church of Hungary and put his country under the protection of St Peter. Pope Silvester II gave him the title king, and Stephen became the 'apostolic king' (1000).

The conversion of the Russians of Kiev

While the Vikings went up the estuaries of the coasts of Western Europe, other Scandinavian groups, the Varangians, who came from Lake Ladoga, reached the Caspian by the valley of the Volga and the Black Sea by the valley of the Dniepr. Engaged in trade, they formed the Slavs of these regions into a nation which from then on was called Rus. At that time they posed a danger to Constan-

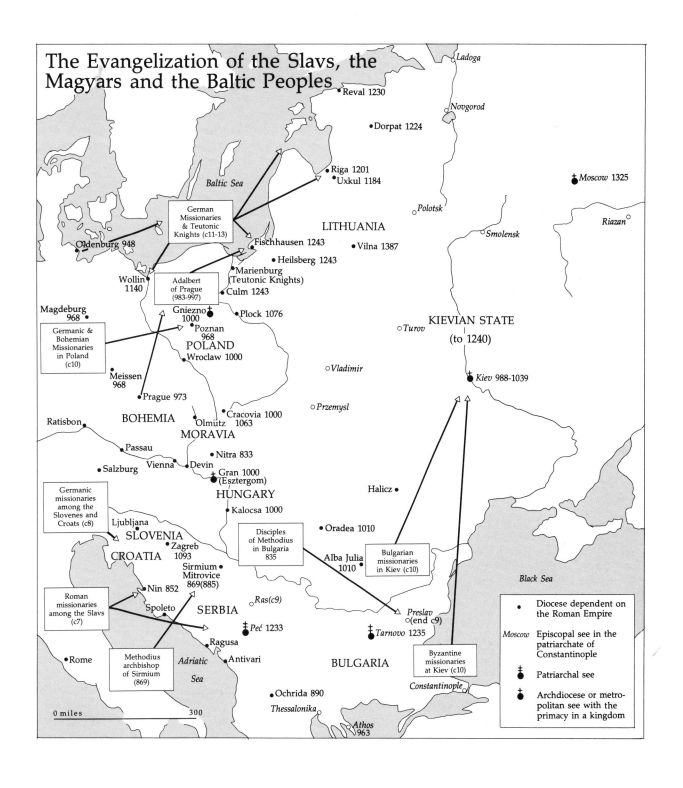

The Evangelization of the Slavs, the Magyars and the Baltic Peoples

Ladoga

● Reval 1230

● Dorpat 1224

Novgorod

Baltic Sea

‡ *Moscow 1325*

● Riga 1201
● Uxkul 1184

○ *Polotsk*

Riazan ○

LITHUANIA

German
Missionaries
& Teutonic
Knights (c11-13)

● Fischhausen 1243

● Vilna 1387

○ *Smolensk*

● Heilsberg 1243

Oldenburg 948 ●━

Wollin ●
1140

Adalbert
of Prague
(983-997)

● Marienburg
(Teutonic Knights)

● Culm 1243

Magdeburg
968 ●

Germanic &
Bohemian
Missionaries
in Poland
(c10)

Gniezno ‡
1000

● Poznan
968

● Plock 1076

KIEVIAN STATE
(to 1240)

○ *Turov*

POLAND

● Wroclaw 1000

Meissen ●
968

● Przemysl ○

○ *Vladimir*

‡ *Kiev 988-1039*

● Prague 973

BOHEMIA

Olmütz
1063

● Cracovia 1000
○ *Przemysl*

Ratisbon ●

MORAVIA

● Passau

● Nitra 833

Salzburg ●

Vienna ● Devin

Halicz ●

Germanic
missionaries
among the
Slovenes and
Croats (c8)

Ljubljana ●

+ Gran 1000
(Esztergom)

HUNGARY

● Kalocsa 1000

SLOVENIA

● Zagreb
1093

CROATIA

Sirmium ●
Mitrovice
869(885)

Disciples
of Methodius
in Bulgaria
835

● Oradea 1010

Bulgarian
missionaries
in Kiev (c10)

Alba Julia
1010

Roman
missionaries
among the
Slavs
(c7)

● Nin 852

Spoleto ●

SERBIA

● *Ras(c9)*

Black Sea

● Rome

Methodius
archbishop
of Sirmium
(869)

‡ Peć 1233

● Ragusa

*Adriatic
Sea*

● Antivari

△ *Preslav*
(end c9)

BULGARIA

‡ Tarnovo 1235

Byzantine
missionaries
at Kiev (c10)

● Ochrida 890

Thessalonika

Constantinople

● *Diocese dependent on
the Roman Empire*

Moscow *Episcopal see in the
patriarchate of
Constantinople*

‡ *Patriarchal see*

+ *Archdiocese or metro-
politan see with the
primacy in a kingdom*

● *Athos*
963

0 miles ━━━━━━ 300

Princess Olga, regent of Kiev, who had gone to Constantinople for political reasons, was baptized there in 957. However, she did not impose Christianity on her subjects and her son, who wanted to remain pagan. Through contacts with Bulgaria, the Kievians were interested in Slavonic culture. It is said that Vladimir, Olga's grandson, sent emissaries in search of a superior religion for his country; his investigators, dissatisfied with Islam, Judaism and Germanic Christianity, were utterly captivated by the Byzantine liturgy of Saint Sophia. Following political and matrimonial negotiations, Vladimir and his subjects received baptism in the Dniepr in 989 and the church of Kiev adopted the Byzantine model through the Slavonic liturgy.

As far as China

We have seen several times that the preaching of the gospel was not limited to the Roman empire and to Europe. Ancient traditions tell us that Thomas and Bartholomew, two of the twelve apostles, went as far as India. The tomb of St Thomas at Meliapur on the east coast of India is a place of veneration. Though we may have some reservations about what apocryphal writings say, we may be fairly certain of a Christian presence in India on the Malabar coast from the fourth century on. A sixth-century Alexandrian traveller, Cosmas Indicopleustes, found a Christian community in Ceylon. Various writings also indicate that there were Christian communities from Persia to China, all along the 'silk route'. The great majority of these communities were founded by the Nestorians of Mesopotamia and Persia, who, cut off from the Byzantine church by the Arab conquest, became orientated on the Far East. The most remarkable testimony to this presence is the stele of Hsianfu in China, written in Syriac and Chinese in the eighth century.

A millennium of Christianity

By the eleventh century, the whole of Europe had become Christian. It is not always easy to discover

tinople. The Byzantines wanted to bring them into their zone of influence through religion. It seems that in the 860s there was a first church of Kiev, but this was soon destroyed by pagan princes. Still, a Christian presence was certainly maintained.

The perplexity of Prince Vladimir, confronted with a religious choice

Influenced from many quarters, Vladimir, Prince of Kiev, hesitates when faced with the range of great religions offered to him.

Vladimir summoned his boyars and the council of the city and said: 'The Bulgars came to me saying, "Receive our law." Then the Germans came and praised their law. After them the Jews came. And finally the Greeks came, censuring all the religions but praising their own, and they spoke for a long time of the creation of the world and the history of the world. They spoke with spirit: it is a marvel and pleasure to hear them. They said: "He who receives our faith will never die; but if he receives another faith he will burn in flames in the other world." What is your opinion and what do you say to this?' The boyars remarked: 'You know, O prince, that no one censures his own views, but on the contrary, each one practises them. If you wish to enlighten yourself carefully, send some of your men to study the different cults and see how each honours God.'

The results of the enquiry

In Germany, they judged that the religious ceremonies of the Christians were too simple, but in Constantinople they were amazed. They were taken to Saint Sophia on a solemn festival and there, under the golden vault of the great church, amongst the clouds of incense and the magnificence of the clergy, the Russian boyars, dazzled by all the splendour of the Orthodox liturgy, thought that they could see in a mystical hallucination young winged people clothed in magnificent costumes, floating in the air above the priests and chanting triumphally, 'Holy, holy, holy is the Eternal One!' And as they asked the Byzantines about this marvellous vision which accompanied them they were told: 'If you were not ignorant of the Christian mysteries, you would know that the angels themselves descend from heaven to celebrate the office with our priests.'

(*Nestorian Chronicle*, eleventh century)

precisely what this meant for the Christians concerned. Who can say how each of them encountered Christ? The history of the expansion of Christianity is not directly a history of spirituality. However, it is worth emphasizing some features of this European Christianity at the beginning of Christendom, features which would have consequences in the future expansion of the Christian faith.

Having become the sole religion of Europe, Christianity constituted the foundation of this Europe. Faith was its social cement. To the degree that new peoples appeared on the scene, their Christian neighbours constantly brought them into the church. These peoples came of age when their leaders received baptism, which often brought them a royal title (as in Poland and Hungary); hence sometimes the conclusion that baptism was necessary to legitimate power and property.

Through the upheavals of six centuries, the church preserved the heritage of the Roman empire, its universalism and its culture, at least in the West. At the same time it integrated Germanic elements, but without being aware of the fact, and the barbarian rulers on becoming Christians first sought to have their share of this Roman heritage, this universalism and this culture, which they deemed superior to their own. It was to take several more centuries in the West for the people to establish their national languages and cultures. Becoming a Christian was to form part of a universal religion linked to a civilization, and the nature of this bond was subsequently to cause problems.

In the West, the empire had disappeared in the turbulence of the Germanic invasions, but the nostalgia for this empire remained. It was restored twice, in 800 for Charlemagne, and in 962, for Otto

The stele of Hsianfu

This stele, dating from 781, which has a bilingual inscription in Syriac and Chinese, was found in an ancient capital of China in the seventeenth century. It attests a first Christian preaching in this country by Nestorians who had come from the Persian empire. The text expounds Christian doctrine and uses a Taoist and Buddhist vocabulary.

Monument commemorating the propagation in the Middle Empire of the illustrious religion of T'ai Tsing.

Eulogy inscribed on the monument commemorating the propagation of the illustrious religion in the Middle Empire, with preface, composed by King Tsing, priest of the monastery of T'ai Tsing, priest and chorepiscopus, pafsi of China.

In truth, He who is pure and peaceable, who being without principle in the origin of origins, incomprehensible and invisible, always existing mysteriously towards every end, who, controlling the hidden axis of the universe, has created and developed all things, mysteriously giving existence to numerous sages, being the one most worthy of praise, is not He our God (allaha), Trinity, one mysterious substance, engendered and true Lord? (*there follows an account of creation and the first sin*).

However, the second person of the Trinity, the Messiah, who is the shining saviour of the universe, veiling his authentic majesty, appeared on earth as a man. The angels proclaimed the good news: a virgin gave birth to the holy one in T'ai Tsing. A shining star announced the blessed event: Persia saw this splendour, and came to pay homage with its gift . . . founding the new ineffable religion, with the Holy Spirit, another person of the Trinity, he gave man the capacity to do good through the true faith. Instituting the rule of the eight precepts, he extricated the world from sensuality and rendered it pure. Opening wide the gate of the three virtues, he introduced life and overcame death.

He ordained baptism in water and the Spirit, which removed the vain pomp of the world and purified it so that it recovered a perfect whiteness. His ministers carry the cross as a seal, which spreads his influence in the four regions of the world and brings together everything without distinction . . . They meet seven times a day to worship and praise, they offer their prayers for the living and the dead. Once, every seven days, they have a bloodless sacrifice.

In the kingdom of the great Ts'ing, there is a man of great virtue called Alopen who, attracted by the shining cloud, brought the holy books; and perceiving the harmony of the zephyrs, he faced the difficulties of the voyage. On the ninth of the years of Tcheng-Koan (636), he arrived at Tch-ang-ngan. The emperor sent the great minister, the lord Fang Huien-Ling, at the head of an escort, to the western suburb, to greet the visitor and introduce him. The books were translated in the rooms of the library; the doctrine was examined in the reserved precinct; its rightness and truth were fully understood, and a special edict gave permission to preach and teach it . . .

the Great, but this was only the temporal aspect of another institution, the church, whose universalism remained when that of the empire disappeared. Of course we must not forget the other empire, that of Constantine, the Byzantine empire which thought that it alone was legitimate and universal. However, when Christendom asserted itself, Byzantium went into irreversible decline.

While evangelization took place at close quarters, the new Christians sought to integrate themselves into a nearby religious and cultural grouping which attracted them, but could things be the same when the gospel was proclaimed at the other end of the world to people caught up in other universalisms? Was the Roman heritage attractive to a Mongol, a Chinese or an Indian? These were all questions which Europe would raise when it organized missions for evangelization in distant lands. Certainly from the beginnings of Christianity there were Christians outside Europe, but they were suspect, regarded by the West as heretics or schismatics. Every time the Christians of Europe encountered them, it would be in an attempt to force them to follow the Latin model.

3
Evangelization in the Period of Christendom (Eleventh to Fourteenth Centuries)

Without giving it a precise date, historians put the beginning of Christendom, that form of religious and political society which characterizes the Middle Ages, at the end of the eleventh century. Faith served to cement together a mass of people who otherwise were much compartmentalized in the framework of feudalism. The Christians of Europe did not stop converting those peoples on their frontiers who had remained pagan, particularly in the north. At the same time, this Christendom became aware of itself as a result of the feeling that it was threatened by an enemy, Islam, encircling it from the East to Spain. Frankish knights came to the support of their Spanish brothers in recapturing the country from the infidels who, moreover, were still threatening the Christians of the East. Having illegitimately occupied the Holy Land, these infidels were preventing the faithful from going on pilgrimage to the holy places of the life of Christ. At the bidding of Pope Urban (1095), Christendom armed itself to recapture the holy places; the Crusades had begun. The term 'crusade' denotes far more than the eight expeditions designated crusades. It above all describes a mentality which for centuries was to shape relations between Christians and non-Christians. The crusade, which initially conjures up the violence of holy war, is apparently diametrically opposed to evangelization. However, even in the Crusades, partly because Christians experienced their limitations, a desire for peaceful evangelization gradually made itself felt. By contrast, the crusader mentality lasted through the evangelization enterprises of the time of the great discoveries in the fifteenth and sixteenth centuries, and put the stamp of its ambiguity upon them.

Evangelization and crusade

The neighbourly evangelization which had characterized the first millennium continued throughout the twelfth century. The Hungarians dreamed of the conversion of the Turkish Cumans on the steppes south and east of Kiev, peoples with whom they had some ethnic links. This evangelization also affected the Balkan peoples (Prussia, Lithuania and Estonia), and the Finns in contact with the Germans and Scandinavians. This conversion was difficult, because it was an element of the *Drang nach Osten*, that thrust eastwards by the Germanic populations of the Holy Roman Empire: Christianization was the logical consequence of the conquest. To consolidate it, the rulers called on the services of the military orders created for the defence of the Holy Land. With the Teutonic Knights, among others, evangelization was transformed into crusade and forcible conversion. Though they could not completely prevent this policy of conquest, the Popes of the thirteenth century affirmed the freedom of the new converts and created among them dioceses and archdioceses with direct connections to Rome rather than to Germanic territories. These included the archdiocese of Prussia, Lithuania and Estonia, which in 1255 became the archdiocese of Riga. The establishment of Cistercian and Premonstratensian monasteries was another important element in this evangelization.

The First Crusade had resulted in the capture of Jerusalem by the knights of the West and the formation in Syria-Palestine of Latin states which were to persist with some difficulty for two centuries. Up to the end of the twelfth century, the Latin Christians of Syria-Palestine hardly dreamed of converting Muslims. On the other hand, by virtue of the fact that up to 1187 the Latins controlled pilgrimages to Jerusalem, they came into contact with a mass of Eastern Christian groups, some of which had not accepted the Chalcedonian Definition and were considered heretical, Monophysite or Nestorian; several penetrated the heart of Asia and speculations began on a mysterious Prester John, who was given different abodes, depending on the author. All this explains how the Latins of the time could believe that 'the entire East, overseas, as far as India and Ethiopia, confesses and preaches the name of Christ' (Burchard of Mount Zion, at the end of the thirteenth century). It was thought that while the Muslims dominated these countries, there were not many of them; it was for Eastern Christians who knew their languages and customs to convert them. Thus the essential task of the Latins was to bring Roman unity to the Eastern Christians, so that they could hand on good Christianity to the Muslims. And great efforts were made in this direction; conversations and arguments were aimed at clarifying disputed points of dogma and above all contributing to the acceptance of Roman primacy. At the level of church leaders, this policy had some effect, as with the Maronites, who

from the middle of the twelfth century announced their union with Rome (1141?).

The new perspectives of the thirteenth century

At the end of the twelfth and the beginning of the thirteenth centuries, a number of events were to change the conditions of evangelization.

The vicissitudes of the Crusades and the formation of the mendicant orders

In 1187, with the capture of Jerusalem by Saladin, the Latins lost a meeting-place with the Eastern Christians. In 1204 the Crusaders captured Constantinople, pillaged it, and installed in it a Latin empire which was to last until 1261. The event hardly helped to encourage closer relations with the Greek church, but it opened up the Black Sea to the West. The religious significance of the Crusades became somewhat blurred. Rather than counting solely on the establishment of a Christian power, the preachers of the gospel took the initiative of following the routes of traders and explorers in the steppes of Asia. The mendicant orders, which came into being at the beginning of the thirteenth century, were to provide a personnel more suited for evangelization. The Order of Preachers (Dominicans) and the Minorites (Franciscans) were not tied to a land which they were to cultivate, as were the old orders. The options of occasional work or begging left them complete freedom of movement. Reference to the *vita apostolica* (the apostolic life) was not only a moral and ascetic appeal, as in the past, but also an apostolic concern to preach the gospel. From the beginning, we can find the 'missionary' dimension in the two founders. Before preaching in Languedoc, Dominic had wanted to evangelize the pagans in northern Europe. When the Order of Preachers was confirmed by the Pope in 1217, Dominic thought of going to convert the Prussians; he grew a beard to indicate his decision. In his place, he sent Hungarian brothers to evangel-

Francis of Assisi preaches the gospel to the Sultan of Egypt

Having tried several times to reach the Saracens, Francis finally succeeded in gaining an audience with the Sultan of Egypt, when he accompanied the Fifth Crusade. The encounter of the two men is surrounded by legend, but the texts are a good indication of the mentality of the times.

Francis was stopped by the guards even before reaching the Sultan. Blows were rained on him but he did not murmur; he was threatened with death, but he was not troubled; torture was promised, but he was unmoved. Having been the butt of so much hatred, he was finally received with much courtesy by the Sultan, who gave him all the signs of favour and offered him numerous presents to try to deflect his soul towards the riches of the world. However, on noting that Francis energetically rejected all these things he remained astounded, regarding him as an extraordinary man; he heard him readily and was moved by his word. But here again the Lord refused to hear the desires of the saint (martyrdom).

(Thomas of Celano, *Vita Prima*, 20, 57)

The Sultan asked him a new question: 'Your Lord has taught you in his Gospels that you should not render evil for evil and should also give up your cloak . . . Then surely Christians should not invade my states?'

The saint replied: 'You do not seem to have read the whole of the gospel of our Lord the Christ; for it is said elsewhere, "If your eye offends you, tear it out and throw it far from you . . ." So he wished to teach us by that that there is no one so dear to us nor parent so close to us as our eye is precious to us, and that if this seems to distract us from the faith and love of Our Lord, we must separate ourselves from it, tear it out and throw it far from us. That is why Christians have been right to invade the countries you occupy, because you have blasphemed in the name of Christ and have deterred from his worship all those you have been able to. But if you want to know our Creator and Our Redeemer, confess them and pay homage to them, Christians will cherish you as they cherish one another.' All those present wondered at his replies.

(The account of Brother Illuminus who accompanied Francis, reported by St Bonaventure, minister general of the order from 1256 to 1274)

---

ize the Cumans; departures of Preachers for the north and east increased during the thirteenth century. And while Francis of Assisi wanted the Minorites, in their travels, to devote themselves to moral preaching throughout Christendom, he also wanted them to preach the gospel to the pagans, and more specifically to the Muslims. Francis himself was often personally involved, particularly in the Fifth Crusade.

Some missionary enterprises in the first part of the thirteenth century

The Cumans, pagan shamanists, who for a long time carried out raids on the Russians and Hungarians, were defeated by the Mongols (Tartars) in 1222. They put themselves under the protection of the Hungarians, who advanced in the direction of Kiev. Now the Dominican province of Hungary had been founded in 1221. The Preaching Brothers were then sent to evangelize the Cumans. Several of them were martyred, but in 1227 Bort, the duke of the Cumans, asked for baptism, and his subjects followed him by the thousand. Pope Gregory IX then designated Brother Thierry, prior of the Dominicans, 'bishop of the Cumans', directly attached to the Holy See (1228). This was a mission territory the eastern limits of which had not been specified. The Hungarian Dominicans wanted to set these limits in the upper valley of the Volga, to convert the inhabitants of Greater Hungary, from where the Hungarians originated. These difficult expeditions

Francis of Assisi, unable to go to Morocco in person, asked some of his brothers to go there in 1220.

When the brothers saw the Saracens assemble they began to preach to them with much impetuosity. On one occasion, when Brother Bérard was preaching to the people from a cart, the king Miramolin passed by the place on his way to visit the tombs of the kings outside the walls. He was struck with amazement at seeing the brother preach and thought that he was mad; the brother refused to interrupt his preaching, whereupon the king ordered the five brothers to be expelled from the city and to be taken immediately by the Christians to the country of the infidels. Don Pedro, leader of the sultan's auxiliaries, gave them some of his servants to guide them towards the country of the Christians. But these five brothers sent them back on the way and returned to Morocco; they re-entered the city and immediately began to preach again to the Saracens gathered in the market place. On hearing this news, the king ordered that they should be shut up in a prison where they remained twenty days without food or drink, and where they had nothing to sustain them but divine consolations . . .

Hardly had they been freed than they wanted to preach the word of God to the Saracens again; however, for fear of the king the Christians did not allow this, and gave them guides charged with taking them back to the country of the faithful. But the brothers sent them back on the way and returned to Morocco. The Christians then took counsel and the above-mentioned Don Pedro shut them up in his house under guard to prevent them from appearing in public . . . One Friday they succeeded in escaping by an unsuspected passage and had the audacity to present themselves to the king when he went to visit the tombs of the kings. Brother Bérard climbed on a cart and began to preach fearlessly in the presence of the king . . . Since the king found that they persevered in the Catholic faith which they confessed and proclaimed it intrepidly, anathematizing the iniquities of Mahomet and his law, he was furious and ordered that various tortures should be inflicted on them and that they should be scourged cruelly . . . All night they were kept under guard, tortured and cruelly scourged by about twenty Saracens.

The next day, when they refused to recant, the king, in a fury, took a sword and separated the saints, and split their heads one after the other: three times he plunged the sword into their brains and thus put them to death by his own hand with the cruelty of a wild beast. They accomplished their martyrdom on the seventeenth day of the calends of February, in the year of the Lord 1220.

(*Chronicle of the Twenty-Five Generals*)

came to nothing. The Mongols attacked westwards; overrun, the Cumans all asked for baptism so that they could take refuge in Hungary. However, since they had not been thoroughly converted, they caused trouble, and a mission within the country had to be organized.

Though they did not have conclusive military results, the Crusades made better religious knowledge of the East possible. The Fifth Crusade, in particular, in 1217–1221, reopened prospects of evangelization. In his *History of the East*, Jacques de Vitry, preacher of the Crusade and then bishop of Acre (1216–1228), gives a detailed description of all the religious groups in the Holy Land and also mentions others of which he has heard: many heretics and even the Saracens would be converted if sound doctrine were preached to them. In the Latin states he himself preached to the Muslims; by letters he urged their leaders to convert; in Egypt he ransomed young children in order to baptize them. Another crusading preacher, Olivier of Cologne (beginning of the thirteenth century), developed an apologetic of Christianity which was based on the Qur'an.

In 1217 the Minorites founded a province in the Holy Land and began to preach to the Muslims. Francis of Assisi, who followed the Fifth Crusade, succeeded in meeting the Sultan. He received Francis well but did not accept the theological debate Francis asked for (1219). The Friars Minor had their first martyrs in Morocco (1220). It has to be said that it was not enough for them to preach Jesus Christ; they thought that insults to Muhammad were essential to Christian preaching. In fact it was impossible to preach in public in Muslim countries, even if the religious could circulate as freely as the merchants. Some planned to bring spiritual help to Christians who were prisoners of the Saracens; new religious orders were founded with the aim of ransoming prisoners: Trinitarians (1198), Mercedarians (1218).

Thus the Latins gradually came to evangelize Muslims and pagans themselves, without leaving this task only to the Eastern Christians. For this purpose Dominicans were sent to Tiflis (1239), to the Georgians who had recognized the Roman primacy. Several popes continued to aim at winning over Muslim leaders to the Christian faith; in 1233, Gregory IX sent Franciscans to different rulers, to the sultans of Konya, Damascus, Aleppo, Cairo, to the Caliph of Baghdad and to the 'miramolin' of Morocco. The religious carried letters containing an exposition of the Christian faith and an invitation to conversion. This approach was not very successful. In 1238 Dominicans and Franciscans were again sent 'into the countries of the pagans and the Saracens overseas, for the conversion of the pagans'. The limited success of this direct evangelization was to lead to the reactivation of the policy of attaching Eastern churches to Rome. The union of the Maronites, in principle established in the twelfth century, only became definitive at the end of the thirteenth. In 1199, the Armenians living in Cilicia (Lesser Armenia) formed a vassal kingdom of the Holy See. The Catholicos, leader of the Armenian church, recog-

nized his direct dependence on Rome, though discussions on dogma and liturgy continued. Other approaches resulted in what was often a formal union with Rome of many church authorities, Jacobites, Copts or Chaldaeans. The desire to evangelize in all its many dimensions really blossomed with Innocent IV. Convening a council at Lyons in 1245, the Pope addressed an encyclical to the prelates of the whole world; Franciscans and Dominicans left as ambassadors to the 'patriarchs, archbishops and bishops in the countries of the Bulgars, Valaks, Khazars, Slavs, Serbs, Alains, Ziks, Goths, Iberians, Georgians, Armenians, Nubians, Nestorians and other Christians of the East'. The Pope called on them to return to unity with Rome, assuring them that he would not infringe their dignity; at the same time he commended his envoys to the Muslim rulers through whose states they would travel, a further occasion for inviting them to convert. Some were sent as far as the Mongols, whose devastating invasions were sowing terror at the same time as they seemed to open up new prospects for evangelization.

The Mongol invasions

It was at the time of the Fifth Crusade (1221) that Christians first heard of the Mongols. It was said that they were Christians and that they had destroyed a number of Muslim kingdoms. So it was hoped to involve them in the Crusades. Disenchantment came when they ravaged the Ukraine and advanced into the heart of Europe (they were defeated by the Hungarians in 1241). This destroyed a number of fields of evangelization, since not only Muslim states but also Christian states fell under their domination: Kiev in Russia, Georgia, Armenia, among others. All Christendom felt threatened, and a crusade was then preached against the Mongols. Pope Innocent IV sought 'a remedy against the Tartars' (another name for the Mongols), and this was one of the objectives of the Council of Lyons (1245). He decided to send ambassadors to the Mongol leaders to call on them to

Exchange of correspondence between a Pope and a Mongol khan

Pope Innocent IV sent a letter to Khan Güyük through his ambassador, John of Plano Carpini, in which he asked the Tartars to explain their destructive conduct and called on them to repent. The naivety of the Pope is matched by the arrogance of the Khan, who thinks that he has a divine mission.

Innocent, bishop, servant of the servants of God, to the great king of the Tartars.

We are surprised to learn that you have invaded and devastated a number of Christian and other countries, and that you continue to strike neighbouring nations with your bloody hands, forgetful of the natural bonds of affinity which unite all human beings, regardless of sex or age. You raise the sword of anger against all indiscriminately.

Following the example of the King of Peace, we desire that humanity should live in peace in the fear of God. Consequently, we advise you, beg you and exhort you to renounce new invasions, to abstain quite specifically from persecuting Christians and, having so offended the divine Majesty and having indubitably provoked his wrath, to expiate your crimes by just penitence . . .

We send our beloved son John (of Plano Carpini) and his companions . . . Let us know clearly what you think of our message, and what you have decided with our envoys on the matter of our peace proposals. Tell us the reasons which have led you to massacre the nations bordering on your territory and finally your plans for the future.

Given in Lyons, 13 March 1245

Güyük's reply

In the power of the eternal heaven, we the Oceanic Khan of the whole people hereby issue our order.

This is an order sent to the great Pope in order that he may know and understand it . . . You have sent us a call for submission which we have heard from your ambassadors. If you act according to your own words, you who are the great Pope, do you come in person with the kings to pay homage to us, and we will lead you to understand the orders resulting from the law. Furthermore, you have said that it would be good for me to receive baptism; you have told me this yourself, and sent me a request. We have not understood your request.

In the power of God, we have conquered all the territories from the rising to the setting sun. How could this be done but through the order of God? Now you must say with a sincere heart: 'We will be your subjects, we will give your our strength.' You in person, at the head of the kings, all together without exception, must come to offer us service and homage. Then we shall recognize your submission. And if you do not observe the divine order, and contravene our orders, you will know that you are our enemies.

(John of Plano Carpini, *History of the Mongols*)

---

cease their destruction and convert to Christianity. The best known of these papal delegations was that of the Franciscan John of Plano Carpini, who left Lyons in 1246. He reached the Great Khan Güyük and was present at his coronation in the heart of Mongolia (August 1246). However, the Mongol leader had no interest in conversion and called for the Pope's submission to him. John, who returned to the Pope the next year, was not very optimistic, but the Franciscan brought better knowledge of the Mongols: there were Christians in the Mongol empire, even if the majority were pagan; their conversion could make them allies against Islam. Furthermore Sartak, son of Batu, the Khan of the Golden Horde (Russia), had received baptism. On learning this, the holy King Louis, from the Holy Land, sent the Franciscan William of Rubruck to congratulate the prince on his conversion; in a

Ecumenical dialogue at the Court of Mangu Khan

The Franciscan William of Rubruck was sent by the French king Louis IX as ambassador to the court of the Great Khan of the Mongols at Karakorum in 1253–1255. The king organized a contradictory inter-religious dialogue.

The khan sent me his secretaries, who told me: 'Your master sends us to you knowing that you here are Christians, Saracens and Tuinans [*an Asian religion, for Rubruck the equivalent of pagan*]. Each of you says that his law is the best and that his scriptures, i.e. his books, are the truest. For this reason, he would like you all to assemble in the same place and for each to write his articles of faith so that he can know the truth.' Then I said, 'I am ready without hatred and fear to give an account of the faith and hope of Christians to anyone who wishes to question me.' . . . The Nestorians were also ordered to write all that they wanted to say, as were the Saracens and Tuinans. The next day the secretary returned, saying: 'Mangu Khan wants to know why you are passing through these countries.' I told them, 'The duty imposed by our religion is to preach the gospel to all men.'

The eve of Pentecost arrived. The Nestorians wrote a history from the creation of the world to the passion of the Christ, and after the passion they said some things about the ascension and the resurrection of the dead and the last judgment . . . We wrote the creed of the mass, 'I believe in one God.' Then I asked them how they wanted to proceed. They replied that they first wanted to discuss with the Saracens. I told them that this was not a good thing, since the Saracens recognize with us that there is only one God: "You will gain help from this side," I said, against the Tuinans . . .'

The conference discusses the oneness of God, then goes on to the origin of evil . . . The moment comes to say farewell:

On the day of Pentecost, Mangu Khan made me his profession of faith: 'We believe that there is only one God by whom we live and die, and for him we have an upright heart.' Then I said to him, 'May God grant you this grace, for without it you can do nothing.' The prince added: 'Just as God has given the hand many fingers, so he has given man many ways. God has made known to you the holy scriptures, and you others, Christians, do not observe them. Surely you do not think that one should censure another?' 'No, Sir,' I said, 'but I have told you from the start that I did not want to have differences with anyone.' 'I am not speaking for you,' he said. 'Similarly, you would not think that a man should renounce justice for money?' 'No, Sir,' I replied. 'God has given you a Testament,' he said, 'and you do not follow us; he has given us soothsayers; we do what they say and we live in peace.' It seemed to me that he drank at least four times before the end of the conversation. And as I waited to see if he wanted to confess any other point of his faith, he began to speak of my return.

(*Travels of William of Rubruck in the East*)

---

mission which lasted for two years (1253–1255), William reached Karakorum and met the Great Khan Mongka. He took part in religious discussions. While the Mongols were tolerant, they remained sceptical. Rubruck brought some spiritual relief to Christians who had been deported into the Mongol empire and got to know Chaldaean or Nestorian Christians better. As well as envoys, many other Europeans reached the Far East: mercenaries, interpreters, officials in Mongol service, and merchants like the two Polo brothers and their son and nephew Marco, who brought a message to the Pope from Khan Kublai, asking him to send one hundred trained men capable of showing that the Christian law was better than that of the Mongols (1269). However, Kublai, who became emperor of China in 1280, opted for Buddhism, the religion of his new subjects, while other Mongol rulers hesitated between Islam and Christianity. Be this as it may, the Mongol conquest had changed the conditions of evangelization.

The birth of a missionary doctrine and organization

The Mongol invasion helped evangelization in several ways, at least after a return to a relative peace. In the religious sphere the Mongols were tolerant; the preachers of all religions could express themselves freely; it became possible for Christians to address Muslims publicly. The disappearance of the Latin states of Palestine had thus been compensated for, as far as missionaries were concerned, by the vast field of evangelization provided by the Mongol empire. Although very soon this empire was divided into several khanates, the circulation of merchants and preachers throughout Asia was greatly facilitated. Furthermore, the Christians of the West acquired a better idea of the extent of the pagan world and a better knowledge of the Eastern Christians whom they wanted to be associated with Rome. Envoys from the Khan were received at the Council of Lyons in 1274, and several of them received baptism then. In 1288, a Chaldaean bishop who came from Peking, Bar Kauma, was entrusted by the Mongol Khan of Persia with an embassy to Rome. After a solemn reception by Pope Nicholas IV, exchanges resulted in the recognition of Roman primacy by the Chaldaean church, and recognition of the authority of the Catholicos of Baghdad. Despite some conversions of Mongol princes, hope had to be abandoned of making this people a Christian nation and recovering the Holy Land through them. In 1295, the Mongols of Persia opted to embrace Islam. Despite these political disappointments, and perhaps because of them, missionary doctrine and organization were made more specific in the course of the thirteenth and fourteenth centuries. Although both aspects are closely linked, I shall treat them separately here for the sake of clarity.

A missionary doctrine

During the period of Christendom, evangelization of distant places was essentially the work of the mendicant orders. As one of them remarked, it was a duty to go to convert the pagans, and not to shrink from the possibility of martyrdom, since Jesus had said, 'Behold, I send you as sheep among wolves.' Several times, when volunteers were asked for among the Dominicans, many presented themselves in tears, particularly during the 'Chapter of Tears' convened by the Master General of the Dominicans, Humbert of Romans (1255). In 1245, the Cistercians decided that the monks should recite seven psalms a day and the laity seven Pater Nosters 'for the Preaching Brothers and Minorites whom the Lord Pope has sent to the most distant lands for matters of faith'.

Several writers from the mendicant orders wrote treatises on missionary method. In various works Humbert of Romans developed a programme for evangelization: there was a need to write treatises which provided missionaries with arguments for converting 'the barbaric nations, the pagans, the Saracens, the Jews, the heretics, the schismatics and others who are outside the church'. Some of St Thomas Aquinas's works look like responses to the desires of the Master General: *Summa against the Gentiles, Against the Errors of the Greeks, The Arguments of Faith against the Saracens, the Greeks and the Armenians*. In an encyclical of 1255, Humbert touches on the question of teaching languages to religious chosen to be evangelists. For this, they need to be sent to countries near to their field of apostolic activity. To prepare for the Council of Lyons (1274), in a work entitled *The State of the Saracens*, the Dominican William of Tripoli, who had lived in the Holy Land for a long time, suggested training for religious missionaries. They had to learn the languages of those whom they were evangelizing, reject force, avoid public controversies and not incur martyrdom for gratuitous provocations; they had to know Islam and base themselves on the Qur'an. Another Dominican,

To refute Islam, it is necessary to know the Qur'an

During a tour of Spain, Peter the Venerable (1092–1156), Abbot of Cluny, visited the Cluniac monasteries founded after the progress of the Reconquista. He thought that it was necessary to have an intellectual plan as well as a military plan for combating Islam. Hence the need for a translation of the Qur'an.

Whether one gives the Mohammedan error the shameful name of heresy or the infamous name of paganism, it must be acted against, i.e. written against. However, since the ancient culture has perished, the Latins and above all the moderns, following the word of the Jews who once wondered at the polyglot apostles, do not know any language other than that of their native land. They have not been able to recognize the enormity of this error nor to bar its way. My heart, too, is inflamed and a fire has burned in my meditation. I am indignant at seeing the Latins ignorant of the cause of such perdition, and their ignorance depriving them of the power to resist it; no one responds because no one knows. So I have sought out specialists in the Arabic language which has allowed this mortal poison to infest more than half the globe. I have persuaded them through prayer and money to translate from Arabic into Latin the history and the doctrine of this unfortunate man and his law which they call Qur'an. And so that the translation shall be entirely faithful and no error shall falsify the fullness of our understanding, I have added a Saracen to the Christian translators. Here are the names of the Christians: Robert of Chester, Hermann the Dalmatian and Peter of Toledo; the Saracen is called Mohammed. This team, having thoroughly scoured the libraries of this barbarous people, has derived from them a large book which they have published for Latin readers. This work was done during the year in which I went to Spain, where I had an interview with the Lord Alfonso, victorious emperor of the Spaniards, that is, in the year of the Lord 1141.

(Peter the Venerable)

Ricoldo of Montecroce (1243–1320), composed a kind of manual, *A Brief Treatise for the Nations of the East*, and a *vade-mecum*, *General Rules*, intended for missionaries. In them he said that Jacobites and Nestorians were not to be condemned *a priori*; he advised against preaching through an interpreter. There was a need to know all of scripture; select extracts were not enough; uniformity of rites was not necessary for the unity of faith.

With Raymond Lull (1235–1315), we meet one of the first missiologists. His whole life is an adventure story. He came from Majorca, and led a more than worldly life at the royal court. A gallant and frivolous poet, he married, but at the age of thirty was converted by a vision of Christ on the cross. He became a hermit and then a Franciscan tertiary, but was never ordained priest. He travelled throughout Christendom, in North Africa and the Middle East. In his numerous works Lull is at the same time a philosopher, theologian, linguist, romancer and mystic. However, one great idea unites all aspects of the life of the 'Enlightened Doctor', 'to lead the infidels and unbelievers to the truth of the holy Catholic faith'.

In the land of the *reconquista* Lull thought particularly of the conversion of the Saracens. In his *Treatise on the Manner of Converting the Infidels* (1292) he reflected on conversion and put forward a method. He himself preached to the Saracens in North Africa and died following a stoning while he was preaching at Bougie. In his reflections, he speaks of the crusade as a failure; beyond question God disapproves of it; one could compare it with the holy war of Muhammad. However, he does not exclude the use of force to obtain freedom for preaching, though conversion can only be a free act; it is a 'work of love accomplished with the intelligence'. The preacher of the gospel among the

A programme of missionary training

Raymond Lull (1235–1315), a Franciscan tertiary from Majorca, preached the gospel several times in North Africa. He tried to keep up with preaching methods, emphasizing the importance of knowing the languages of the peoples encountered. However, the Crusader mentality remained.

A list of the different sects opposed to the Catholic faith first needs to be drawn up, and much study is required to come to know the language of the infidels. Such work should be entrusted only to holy and pious men, ready to die for Christ, learned in philosophy and theology, and with well regulated habits. Then they should be sent to preach and discuss among the infidels. Their polemic should use the necessary reasons and arguments, and should also reinforce the doctrine and responses of the faithful. These elements of argument are disseminated in the pages of holy scripture and in many learned authors: writers are needed who are capable of composing treatises based on arguments of this kind and translating them into different languages, so that the infidels can study them and become aware of their errors. Similarly, books need to be written on the errors of the schismatics, who are to be combated by necessary reasons which are easy to find . . . The Pope and his brethren must work hard at this cause of the union of schismatics. Think how much it would help towards gaining victory over the Tartars and the other peoples! A centre of study is to be organized in Rome, the heart of the church, and another in Paris, where science is more honoured than anywhere else. A large number of students flock there who could also initiate themselves in the kind of methods, conceptions and arguments that they will encounter among the infidels. One of these faculties is to be created in Spain because of the Saracens there, one in Genoa and another in Venice, whose citizens in particular travel among the Saracens and the Tartars; others in Prussia, in Hungary, at Capha in Armenia, in Taurus, and in some places favourable to the acquisition of the different languages and to discussion with the infidels. Studies in a Latin sphere are more advisable than among the infidels, for reasons of security, perseverance and the control of those being taught. In these schools, children will also be prepared for knowledge of the languages of the infidels and the desire will be inculcated in them to die for Christ. The Saracens bring up their young people for diabolical ends and worldly vanities. What is extraordinary about Christians bringing up young people for the cause of Christ who was crucified and died for us, who will lavish glory and blessing on the disciples who follow in his footsteps and is also our judge?

(Raymond Lull, *Treatise on Converting the Infidels*, 1292)

Saracens must primarily convince the sages and the intellectuals. He must combine an encyclopaedic knowledge with a method which compels conviction; reason must lead to faith. It is necessary to know the beliefs, customs and philosophy of the area in which one wants to preach. To achieve that, it is imperative to learn the Eastern languages, Arabic, Hebrew, Syriac and Greek, and to found schools for studying them. Lull took up earlier intuitions and systematized them: in the twelfth century Peter the Venerable had had the Qur'an translated, and in the thirteenth century the Dominican Raymond Martin had been a remarkable specialist in Arabic. In 1274, Lull secured the establishment of a language college for the Minorites at Miramar, on Majorca. Several times he asked the Popes and universities to create chairs of oriental languages; canon XI of the Council of Vienne (1311) supported him here: it provided for the foundation of five language colleges. But were they actually founded? In his *Request to Celestine V*, Lull is interested in the Tartars: they must be converted by the Eastern Christians associated with Rome. Finally, he suggests that a cardinal should be put in charge of the papal missionary policy.

A rule of life suitable for preachers of the gospel

Honorius III (1216–1227) allowed members of the mendicant orders certain dispensations in the application of their rule to make it easier for them to work in Muslim countries. These exceptional permissions were subsequently generalized.

Honorius, servant of the servants of God, to his dear sons, Preaching Brothers and Minors, sent at the order of the Apostolic See to the kingdom of Morocco, greetings and apostolic blessing.

We have been informed that having voluntarily, at the call of the Apostolic See, exposed yourselves to the greatest of perils for the purpose of assuring the salvation of a large number of people, you have thought it wise to modify your costume to some degree and to wear a beard and long hair, not in order to escape the ferocity of this people which is frenetically unleashed against Christians, but in the hope of being useful to a greater number, to have more freedom to visit the Christians in their torments and to bring them salvation and the sacraments of the church. Since it is not possible for you to obtain your food without payment in the country in which you are, because it is not the custom to give bread to the poor in those countries, but rather money, and since necessity drives you to receive alms, keep the money in your possession and buy supplies and clothing. Since this goes against the precepts of your orders, you are excused from them as by an inevitable necessity, so that you can be of more use to others . . . While you are in these regions, you will be constrained by necessity and utility, so we dispense you with compassion from observing your rule, provided that neither fraud, stratagem or cupidity lead your good faith astray.

Given at the Lateran, 17 March 1226.

A specialized organization

Even if for convenience we tend to talk about 'mission' and 'missionaries' in connection with the proclamation of the gospel, the idea of centralized organizations sending specialists as a particular project appears only during the thirteenth century. Beyond question there was always an element of spontaneity and chance in evangelization. Lay people, merchants, deportees played a role as interpreters and messengers. The goldsmith William Boucher gave Rubruck a good deal of help. The Polo brothers proved useful intermediaries. However, from the thirteenth century on, the evangelization of distant places had become the speciality of the mendicant orders, Dominicans and Minorites; the Master General of the Dominicans or the Minister General of the Franciscans had a policy of evangelization; they designated missionaries and defined a form of training. The papacy addressed the generals responsible when it planned any evangelization. The essential element of training was the study of languages. As we have seen, some language schools were opened in the West; young people from the countries to be evangelized might also be sent to the West to study theology, but more often it was in a house of his order that the missionary was trained in the dialect he was to use.

To begin with, Dominicans and Franciscans designated for evangelization were given a place in the ordinary framework of their orders, in houses nearest to the places of their apostolate, often themselves integrated into provinces. Little by little, however, in both orders a special organization for mission in distant lands was developed. Instead of the traditional houses, local, missionary posts with only a few religious were founded; establishments came to be grouped together in a new way. Among the Minorites, around 1290, mission posts were organized into two vicariates, Aquilonian Tartary (north of the Black Sea) and Eastern Tartary (Asia); a third vicariate, that of Cathay, was detached from the former of these around 1320. The vicars responsible were directly under the Minister General; each vicariate was subdivided into custodies. Organization among the Dominicans was more original. Around 1300 they set up a 'Society of Brothers Peregrinating for Christ among the Nations'; this regrouped brothers sent on missions and elected its vicar general in direct association with the Master General. The Society was dissolved in 1363, but re-established ten years later. For several years the Franciscans also had their own Society of Peregrinants. The regular rules were relaxed for brothers involved in evangelization: they might wear a beard, dress in secular clothing, and have covered shoes instead of sandals, which was appreciated in Central Asia! They might carry money and did not have to celebrate mass regularly. Of course every now and then we come across abuse of these privileges.

The role of the papacy

More significant for the future of evangelization is the beginning of a degree of Roman centralization in this sphere. Though the missionaries were sent by their superiors, this was primarily by the 'decision' or 'permission' of the Apostolic See; the orders were only mandated intermediaries. Furthermore, it was often papal legates in the Holy Land, Greece or Hungary who organized the apostolate among the pagans or non-Catholics. Many missionaries, like John of Monte Corvino, received the powers of a legate. Thus the papacy would seem to have been the linchpin of evangelization: it called for investigations of missions and missionaries; it received the requests of missionaries and passed them on to the superiors of the orders. The Popes gave recommendations to rulers and tried to extract funds for travel and buildings. Without creating a special organization of the kind that Raymond Lull wanted, in 1373 Gregory XI designated a commission of six theologians to respond to questions submitted by 'those who preach the word of God among the infidels, heretics and schismatics'. This ephemeral commission was a foretaste of the Congregation of Propaganda.

There was only a real 'new implantation' of the church when dioceses were formed under a bishop. If a recently converted people had a Christian ruler, the papacy soon recognized the existence of new episcopal sees. In countries in which the majority of the population belonged to Christian churches separated from Rome or were pagans, the situation was quite different. There might be hopes that local prelates would attach themselves to Rome, or Roman Christians might be put under the nearest dioceses on Christian territory. An interim solution was for the Pope to grant a certain number of episcopal prerogatives to the missionaries. These prerogatives above all had legal aspects, which were finally secondary. In the fourteenth century, the Popes of Avignon set up a real missionary episcopate in countries with Muslim or pagan rulers in which Christians were in a tiny minority.

The birth of a missionary episcopate

Out of a complex history, I have selected the three major areas where the church was planted: the archdiocese of Khanbalik in China, the archdiocese of Sultaniyet in Persia, and the settlements north of the Black Sea.

The creation of the archdiocese of Khanbalik (1307)

The first (Latin) evangelization of China is one of the most extraordinary events in the history of mission. Pope Nicholas IV had responded to a new request for missionaries from the Great Khan Qubilaï by sending John of Monte Corvino, from the province of Salerno (1289). John had carried out missions in Armenia and Persia; he left as a legate with pontifical letters destined for different princes and heads of churches; the Mongol princes were invited to become Christians. He set out from Rieti in July 1289, crossed Asia Minor and reached the Persian Gulf; he then stopped in South India where he performed several baptisms and arrived at Khanbalik (Peking) in the last days of 1293. Kublai died in February 1294. His successor, Temür,

48

A Franciscan at Peking (Khanbalik)

John of Monte Corvino, who had left Italy sixteen years previously (1689), finally gives his news.

From Khanbalik, in the kingdom of Cathay, 8 January 1305.

I, Brother John of Monte Corvino, of the order of the Friars Minor, in the year of the Lord 1291, left the city of Tauris, in Persia, and went into India. I stayed in this country and in the church of the apostle St Thomas for thirteen months and here and there baptized around one hundred persons... Resuming my journey, I reached Cathay, the kingdom of the emperor of the Tartars, who is called the Great Khan. Delivering to the said emperor the letter of the Lord Pope, I preached the law of our Lord Jesus Christ. The emperor himself is too rooted in his idolatry, but he is full of goodwill towards Christians. I have been with him for twelve years.

The Nestorians who claim the title of Christians but are far removed from the Christian religion have gained such power in these regions that they do not allow a Christian of another profession to have even the smallest oratory or to preach any doctrine other than their own. No apostle or disciple of an apostle has come to these parts. So it was that the Nestorians, and others whom they hired with money, launched the gravest persecutions against me, claiming that I had not been sent by the Pope but was a spy, a magician and an impostor... This lasted for five years.

Isolated in this distant peregrination, I was eleven years without confession, until the arrival of Brother Arnold, a German from the province of Cologne, who has been here two years. Six years ago I finished building a church in the city of Khanbalik, adding to it a campanile with three bells. In it, I think, I have baptized almost 6,000 persons, and but for the campaign of calumny which I have mentioned, I would have baptized 30,000. I am often busy administering baptism. I have also bought, one by one, forty pagan children between seven and twelve years of age. As yet they know no law; I have baptized them and taught them Latin letters and our worship. I have transcribed psalters for them, with thirty hymn books and two breviaries. Eleven of them already know our office; they sing in our choir as in a convent, whether I am present or not; several of them are transcribing psalters and other useful things. The emperor takes great pleasure in hearing them sing. I ring the bells for each hour and celebrate the divine office with them.

A king of these regions, of the sect of the Christian Nestorians, and who was of the race of the great king called Prester John of India, joined me in the year following my arrival here and was led by me to the truth of the true faith; from me he received minor orders. Clothed in sacred vestments, he serves mass for me, to the point that the Nestorians accuse him of apostasy; nevertheless, he has led a large part of his people to the Catholic faith. He is building a fine church worthy of his munificence as king.

I beg you, brothers whom this letter may reach, to see that its content is brought to the attention of our Lord the Pope, the cardinals and the procurator of our order at the Roman court. Of our minister general I ask alms of an antiphonary and readings from the lives of the saints, a gradual and a psalter with notation to serve as a model for us.

At the moment I am in process of building a new church to share with children in many places. I am getting old and my hair is quite white, not through age (I am only fifty-eight) but through fatigue and worries. I have learned to speak and write Tartar, the customary language of the Mongols, reasonably; I have translated the whole of the New Testament and the Psalter into this language. I have had them transcribed in superb calligraphy and I show them, I read them, preach them and make them known publicly as a testimony to the law of Christ.

proved well disposed to the Franciscan but was not interested in Christianity. John of Monte Corvino converted several thousand people, and built churches and a monastery in which he installed young

A letter from Peregrine of Castello, Bishop of Zaitun (Ch'uan-Chou), 18 December 1318

Peregrine is one of the bishops sent by Clement V to consecrate John of Monte Corvino Archbishop of Peking. At the beginning of his letter he takes up what we know from John of Monte Corvino. However, he is much less optimistic.

For all the Christians (of different languages and races) we can preach and administer the sacraments of the church. As for the infidels, we can preach freely and we have preached several times in the mosques of the Saracens to convert them; similarly for the idolaters in their great cities, through two interpreters . . . The harvest is abundant but we brothers are few, very old, and incapable of learning languages. I have become bishop of Zaitun; with three pious brothers I can rest peacefully and with tranquillity in God . . . In the city of Zaitun we have a good church with land which an Armenian lady left us . . . We need nothing so much as the brothers whom we desire. Brother Gerard, the bishop, is dead, and as for the rest of us brothers, we cannot live long and no others have come. The church will have no baptisms and no congregation . . . The great city of Zaitun where we are is on the sea; it is almost three months' journey from the great city of Khanbalik.

all Franciscans without any particular title when they set out. The six were given episcopal consecration and left for China. Of the six, only three arrived in Khanbalik in 1313. However, they were enough to consecrate John archbishop. The suffragans took up residence in southern China at Zaitun (Chu'an-Chou), where an Armenian benefactor had built a church and convent; the three bishops quickly succeeded one another there, Gerard Albuini, Peregrine of Castello and Andrew of Pérouse. We know about the life of the Christian community through letters from these bishops and from the travel account which the Franscican Odoric of Pordenone wrote between 1318 and 1330. It would be better to speak of several communities: a certain number of Tartars (Mongols) and Chinese were converted; the Nestorians came over to Rome and John of Monte Corvino provided a Latin liturgy translated into their own language for them.

There were also survivors of the Alans, a Christian people from the Caucasus who had been deported to the Far East by the Mongols; Armenians; other Eastern Christians; and some Latins, for example Italian merchants. It seems that the majority of Christians were expatriates rather than indigenous Chinese, whom the French could not address: Peregrine tells us of his inability to learn Latin. We can understand the fragility of this church.

John of Monte Corvino died shortly after 1330. Pope John XXII learned of his death in September 1333 and nominated a successor, but we do not know whether he reached Khanbalik. A new request from the Khan and Christians prompted the sending of an embassy by Pope Benedict XII. Led by the Franciscan John of Marignolli, it took a voyage of fourteen years (1338–1352) to get there. The gift of a 'heavenly horse' (a large horse) to the Great Khan from the Pope made a deep impression on Khanbalik. Another ambassador was nominated in 1370, but the Christian community in China disappeared right at the beginning of the fifteenth century in obscure circumstances. Several factors might explain this disappearance. The church did

slaves whom he had ransomed. He met Nestorians who caused him a good deal of trouble, but succeeded in winning over a prince of this confession to the Roman church. The only priest, and harassed by his task, John asked for help from the West in a letter of 1305 in which he recounted his sixteen years of apostolic peregrinations.

Amazed at such results, Pope Clement V established Khanbalik as an archidocese with John as its first archbishop; the archdiocese covered the whole Tartar empire, virtually the whole of Asia beyond the Levant. John was given six suffragan bishops, not have enough human resources to subsist by itself without new support from Europe; the overthrow of the Mongol dynasty in China in 1368 and its replacement by the Chinese Ming dynasty could explain why Christians fell out of favour, but even more, the conversion to Islam of the khans of Djagataï cut Khanbalik off from the West. The diocese of Almaligh in Djagatai, created around 1320 and dependent on Khanbalik, had a difficult existence. In 1339 the bishop of Almaligh and a number of religious and Christians were martyred by a Muslim khan.

The archdiocese of Sultaniyet (1318)

It took time for people in Europe to understand that the Mongols were no longer a single empire under the rule of the Great Khan who resided in Khanbalik. Pope John XXII was impressed by several writings, including *On How to Exterminate the Saracens*, written by the Dominican William Adam. Adam, who had travelled in Persia, in the Indian Ocean and in Ethiopia, stated: 'We who are true Christians are not a tenth, nor even a twentieth part of humankind.' This prompted the Pope in 1318 to create the archdiocese of Sultaniyet, the capital of the Mongol khans of Persia. The new province was entrusted to the Dominicans, who thought that the Franciscans were monopolizing missionary responsibilities in Asia. The jurisdiction of the new archbishop extended over the khanates of Persia and Djagataï, India and Ethiopia. Six bishops consecrated by the Pope left to give episcopal consecration to the first archbishop, Francon of Pérouse, vicar of the Society of Peregrinating Brothers. The convents of the preachers were the basis of diocesan and metropolitan organization; the bishops of the province had to ensure the continuity of the institution by electing a successor after the death of the archbishop and giving him the pallium, the special insignia of white wool embroidered with black crosses, of his predecessor. The archbishop organized his province, dividing it between the suffragans and providing for their replacement. It seems that these procedures were not perfectly followed, since several times the Pope himself had to designate new bishops at the request of the religious of the province. Vacancies in the see of Sultaniyet were also quite frequent.

The first six suffragan bishops were distributed over Azerbaijan and Georgia. Other dioceses were founded later, like Samarkand (Djagataï) and Quilon (India) in 1329. Bishops and missionaries of the vast province planned, as in the other Mongol territories, to bring the khans to the Christian faith, to convert the more or less nomadic pagan peoples, and to unite the Eastern Christians with Rome. Despite the adherence of some khans to Christianity, Islam won the day; the hopes of Christian dynasties and mass conversions had to be abandoned. It is worth noting a few significant events and persons who played an important role.

The Italian Dominican Thomas of Mancasola, who had been transferred to the Society of Peregrinants because of disobedience, proved particularly active. He established Christianity in Samarkand, converted Eldigidaï, the khan of Djagataï, who built a church dedicated to John the Baptist, and sent the Dominican as an envoy to John XXII. He designated Thomas bishop of Samarkand (1329).

Another illustration of evangelization: India, where Christianity had been established from antiquity, was dependent on Sultaniyet. For the Latins, India was a stage on the route to Cathay (China). Four Franciscans and a Dominican, Jordan of Cathala, stopped at Thana, near Bombay, in 1321; they addressed the Chaldaean Christians (Nestorians). The Franciscans, led by Thomas of Tolentino, became involved in a debate with the Muslims and, as was usual in such cases, not only tried to prove the divinity of Christ but insulted Muhammad, which led to their being martyred. The Dominican remained in India; the difficulty of preaching to the pagans led him to settle on the Malabar coast where the local Christians, and itinerant merchants, lacked spiritual support. Filled with hope, Jordan returned to Europe to seek reinforcements in 1328. In Avignon he recounted his travels and missionary experience in a work *The Wonders of Asia*. John XXII thereupon decided to establish a see at Quilon in southern India, with Jordan as its first incumbent.

The Dominicans of Sultaniyet gained further distinction in trying to bring the Armenians of Greater Armenia over to Rome; they spoke in particular to monks. The union of Qrnai was proclaimed in 1330, named after a monastery in which the monks, who were very interested in Latin thought, founded the congregation of the Uniting Brothers attached to the Dominican Order. They had considerable influence for some decades, but their zeal in Latinizing – they practised rebaptism – rebounded against them in the 1380s.

Evangelization north of the Black Sea and the Caucasus

After the Mongol invasion, the countries north of the Black Sea came under the khanate of the Golden Horde. The announcement of the conversion of Sartak, which was the origin of the mission of William Rubruck, aroused many hopes. In 1287 the Franciscans instituted the custody of Gazaria in the Crimea, which was controlled by a Hungarian, Ladislas. The progress of Christianity made reinforcements seem desirable, preferably Englishmen or Germans, who had a better aptitude for the study of languages. Franciscans organized themselves into mobile communities on waggons and followed the nomads as they moved around. The religious succeeded in converting Khan Toqtaï and his family in 1311; the ruler died the next year in the Franciscan habit, and he was spoken of as 'blessed brother John'. However, in 1342 the dynasty of the Golden Horde definitively passed over to Islam.

The Italian traders who had settled around the Black Sea – Kaffa, in the Crimea, was a veritable Genoan city – provided support for the missionaries. However, as always, customs did not follow faith. The Genoese made their fortunes by trading in slaves, which they acquired in the Caucasus and sold throughout the Mediterranean; Popes and bishops had great difficulties in ensuring that Christians were not sold to Muslims. John XXII and his successors created several dioceses in the region: in 1318, Kaffa in the Crimea and Saraï on the Volga (which became an archdiocese in 1362). An inhabitant of the Ziquia (the east coast of the Black Sea), who had been carried off to Genoa as a slave and became a Franciscan under the name of John of Ziquia, returned to evangelize his native country with considerable success; in 1349 the Pope nominated him Archbishop of Matrega on the Black Sea.

Stocktaking of an era

At the beginning of the fifteenth century, evangelization of distant lands had undoubtedly slackened. However, for Archbishop John III of Sultaniyet, who in 1404 wrote a work the title of which one could translate as *Survey of the World*, the situation was not desperate: he lists all the places where Christians were present, from distant Cathay to Ethiopia, passing through the vast lands of the Mongols. Still, although he agreed to become ambassador to Europe for Tamberlaine (1336–1405), the leader of the Mongol clan whose expeditions were ravaging Central Asia, Asia Minor and Russia, he could not help noting the irremediable devastations of the conqueror of Samarkand in the last years of the fourteenth century: Christians massacred or reduced to slavery, churches destroyed, journeys in Asia made impossible. Fifty years later, the thrust of the Ottoman Turks made the shores of the Black Sea inaccessible.

Furthermore, these distant missions always needed men to go on them. The Franciscans and Dominicans to whom they were entrusted were only a handful for the vast territories, and an epidemic like that of the Black Death in the middle of the fourteenth century carried off almost all the religious in the province of Sultaniyet. In these conditions, the arrangements made by the papacy for these 'new plantings' to be self-sufficient did not work; reinforcements were constantly called for from the Apostolic See.

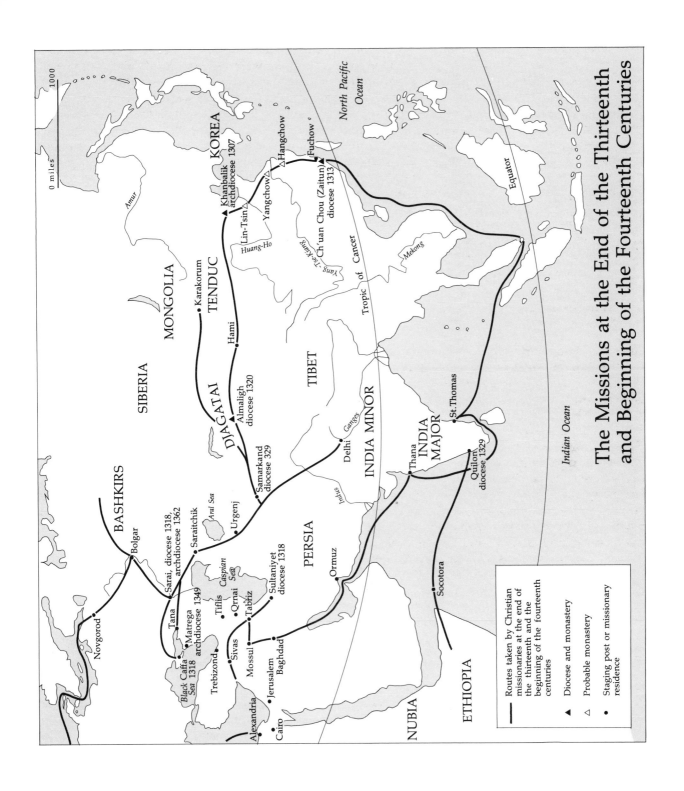

The Missions at the End of the Thirteenth and Beginning of the Fourteenth Centuries

Legend:
— Routes taken by Christian missionaries at the end of the thirteenth and the beginning of the fourteenth centuries
▲ Diocese and monastery
△ Probable monastery
• Staging post or missionary residence

Place labels on map:

1000
0 miles

North Pacific Ocean

Amur

KOREA

Khanbalik archdiocese 1307

Karakorum

TENDUC

Lin-Tsin

Yangchow △

△ Hangchow

Fuchow

Ch'uan Chou (Zaitun) diocese 1313

Huang-Ho

Yang-Tsï-Kiang

Mekong

Tropic of Cancer

Hami

MONGOLIA

SIBERIA

DJAGATAI

Almaligh diocese 1320

TIBET

Equator

Samarkand diocese 329

Urgenj

Aral Sea

BASHKIRS

Saraitchik

Sarai, diocese 1318, archdiocese 1362

Bolgar

Ganges

Delhi

INDIA MINOR

St.Thomas

INDIA MAJOR

Thana

Quilon diocese 1329

Indus

PERSIA

Ormuz

Matrega archdiocese 1349

Tana

Caspian Sea

Tiflis

Qrnai

Tabriz

Sultaniyet diocese 1318

Novgorod

Black Sea

Caffa 1318

Trebizond

Sivas

Mossul

Jerusalem

Baghdad

Alexandria

Cairo

NUBIA

ETHIOPIA

Socotora

Indian Ocean

The bold policy of establishing ecclesiastical provinces in countries in which the majority were not Christians is to be attributed to the Avignon Popes. We need to recognize that they did some good things! However, the policy was difficult to maintain, not only because of the lack of personnel but even more because the Latin dioceses were often competing with the Eastern churches and the quest for unity was not without ambiguity; the Latins were not content with trying to obtain recognition for the Roman primacy, but also wanted to Latinize rites and customs.

If hardly any missionaries left Europe during the fifteenth century, isolated Christianities nevertheless survived in distant lands. The arrival of pilgrims from India and Ethiopia in Rome and Compostella bears witness to an awareness of the universality of the church. Many agreements between the Latin church and the Eastern churches proclaimed at the Council of Ferrara-Florence (1438–1439) were the fruit of missions in previous centuries.

Whatever the statistical results may be, the last centuries of the Middle Ages were an important stage in the history of evangelization, which became a specific activity in the church: from now on it had its personnel, the mendicant orders, and the papacy had universal responsibility for it. Nevertheless, the preachers of the gospel usually had only feeble resources. We can only admire their courage and their faith when they launched out alone and without support into completely unknown countries, more often than not with no hope of return and with the possibility of martyrdom.

4

Conditions and Motivations for the Great Missionary Upsurge in Modern Times (Fifteenth to Eighteenth Centuries)

We should not minimize the importance and symbolic significance of 12 October 1492, the date of the 'discovery' of America. At the beginning of the sixteenth century, after the great discoveries, the gospel was proclaimed all over the world, and the church became truly 'catholic'. However, there can be no question of a complete break with the previous period. In the expeditions of Christopher Columbus the mediaeval heritage was combined with new motives and with scientific and technical progress. Before describing the geographical expansion of the church during this period, we need to illuminate the context of this evangelization, and to locate it within the complex interplay of the conditions of expeditions to distant lands and the motives for them. The concern for evangelization cannot be dissociated from this cultural context, which meant that people took the political decision to cross oceans, to travel far afield and to colonize new lands.

The conditions for the discoveries and for evangelization

The progress in navigation

The messengers of the gospel used the ships of traders and the military. In fact navigation made notable progress during the Middle Ages. The humanists took up the idea that the earth was a globe from Ptolemy, the geographer of antiquity. The rudder, the sextant, the addition of further masts and sails, allowed ships to become fleets of discovery. The European fleets, initially those of Spain, launched out on all the seas in a navigation which was always dangerous and slow. The consequences for evangelization can easily be understood: at least six months had to be allowed for a return trip from Spain to America, eighteen months for a return trip from Spain to Goa, and five years for a return trip from Europe to the Philippines or Japan; for this last voyage, the navigator had only a fifty-fifty chance of returning. Many perished in shipwrecks, epidemics or fights; missionaries were obviously subject to the same constraints. Anyone leaving his country to proclaim the gospel did so without much hope of returning. In a church where centralization was emphasized, relations with Europe were difficult: that explains the long vacancies in episcopal sees, the holders of which were designated in Spain, Portugal and Rome. We can also understand why conflicts like the Rites Dispute dragged on: letters never arrived. However, very quickly the missionaries learned to send the same letter several times by different routes and different ships.

The commercial capitalism of the cities and states

The organization of expeditions to distant lands called for substantial capital investment. Commercial capital raised in the Italian ports made it possible to gather funds and organize syndicates for expeditions. The most rapid and most practical means of payment were used. Many Italian navigators put themselves at the service of Spain, Portugal or France. On the Iberian peninsula it was the states which financed and organized expeditions. In Portugal and Spain, state organizations controlled the whole of colonial commerce. The missionaries had to join expeditions and pay for their transport. To keep their missions alive they sometimes launched out into commerce, as was the case in Japan. The famous Lavalette affair in the eighteenth century, in which Fr Lavalette, superior of the Jesuit Mission in the Antilles, was made bankrupt in a commercial operation, shows the problems in such operations.

The complex motives: gold, pepper and souls

Expeditions to distant lands involved only an active minority, that of the ports and their hinterland: some tens of thousands of people at the end of the fifteenth and beginning of the sixteenth centuries. But at the same time it could be said that what set out from Christendom was a whole society. The missionaries were only some of the people engaged

in this great movement. We cannot isolate the apostolic zeal of the evangelizers from the lure of profit for the navigators. We need to consider the global motives of the discoverers, as they must have been perceived by those whom they discovered.

The economic motivations

A number of historians have tried to explain why Europe turned towards Asia rather than Asia towards Europe; it seems that vegetarian China, which fed four or five times more people than Europe on the same amount of land, had no need of space. On the one hand, by contrast, Europe was orientated on meat-eating and used the power of animal muscles. It lacked space to cultivate and had far more motive power than China. On the other hand, the rich minority of Europe acquired a taste for exotic products which had to be sought in far-away places.

Mediterannean Europe, in which prices were high, was involved in the mechanisms of a monetary economy. Portugal imported corn from the Maghreb and lacked labour. Gold was needed to buy luxury products from the East, like silk and spices. In the fifteenth century the lack of gold led to a slow-down in trade; that is why the Mediterranean peoples launched out in passionate exploration. They sought the source of the precious metal, first in Africa and then in America. For Christopher Columbus, the word 'gold' had a magical and mythical resonance. People wanted to go to the source of spices so as not to have to pay for them in gold; spices were essential for giving taste to meat and preserving it. Africa did not provide good spices, so it was necessary to go further, to India, either round the Cape of Good Hope or by the western route.

Conquest was also a quest for labour. From the middle of the fifteenth century, the slave trade provided workers for Portugal; historians reckon that around 1500, ten per cent of the population of Lisbon was made up of slaves. Finally, land had to be found for planting sugar cane and then coffee.

The cultural and religious motives

Travel accounts fired people's imagination. They read and reread the legendary account of the navigation of St Brendan to the West, the adventures of Marco Polo and the purely imaginary prowess of Jean de Mandeville (who died in 1372). In addition to these somewhat uncontrolled narratives there were the more 'scientific' reflections of Pierre d'Ailly and Piccolomini. In any case, many people wanted to verify the information that had been gained.

The crusades had been a failure in the East, but the idea of the crusade continued to haunt the Christians of the fifteenth and sixteenth centuries, and the Popes attempted to call further ones. Pope Pius II died of chagrin over his failure at Ancona (1464); in the East, Islam advanced inexorably with the capture of Constantinople (1453) and the conquest of Balkan Europe by the Ottoman Turks. On the other hand, in the West the struggle against Islam brought undoubted success. In 1415 the Portuguese took Ceuta on the coast of Morocco from the Muslims; this was the starting-point for Portuguese expeditions along the coasts of Africa, particularly those led by Prince Henry, called the Navigator. On this occasion the Portuguese secured crusading bulls, the best known of which is that of Nicholas V, *Romanus Pontifex* (1455). The destruction of Islam was associated with new Christian settlements. Christopher Columbus always saw a close link between the capture of Granada, the last Muslim bastion in Western Europe, in 1492, the expulsion of the Jews in the same year, and his commercial and apostolic expeditions. Prester John was now located in Ethiopia, and an alliance with him was always hoped for in order to attack Islam from the rear. So there was always a touch of the crusade about evangelization, with the idea of extending the kingdom of God – in the event the sphere of the church – if need be by force. This perspective explains certain modes of behaviour towards the peoples who were encountered: the crusading bulls asserted that the infidels could be reduced to slavery and their goods confiscated by Christians, who would 'make good use' of them!

At the same time there was quite clearly a simple desire to make Christ known to the pagans and to bring them salvation. This concern to convert the pagans was not limited to the preachers. It was to be found in all the Portuguese, Spanish, French and Italian conquerors: Eanes da Zurara, Christopher Columbus, Cortes, Verazzano, Jacques Cartier and others. The view of salvation according to which pagans and even heretics were damned was the one that was most commonly held at the time. That is why it was urgent to baptize the greatest possible number of pagans in the shortest possible time, just as it was important to bring the heretics and Christian schismatics into the 'true church', that of Rome.

One of the reasons for the urgency of the evangelization was that many people believed that the end of the world was near. We can find here a legacy of the speculations of the Calabrian monk Joachim of Fiore (1130–1202), whose doctrines had been passed on by the Franciscan milieux with which Christopher Columbus was in contact. Apart from holding a theory of the three ages of the Father (Old Testament), Son (New Testament, church) and Spirit, the latter beginning about 1200, Joachim thought that the world would end after seven thousand years, a week of millennia, since for God a thousand years are as a day. Christopher Columbus calculated in 1501 that the end of the world would come in 1656. The kingdom of God would definitely be established on earth in connection with a new world in which everyone would be Christian, and a restored Jerusalem in which the Jews had been converted. The gold that was discovered was to be used towards the recapture of the holy city. The sixteenth century was the eleventh hour. That explains the mass baptisms, and also the use of force, which was based on the parable of those invited to the marriage feast (Luke 14.23), a passage which had already been used to justify the Inquisition. It was thought possible, though not by

The beginnings of the Portuguese patronage: the bull *Romanus Pontifex* of Nicholas V (8 January 1455)

After the capture of Ceuta from the Muslims in 1415, the Portuguese, under the impetus of Prince Henry the Navigator, launched out on the discovery and conquest of the African shoreline. On several occasions they asked the papacy for crusading bulls to legitimize their expeditions, the appropriation of land from the infidels and the reduction of the populations to slavery. Following the expeditions, rulers were given the right to organize the church in these conquered lands. We can grasp the ambiguity of these texts when we see that they eventually served as a point of reference for colonial conquest.
(The bull takes up the history of Henry's expeditions) . . .

After these expeditions, numerous Guineans and other negroes who were captured, and some who were even exchanged for authorized merchandise or bought in regular trading, have been brought to Portugal, where a large number of them have been converted to the Catholic faith. With the favour of the divine clemency, we can hope that if progress continues to be made with them in this way, whole peoples will be converted to the faith, or at least that many of them will one day belong to Christ . . .

By other letters we have already granted to the aforesaid King Alfonso, among other things, the freedom to fight against and subject the Saracens, the pagans and other enemies of Christ wherever they are, and the faculty to conquer the kingdoms, duchies, principalities and take the properties and goods in their possession, and to reduce the populations of these territories to perpetual servitude. We have given the king the right to transmit all this to his successors.

We desire that Ceuta and all other places which have been acquired previously, and any which may be acquired in the future in the name of King Alfonso, his successors, or the Prince, in the same countries, neighbouring countries or more distant lands which are in the hands of pagans or infidels, that the provinces, the isles and all the seas are definitively given to the said King Alfonso, his successors and the Prince: the conquests made from Cape Bojador to Guinea and beyond toward the south we declare to be the possessions of this country. Let them be seen clearly to belong to King Alfonso, his successors and the Prince, and let them appear perpetually as rightfully belonging to them . . . King Alfonso, his successors and the Prince will found and build in the provinces, islands and places already acquired or to be acquired, all churches, monasteries and other pious foundations; and similarly they will send all volunteer secular priests and those of the mendicant orders who have received permission from their superiors; we decree that these persons shall remain there until their death, to hear freely and lawfully the confessions of the inhabitants of these countries which are in their charge and, except for cases reserved to the said Holy See, to grant absolution and pronounce salutary penances, and equally to administer the sacraments of the church. All this we benevolently grant to King Alfonso, his successors the future kings of Portugal, and the Prince.

everyone, to compel people, if not to convert, at least to hear the preaching of the gospel, and for that, conquest was necessary.

Finally, after the Council of Trent, the conversion of pagan peoples seemed to be a providential compensation for the losses which the Roman church had undergone as a result of the Protestant Reformation: 'God chose this brave captain, Don Fernando Cortes, by his zeal to open the gates of this great country of Anahuac (Mexico) and to prepare the way of those proclaiming the gospel in this new world where the church would be able to renew itself in order to create a counterbalance by the conversion of so many souls, and to repair the great damage and loss which Luther provoked at that time in ancient Christendom.' So wrote Juan de

The five reasons which prompted Prince Henry to the discovery of the coasts of Guinea

Gomes Eanes da Zurara, equerry to Prince Henry 'the Navigator' (1394–1460), is charged by his master to relate the Portuguese epic. The panegyrist gives a good summary of the many motives of the discoverers.

After taking Ceuta (1415), the Prince did not cease to arm ships against the infidels, because he wanted to know what territories extended the other side of the Canary Islands, beyond Cape Bojador. At this time there was neither writing nor tradition which made it possible to identify what kind of country lay beyond the Cape. Certainly it was related that St Brendan had adventured that far; it was even added that two galleys had never returned . . . The Prince wanted to shed light on all this, so he decided to send his ships towards these countries with the thought of serving God and his brother who was reigning at the time. This was the first reason for his decision.

The second was that if he discovered in these regions countries populated by Christians, or sheltered ports which it was easy to put into, one could bring back to this kingdom a large quantity of merchandise which no doubt would be purchased at a low price . . .

The third reason was that people spoke of the power of the Moors of this country of Africa . . . and the absence among them of Christians or other races. And since it is the duty of a wise and prudent man to seek to evaluate the power of his enemy, the Lord Prince wanted to know this, so as to determine precisely where the authority of these infidels extended.

The fourth reason was that during the thirty years in which he was waging war against the Moors, he was never aided in this war for the love of our saviour Jesus Christ either by a Christian king or a lord foreign to our kingdom; he wanted to know if in these countries there were Christians sufficiently steeped in the charity and love of Christ to want to help him against the enemies of the faith.

The fifth reason was his great desire to spread the sacred faith of our Lord Jesus Christ and to win to it all souls desirous of salvation; for he was not unaware that the sole need of the mystery of the incarnation, the passion and the death of our Lord Jesus Christ is the salvation of souls which have gone astray, souls which the Lord Prince wanted to lead on the way of truth by his works and his expenditure, since he knew that he could not make a better offering to the Lord.

(Gomes Eanes de Zurara, *Chronicle of Guinea*, 1453)

Torquemada, a Spanish chronicler, at the beginning of the seventeenth century.

All these motives were mixed in each of the conquerors. The religious motives might sometimes seem to us no more than the colouring of worldly, if not base, motives, but it would be wrong to speak sweepingly of hypocrisy. The discoveries and the conquistadors, like the kings who sent them, are full of contradictions. They had faith, but not always morals. Christopher Columbus was a mystic in his own way; Pius IX wanted to canonize him. The discoverer associated the conversion of the peoples he encountered with the destruction of heresy and trade. He wanted both to save the peoples and to sell them as slaves to finance a crusade and the recapture of Jerusalem. Before taking Indian women as concubines, the conquistadors had them baptized; even worse, before strangling the Indian emperors, they took care to have them baptized to ensure their eternal salvation.

The evangelizers had to work in this context. Even if they were inspired by the purest motives, they could no longer set off by themselves, as

The motivations of the discoverer

The logs and the letters of Christopher Columbus reveal the extraordinarily mixed motives of the discovery, which were those of a mystic and a slaver.

In this present year 1492, Your Highnesses (Isabella and Ferdinand of Spain) put an end to the war against the Moors who were dominant in Europe and concluded it in the very great city of Granada . . .

Your Highnesses, as Catholic rulers, both devoted to the holy Christian faith and propagators of it, enemies of the sect of Mohammed and all idolatries and heresies, resolved to send me, Christopher Columbus, to the said regions of India to investigate the princes and peoples, not to mention the disposition of the lands and all the rest, and to advise on the way in which one could convert these peoples to our holy faith. And they ordained that I should not go to the East by the customary way, but by a westward route, a way which we believe no one has taken until the present. So having expelled from your kingdom all the Jews who were in it, Your Highnesses resolved to send me to these countries with a sufficient armada.

Cuba, November 1492

I regard it as certain that if religious and devout men knew the language of these natives, they would immediately make them Christians. I hope that Your Highnesses will use the utmost diligence to give such numerous peoples to the church and to convert them, just as they have destroyed those who were not willing to confess the Father, the Son and the Holy Spirit. In this way they will learn our language and adopt our customs and the things of faith; for I see that these people have no sect and are not idolaters . . . They know that there is a God in heaven and are persuaded that we come from heaven. They repeat every prayer that we say and make the sign of the cross.

In these countries there could be a place of trade for all Christendom and principally for Spain, to whom all should be subjected. Only good Catholic Christians should set foot here, since the initial aim of the enterprise has always been the increase of the glory of the Christian religion.

1498, third voyage

It is the Holy Trinity in his infinite goodness who has led Your Highnesses to this enterprise of the Indies. The Trinity has made me his messenger. I was certain that all would be accomplished, since in truth, 'all things pass away but the word of God will never pass away', the word which has spoken so clearly of these lands by the mouth of Isaiah, in so many places in Holy Scripture, affirming that it is from Spain that the spread of God's Holy Name will go forth . . . From here in the name of the Holy Trinity one could send as many slaves as one could sell, and also from Brazil . . . It is the custom to employ many black slaves in Castile and in Aragon, and I think that a great many of them come from Guinea; now one of these Indians is worth three blacks . . . From these two commodities it seems to me that one could gain 40 million, if there were enough ships to bring them here. Although at present the Indians are dying, that will not always be the case, since that is what happened to the blacks and the people from the Canaries to begin with.

There is no colonist who does not have two or three Indians in his service, dogs to hunt and, something which goes against the grain to say, who does not have several wives, so beautiful that it is a wonder . . . That is why some religious devotees would be very useful to us, more to reform the faith among the Christians than to bear it to the Indians.

1500, letter to Jeanne de Torres

I am making myself the messenger of the new heaven and the new earth of which Our Lord speaks in the Apocalypse by the mouth of St John, having done so by the mouth of Isaiah, and I am returning from these regions.

1502–1504, fourth voyage

Gold, what an excellent product! It is from gold that riches come. He who has gold can do whatever he pleases in this world. With gold one can even bring souls into Paradise.

Jerusalem and Mount Sion must be rebuilt by the hands of Christians. God says it by the mouth of the prophet in Psalm 14. Abbot Joachim says that they must come from Spain. The emperor of Cathay has long asked for wise men to instruct him in the Christian faith. Who will offer themselves for this task? If Our Lord brings me back to Spain, I commit myself to take him down there safe and sound.

The objective of the mission to Ethiopia: the return of schismatics to the Roman church

For preachers who set off for distant lands, it was as important to bring schismatics back to the Roman church as it was to convert the pagans. Since the conversion of Muslims was impossible and sometimes punished by death, the missionaries in the Middle East were essentially interested in separated Christians. This is the aim that Ignatius proposes to the Jesuits sent to Ethiopia.

Rome, 7 April 1555

Advice which might be useful for the return of the kingdom of Prester John to union with the church and the Catholic religion, sent to Fr Joan Nunez.

Since the main aim of the enterprise which we seek to realize lies, humanly speaking, in the person of Prester John, king of Ethiopia, and after him in his people, here is some advice, first of all on the means which would seem useful to win over the Priest, and then on those which will win over the people at the same time as the king . . .

The patriarch (Fr Nunez) and those who are sent should employ their efforts in making the acquaintance of Prester John and, by every kind of honest means, in gaining his affection. When it becomes possible and he is well disposed, they should make him understand that there is no hope of being saved outside the Catholic Church and that to be saved it is necessary to believe what it defines for faith and morals. If he can be convinced of this general truth, it will be possible to go on to a number of particular points which depend on it and can be deduced from it little by little. If it is possible to persuade several great figures whom Prester John holds in high esteem, or the Priest himself, to perform the *Exercises* and have a taste for praying, meditation and spiritual things, this, it seems, will be the most effective way of lessening the exaggerated esteem they have for bodily mortifications and may even lead them to abandon excesses.

They have a prophecy according to which around this time a king of the Western countries, one whom we believe they think to be none other than the king of Portugal, must destroy the Moors. That being so, they can be persuaded that to win the friendship of the king it would be better to attain uniformity of faith, since if there is no contradiction in the religious sphere, there would be a greater union of charity between them.

It seems that they would find a precious help in giving up their abuses in evocative festivals like the processions of the Body of Christ our Lord or others in force in the Catholic Church, in place of their baptisms and other ceremonies . . . Attempts should be made to lead them to make the hosts of the Blessed Sacrament in the manner customary here . . . Everything proposed here is a matter of opinion. The patriarch need not feel obliged to go by it. He should hold, rather, to what discreet charity, taking account of the situation of the moment, and the unction of the Holy Spirit, which must be his main guide in all things, dictate to him.

(Ignatius of Loyola, *Letter* 148)

St Paul and his companions had once done, their small bundles on their shoulders. They had to go through princes, navigators and soldiers to obtain their transport. Without always making a providentialist reading of conquests, the missionaries had to accept that the conquerors had crossed the oceans 'to serve God and to enrich themselves'. Francis Xavier held out great prospects of gain to the navigators who took missionaries on board: 'For some to be able to win souls to God, it is necessary for others to be able to win gold.' However, the Christian conscience of the missionaries could not accept all the violence of conquest.

The foundations of conquest and the organization of evangelization

Crusading bulls and demarcation bulls

In the past, and all through the fifteenth century, the papacy had granted the Portuguese rulers crusading bulls which gave them possession of the lands they had conquered from the infidels, with the right and the duty to set up Christian establishments (churches and monasteries) in these same places. Crusade, colonization and evangelization were clearly associated. To meet possible challenges from the Portuguese, the Spanish rulers, Ferdinand and Isabella, obtained several bulls from Pope Alexander VI Borgia, who was of Spanish origin. These recognized Spanish sovereignty over the lands discovered by Christopher Colombus and entrusted them with the charge of evangelizing the inhabitants. In a more precise way, the bull *Inter cetera*, dated 4 May 1493, drew a line of demarcation one hundred leagues west of the Azores and the Cape Verde islands. All the lands discovered on the far side of the line would belong to Spain; all lying on the other side would belong to Portugal. The two states shifted the line 270 leagues westwards by the treaty of Tordesillas (June 1494). Thus Brazil became Portuguese territory after its discovery around 1500. The difficulty of calculating longitudes led to disputes in Asia over the Philippines at the end of the sixteenth century. According to widely challenged mediaeval conceptions, the Pope had a universal power over the world, which he delegated to rulers for the salvation of the peoples set under them. From this perspective, only baptism conferred a legitimate right to property.

The patronages

On the basis of this division, new agreements resulted in the legal definition of the Spanish (*patronato*) and Portuguese (*padroado*) patronages. The main bulls were issued in 1508 for Spain and 1514 for Portugal. For several centuries, the papacy had considered that it had responsibility for the evangelization of the world. By these bulls of patronage, the Pope left to the two kings the organization of the church in the countries which had been discovered and conquered. They were the 'patrons', the heads of the new churches. The royal treasury paid for the living costs of the clergy, the building of the churches, the expenses of worship, and so on. The authorities provided transport for bishops, priests and religious. The king founded dioceses and appointed bishops. Certainly papal ratification was needed for the nominations, but the Pope did not intervene directly. The system of patronages provided an immediate solution for the organization of evangelization, but the disadvantages soon appeared. At the time of the share-out, Spain and Portugal were the only rivals. When France joined the ranks of colonial conquerors, Francis I ironically remarked: 'I would like to read the clauses in the testament of Adam which exclude me from the division of the world.' France gained territory in both the Spanish and the Portuguese domains. As for England and Holland, after the Reformation they no longer felt bound by the papal bull.

Within the framework of patronage, evangelization was often subject to the vicissitudes of colonial and European politics. This meant that sometimes there were considerable delays in decisions and nominations. The two countries proved extremely concerned to preserve their rights, though they had difficulty in fulfilling their duties. Portugal, with a million and a half inhabitants in the sixteenth century, could not meet the needs of the church in half the world; it had to appeal to foreign personnel, for example to Jesuits of all nationalities who had to pass through Lisbon. There were numerous vacancies in episcopal sees, and the Portuguese rulers rejected any direct intervention from the Holy See.

The missionary personnel

I shall make only some general comments here, since we shall have to return to each sector of evangelization. Secular priests left to go overseas; they were often somewhat footloose adventurers, seeking their fortune as colonists and limiting their ministry to their fellow-countrymen. This was originally the case with de Las Casas.

The first evangelization was essentially the work of the old religious orders, particularly the mendicant orders, who as we have seen had gained experience in previous centuries. Though we should not forget the Augustinians, the Carmelites or the Mercedarians, it was the Franciscans and the Dominicans who were in the forefront of the evangelizers. The first Franciscans who came to Mexico were from a reformed house in which Joachimite speculations had met with a wide response.

With the departure of Francis Xavier for the Far East in 1540, the Jesuits engaged in evangelization. The Basic Rule of the Jesuits called for them to be at the disposal of the Pope for any mission he proposed, particularly one which concerned the propagation of the faith. The Society of Jesus thus became the first missionary order of modern times. The Society was always to have an important proportion of its members outside Europe: 15.5% of the Society in the eighteenth century; the proportion was greater in the maritime provinces.

With the Jesuits, a missionary spirituality and method emerged. In the seventeenth century the words 'mission' and 'missionary' took on the 'technical' sense that they have today. The missionary was sent by a superior for a specific task of evangelization. This could be evangelization overseas, but also evangelization within Europe in the context of religious renewal which followed the Council of Trent. Furthermore, there were numerous links between these missionaries within Europe and missionaries abroad. They often belonged to the same orders or societies of priests.

Evangelization, colonization and Christian conscience

Thus from the beginning of the discoveries and the conquests, evangelization started. The first dioceses were founded less than twenty years after the landing of Christopher Columbus in the Antilles. The religious orders sent remarkable figures as missionaries. At the same time, in the Spanish world, all the questions now prompted by consciences about the legitimacy of colonial conquest and the link between colonialization and evangelization were expressed forcefully. As one historian has remarked, 'The Spanish conquest of America was one of the greatest historical attempts to make Christian principles prevail in international relations. In comparisons with other colonizing nations, if anything distinguishes the Spanish conquest, it is not the proportion of crimes over which one of these nations has to envy another, but the proportion of scruples.'

The violence of the conquest

The history of the conquest of the West Indies (America) cannot fail to horrify us if we believe the accounts of Las Casas. Though they are sometimes judged excessive, they are confirmed by many other sources. Less than thirty years after the discovery of the Antilles by Columbus, the Indians on the islands had almost disappeared as a result of wars, forced labour and terrible epidemics. In this connection one historian has called this the 'first bacteriological war'.

The Indians were not good slaves, as Columbus had thought. After 1500 they were replaced by blacks imported from Africa. The trade, which had begun in the middle of the fifteenth century between Africa and Portugal, took on considerable proportions when it was regulated by Charles V in 1518. The Spanish government gave an import licence, the *asiento*, to companies: Englishmen, Dutchmen and Frenchmen took part in the traffic. The African coasts became a hunting-ground for slaves. The local chiefs were generally used as intermediaries for selling the blacks of the interior.

With considerable ease, the Spanish conquerors destroyed the great empires of the American continent. Cortés put to death the Aztec emperor Cuauhtemoc in 1525; Pizarro and Almagro executed the Inca emperor Atahualpa in 1533. A last Inca, who revolted in 1572, was baptized in his turn and beheaded on the orders of Francis of Toledo, the viceroy of Peru. The conquerors destroyed idolatry by pillaging the gold in the temples. The Indian lands were divided between the Spanish lords in

You are all in a state of mortal sin

This sermon, given by the Dominican Montesinos to the colonists of Hispaniola (San Domingo) in 1511, marked the start of the struggle for justice in which Las Casas distinguished himself.

You are all in a state of mortal sin; you live in this state and you will die in it, by reason of the cruelty and the tyranny which you show to these innocent peoples. Say by what right and by virtue of what justice you hold these Indians in such cruel and horrible servitude. Who could authorize you to wage all these detestable wars on people who were living in peace and tranquillity in their country, and to exterminate them in such vast numbers by murder and carnage unprecedented? How can you oppress them and crush them thus, without giving them food or tending the diseases to which the excessive tasks that you demand of them expose them so mortally? It would be more correct to say that you kill them to extract and accumulate your daily gold. And what concern do you have to assure their conversion, and to see that they know their God and Creator, that they are baptized, that they hear the mass and observe the festivals and Sundays? Are these people not human? Do they not have a soul, a reason? Are you not obliged to love them as yourselves? Don't you understand? Don't you feel? How can you sleep such a profound, lethargic sleep? Be persuaded that in the state that you are you will not gain your salvation any more than the Moors and Turks who do not know, or scorn, the faith of Jesus Christ.

accordance with the *encomienda* system (a kind of feudalism): the Indians who were 'recommended' became virtually slaves. By contrast the *encomenderos* had the duty to evangelize their Indians, but this was not the first of their preoccupations.

The struggle for justice

Christian consciences did not remain silent. Given expression by several religious, they began to

The slavery of the Indians is illegitimate

In the bull Sublimis Deus *(9 June 1537), at the request of several religious from Spanish America, Pope Paul III solemnly recognized the freedom of the Indians, thus breaking with the crusader mentality of earlier pontifical documents like* Romanus Pontifex, *quoted above.*

Man is, by his nature, capable of receiving faith in Christ, and all those who participate in human nature have the capacity to receive this same faith . . .

The enemy of the human race has devised a hitherto unknown means of preventing the word of God from being preached to the nations for their salvation. He has raised up certain of his minions who, in a desire to assuage their appetites, have had the audacity to affirm everywhere that these Indians who have been discovered in our time must be reduced to slavery on the pretext that they are brute beasts and incapable of receiving the Catholic faith. They are more destructive towards them than to the animals without reason which they use . . . Considering that these Indians, which on all the evidence are true human beings, are not only capable of receiving the Christian faith but, as we have learned, are prompt in receiving this faith, in a desire to provide appropriate remedies in this matter, by virtue of our apostolic authority we declare that these Indians, and all other peoples who come to the knowledge of Christians in the future, although they are still outside the Christian faith, must not be deprived of their freedom nor of the enjoyment of their goods. On the contrary, they must be able to make use of this freedom and these goods and enjoy them freely; they must not be reduced to servitude. It is necessary to invite these same Indians and the other nations to receive the Christian faith by preaching the word of God and giving the example of a virtuous life.

---

extract from royal power a legislation which sought to be inspired by justice. It is interesting to note the logic of the standpoints of the religious and the legislative measures, if we are to understand their relative failure. In 1511 the Dominican Montesinos on Hispaniola (San Domingo) protested in a sermon against the exploitation and slavery of the Indians. The king of Spain responded with the Laws of Burgos (1512): the Indians were free men; there were regulations about working hours, food, habitation, religious teaching, and so on. Since some had questioned the legitimacy of the conquest, in every expedition a notary solemnly proclaimed to the natives the rights of the Pope and the king of Spain; this was the Requerimento, which was usually read only to the parrots in the jungle. Things hardly changed.

In 1514, the colonial priest Bartolomeo de Las Casas repented of his injustice towards the Indians. From now on, for half a century, the fight for justice was to inspire his life. He proposed concrete means for stopping the exploitation of the Indians. He was later to regret a bad suggestion of his that black slaves should be imported, but the trade had begun before him. He tried to settle Spanish workers and their families in the New World; they joined forces with the Indians to exploit the country. The workers certainly wanted to come, but to look for gold! With the conquest of Mexico, the exactions were worse than ever. Las Casas became a Dominican and acquired a theological education during a number of years in retreat. In 1523 the Spanish government reaffirmed that the Indians were free men, but the slaughter continued. In 1531 Las Casas addressed the Council of the Indies: 'The cry of so much spilt blood is now rising to heaven'; the reason for the presence of the Spanish in the Western Indies was to proclaim the gospel. Alerted, Pope Paul III recognized the freedom of the Indians in the bull *Sublimis Deus* (1537). Las Casas thought that it was necessary to suppress the *encomienda*, which was the root of the evil; the preachers had to come before soldiers and colonists. To illustrate his suggestions, Las Casas

Idols cannot be eradicated in a day

In this passage Las Casas opposes the expeditious Christianization practised by the Conquistadors and particularly Cortés.

Gomara has written in his *History* that Fernand Cortés decided to remove the idols from this people and to set up crosses on this island (Cozumel, 1519). That is one of those errors, one of those nonsensical things that many have done in these countries; for unless first over a long period Christian doctrine has been taught to the Indians, as to any other idolatrous nation, it is quite absurd to suppose that one can make them abandon their idols. They never do this of their own accord; for there is no one who will voluntarily and with a good heart abandon the god whom for many years he has thought to be true, the beliefs that he has been taught at his mother's breast, and all that his ancestors have venerated. There is a need to have understood that what is proposed in place of one's gods is the true God. And what Christian teaching can the Spaniards have brought to these people over the two, three, four or ten days that they spent among them? It is evident that they cannot have been able to talk to them of the true God in such a way as to make them abandon the erroneous trust which they had placed in their gods, and that once they had gone away, these people would begin to worship idols again. First it is necessary to efface the idols from their hearts, i.e. to efface the faith which they have in them, regarding them as true gods; teaching them day by day with diligence and perseverance, it is necessary to imprint on their hearts the real, true concept of the true God. Then, of their own accord, they will recognize their error and begin to destroy with their own hands, in complete freedom, the idols which they venerated as gods.

To set up crosses and to invite the Indians to pay their respects to them is a good thing, on condition that one can make them understand the significance of this gesture; but if one does not have the necessary time, or one does not speak their language, it is useless and superfluous, since the Indians can imagine that here they are being offered a new idol which depicts the god of the Christians; and in this way they will be invited to worship a piece of wood as a god, which is idolatry.

The surest conduct, the only rule, which Christians should observe when they find themselves in pagan lands is to give them a good example by virtuous works so that, according to the words of our Redeemer, 'they may see your good works and praise and glorify your Father', thinking that a God who has such followers cannot but be good and true.

(Las Casas, *History of the Indians*)

described the horrors of the conquest in his *Very Brief Account of the Destruction of the Indians* (1540). His moves resulted in the publication of the New Laws (1542), 'the pride and the humiliation of Spain'. The *encomiendas* were suppressed. But in America, if the law was respected, it was not applied. Nominated bishop of Chiapa in the south of Mexico in 1543, Las Casas tried to apply his principles. He had some success in peaceful evangelization, but the colonists would hear nothing of the New Laws. Las Casas returned to Spain once and for all. For him, from now on there could be only one solution: the king had to be made to stop the wars of conquest.

A theological essay on colonization and evangelization

At the same time, a theologian from Salamanca, the Dominican Francisco de Vitoria, echoed what was related about the conquest: 'We hear talk of so many men massacred and plundered, when in reality they are innocent, and so many masters driven from their possessions and deprived of their power. So we can reasonably ask ourselves whether or not this is done justly.' He was to reply to these questions in his *Lessons on the Indians and on the Right of War* (1539). Vitoria has been praised as one of the founders of international law. In fact he firmly abandoned the mediaeval perspectives of the bulls of crusades and demarcation: neither the Pope nor the emperor have universal power over the world; sin, idolatry and heresy do not destroy natural law; the Pope's donation has no temporal validity but only spiritual validity; the Indians are the legitimate possessors of their land, and one cannot make war on them because they refuse to convert.

However, Vitoria wants to define the legitimate title to the Spanish presence in the Indies. For him, an original solidarity unites all men; it is normal for there to be exchanges between them. So the Spanish have the right to go the Indies and preach the gospel there. If the Indians oppose them violently, a just war can be engaged in against them. Without noticing it, Vitoria takes away with one hand what he gives with the other, since this right of exchange is purely theoretical, unilateral and without reciprocity. After all, the Eskimos have not asked to fish in the Lake of Geneva, or the Pygmies to hunt in the forests of Rambouillet! Vitoria envisages a kind of mandate from the king of Spain over the Indian rulers, thus preparing them to enter the international community. In this way Vitoria left in reserve for the Spanish plenty of possible justifications for the conquest.

An unfinished debate

Las Casas did not put the pontifical donation in question. However, for him it had only one goal, evangelization. In a number of treatises which were not published in his lifetime, like *On the Only Way of Evangelizing the Whole World*, Las Casas suggested several rules for proclaiming the gospel. It was not a question of replacing idols with the cross from one day to the next; one does not change hearts in that way. Evangelization is slow work and respects indigenous customs. Christians must make faith desirable by the example of their conduct. The proclamation of the gospel cannot be subordinated to the submission of the Indians to Spain. The powers of the Indian rulers are legit-

imate; all the wars waged against the Indians are unjust: the conquest must be stopped. The Spanish court took this seriously: the colonial expeditions were stopped pending the result of a great debate between the partisans of the legitimacy of the conquest (Sepulveda) and those who rejected it (Las Casas). This debate at Valladolid (1550–1551) did not come to any decisive conclusions. The *encomienda* remained. The Council of the Indies issued new regulations. The word 'conquest' was replaced by 'pacification', but the reality hardly changed. It is true that quite sincere religious like the Franciscans of Mexico stubbornly opposed Las Casas: in an eschatological perspective, there was a need to make haste to baptize the Indians. To delay the conquest was to compromise their salvation. The death of large numbers of Indians was perhaps only the punishment of the idolaters spoken of by the Old Testament, and the survivors did not have a rougher life than the Spanish peasants. Subsequently, the Spanish bishops of America took seriously their title of 'protectors of the Indians'. Synods and provincial councils were still protesting against the exploitation of local populations in the seventeenth century, particularly against the abuses of *mita*, forced labour in the mines. These texts, which had only a limited effect, annoyed the authorities, since they banned publication of them.

Slavery and the trade in blacks

Christian consciences were far less aroused by the problems of the trade in black Africans and their slavery. Economic imperatives made thinkers and philosophers very timid on the subject. Bernadin de Saint-Pierre made a famous remark: 'I do not know whether coffee and sugar are necessary for the happiness of Europe, but I do know that these two plants have caused unhappiness in two parts of the world. America has been depopulated to plant them, and Africa has been depopulated to have a nation to cultivate them.'

Las Casas did not put the energy which he

The debate at Valladolid (1550–1551): are the Indians slaves by nature?

Yes, it is just to reduce the Indians to slavery

Sepulveda:

Compare, then, the benefits which the Spaniards enjoy: prudence, invention, magnanimity, temperance, humanity and religion, with those of these mediocre examples of humanity, deprived of all science and art, without monuments from the past other than some obscure paintings. They have no written laws but only customs, barbarous traditions. They do not even know a property law . . . How can we doubt that people so little civilized, even barbarian, soiled by so many impurities and impieties, have been justly conquered by such excellent, pious and just sovereigns as Ferdinand the Catholic and the emperor Charles, and by a nation so human, so rich in all kinds of virtue? . . .

No, since human nature is one

Las Casas:

All human beings are men; all possess understanding and will, the five outward senses and the four inward senses, and are driven to satisfy them; all love the good, enjoy the good and the beautiful, and censure and abhor evil. There is not and cannot be a nation so ferocious and so depraved that it cannot be converted to all the political virtues and all the humanity of domestic, political and rational man . . . Examples both old and new clearly show us that there is no people so rough, uncultivated, crude and barbarous which cannot be convinced, led to the right way, to truth, gentleness and obedience, by an appropriate and naturally human way, in other words by courtesy and affection.

deployed in defending the freedom of the Indians at the service of the blacks. At the end of his life he much regretted the advice he had given in 1516 that some black slaves should be imported into the Antilles. If, finally, his condemnation of the trade was radical, it only slowly impressed itself on his mind: 'This advice to give a licence to import black slaves into these lands was given by the young priest Las Casas at an early stage, without taking account of the injustice of their capture by the Portuguese and their reduction to slavery . . . He has greatly repented of this advice which he gave, judging himself guilty by inadvertence. In fact, he later had evidence that in truth the captivity of the blacks was no less unjust than that of the Indians' (here Las Casas is speaking of himself in the third person). We can see both the sincerity of Las Casas' repentance and the weakness of an argument derived from mediaeval conceptions. In fact the Christian tradition, while not regarding slavery as natural to human beings, saw in it the consequence of sin or punishment for sin. Theologians like St

Thomas justified slavery in several cases. In particular the reduction to slavery of prisoners captured in a just war was regarded as legitimate. These were essentially prisoners who had been captured in wars with Muslims or pagans. This was reciprocity for the fate of Christians captured by the infidels. The crusading bulls (*Romanus Pontifex*, 1455) legitimated this reduction to slavery and even saw it as an opportunity given to captives to become Christians. Reference could also be made to Aristotle's argument that there are men who are slaves by nature and to the cursing of the descendants of Shem (Gen.9.25) which lay on the blacks.

This kind of argument continued until the eighteenth century. It was the manner of capture which decided whether or not slavery was legitimate. Account was taken of the fact that the millions of blacks (between twelve and twenty million) who were taken from Africa had not been captured in a just war. Then appeal was made to economic necessities or the obligation for societies to tolerate a certain number of abuses like usury, prostitution and the slave trade. Furthermore, the blacks were baptized before being embarked for America, and the Catholic missionaries above all feared that they would be sold to heretics, Dutchmen or Englishmen, since for these poor slaves that was an assurance of damnation. Moreover missionaries took part in the trade. Many religious establishments had slaves. According to Jesuit travellers, the houses of the Society in Angola (St Paul of Luanda) had twelve thousand of them.

Without doubt the possession of slaves did not necessarily imply that they were maltreated. But the legislation relating to them, like Colbert's Black Code of 1685, shows very few Christian sentiments. The evangelization of the blacks was thus completely falsified by the slave trade and slavery; it is terrible that for the blacks baptism signified the loss of their freedom. Rather than fight against slavery, charitable souls, of whom the saintly Jesuit Pierre Claver in seventeenth-century Colombia is the finest example, tried to mitigate their lot.

Cultural shock

These questions posed to the Christian conscience were not limited to conflicts of interests. Certainly cupidity often explains the way in which the conquerors treated the populations they encountered. But there is a deeper element which is of prime importance for evangelization; the debate between Sepulveda and Las Casas is an illustration of this. The Europeans of Christendom came abruptly into contact with civilizations of which they had not had the least prior idea. The shock was brutal in both directions. Conquerors and missionaries brought with them a Christianity which had been fifteen centuries in the maturing. In preaching the gospel they wanted to hand down at a stroke a Christian civilization whose norms were very different from those of the peoples whom they encountered. For a European, a Christian wears clothes even when it is very hot; he cultivates the land; in principle he has only one wife; he has a sense of private property, and so on. But these

peoples behaved in a very different way. Certain aspects of their religions, like the human sacrifices of the Aztecs, were particularly shocking. Hence there was a temptation not to consider them as equals but as subhuman. Hence also the desire to impose on them the norms of the Christian populations of Europe: sedentarization, monogamy, modes of dress and so on. Their evangelization implied the disappearance of the traditional religions. People talked of the 'clean sheet' (tabula rasa). But the ruin of the traditional religions was also that of cultures and societies. Las Casas had already sketched this out. The encounter with the great civilizations of India and the Far East suggested the hypothesis of an adaptation of Christianity to non-European cultures.

The Congregation for Propaganda

Even if by law the papacy kept overall control of the evangelization of the world, in fact it had abandoned it to the Iberian rulers through patronage, and hardly had the means to mitigate its inadequacies and correct its abuses. In the years which followed the conclusion of the Council of Trent (1563), the Popes gradually became aware again of their role as defenders and propagators of the faith. This development had many aspects, the most visible of which was the crusade (Battle of Lepanto, 1571). However, above all the Holy See wanted to recapture the Christian masses which had left the Catholic Church and to improve the organization of distant evangelization. In 1568 a commission of four cardinals had been created, charged with promoting the Catholic faith. It faded away at the end of the century. At last, in 1622, Gregory XV founded the congregation *De Propaganda Fide*, the Sacred Congregation for the Propagation of the Faith (or Propaganda, for short). Since 1968 it has been called the Congregation for the Evangelization of the Peoples. It was added to the fifteen congregations created by Sixtus V in 1588, kinds of collegiate ministries: 'The new congregation is intended to safeguard the salvation of souls and above all the care of the Catholic faith, preserving it among the faithful and spreading it among the infidels.' It was presided over by Cardinal Ludovisi, but for twenty-seven years the linchpin was his secretary, Francis Ingoli.

The Congregation was just as much concerned to bring heretics and schismatics back to the Catholic faith as to convert pagans. The formation of the Propaganda corresponded to and contributed to a change of mentality about mission; it was to take into account all the problems which had been accumulating for more than a century of evangelization overseas: political interventions, violence, attitudes towards cultures. The Congregation wanted to convince those responsible for evangelization that only the arms of persuasion should be used, and it put new means at the service of missions. In 1626 a polyglot printing house was created; in 1627, Pope Urban founded an international college intended to train both secular priests for mission countries and also candidates for the priesthood coming from the mission field; this was the Urban College (now the University) of Propaganda. Secretary Ingoli started a great world-wide survey of evangelization. The replies showed a certain number of weaknesses and abuses: conflicts between religious orders, between bishops and religious; missionaries who thought only of enriching themselves by trade. They emphasized all the inadequacies of the patronages: vacancies in episcopal sees, exploitation of the populations and so on. Ingoli put forward remedies, insisting on the training of missionaries and the control of recruitment before they set off overseas; he called for the training of an indigenous clergy at all levels. The Congregation in principle had rights over all missions and could nominate missionaries. However, the patronages held on to their privileges. The

Congregation sent a certain number of missionaries directly, but conflicts with those who depended on the patronages increased, as we shall see later, and the Propaganda was often impotent.

The formation of the Propaganda coincided with the birth of a true priestly spirituality, independent of the religious life; for the authors of the 'French School', the priestly mission was rooted in the mission of the Word incarnate. That explains the link, already mentioned, between missions at home and missions abroad. In founding the Urban College (1627), instituting vicars apostolic (1658) and encouraging the foundation of the seminary of the Society of Foreign Missions in Paris (1663), the Propaganda endorsed the secular priesthood; the recruitment of missionaries was no longer limited to the religious orders.

The Congregation for Propaganda tried to detach mission from the framework of politics and commerce. But did it have the means for doing so? It is certain that this evangelization which was rooted in the great discoveries is hard for Christians to bear, since it is so bound up with conquest and colonial exploitation. The good will of the missionaries, often taken to the point of heroism, is not in question, but it is disturbing to note that the evangelization of the Indians of America came about through a demographic catastrophe which removed three-quarters of them, and that the evangelization of Africa came about through the slave trade and slavery. Certainly the gospel is not responsible for this, but it must be noted with regret that there are realities which religions cannot master. Christianity never mastered modern European expansion, even ethically; it tried to act in it and profit from it. But history cannot be begun all over again. It is through this imperfect heritage that the church has to continue to bear witness to the gospel.

5

The Mission Field in Modern Times (Fifteenth to Eighteenth Centuries)

The previous chapter already mentioned a certain number of missionary events in different parts of the word, primarily taking into account the general aspects of evangelization. Now I shall attempt to give a panorama of apostolic action across the different continents for the three centuries of modern times.

Africa

Crusades, explorations and missions

A continuation of the crusades, Portuguese expansions in Africa began with the capture of Ceuta (1415). The 'scientific' preoccupations of Prince Henry the Navigator led him to organize expeditions of discovery along the coasts of Africa. In 1434 Gil Eanes circumnavigated Cape Bojador; in 1444 the mouth of the Senegal was reached; this was the discovery of the black countries. The first public sale of slaves took place in Lisbon. In 1482, Diogo Cao explored the estuary of the Zaire. In 1486 the fort of Elmina (in present-day Ghana) was established; in the same year Bartolomeo Diaz discovered the Cape of Good Hope, and in 1498 Vasco da Gama made port in Mozambique. Thus the Portuguese set up trading posts all round Africa:

these were places for commercial dealings, defended by a fort and a small garrison. They were also the starting points for an evangelization which was often ephemeral; the first missionaries were the garrison chaplains.

A hope disappointed: the evangelization of the Congo

After a Congolese delegation asked Portugal for missionaries, in 1490 King Juan sent a real missionary expedition: priests, monks, soldiers, farmers, masons and carpenters along with devotional objects. It was a microcosm of European society, which thus was exported so as to be able to shape the society and civilization of the Congo in its own image. The Manicongo (the king) was baptized in 1491. A church was built within a year. The new religion was well received because of its effectiveness. The Portuguese helped the king against tribes in revolt and thus strengthened the central power. The royal banners bore the cross. After some difficulties – the king did not want to give up polytheism – Christianity triumphed with Afonso I, a very Christian king (1506–1544). The king deliberately opted for the new religion and modernism; he wanted to model his state on Portugal. He

The beginnings of Christianity in the kingdom of the Congo

Duarte Lopes, a Portuguese trader and a Negro, was sent as an ambassador to Pope Sixtus V by Alvaro I, king of the Congo. In Rome he met the humanist and traveller Filippo Pigafetta (1533–1604), who transcribed in Italian what Lopes told him about Africa and the evangelization of the Congo. The work appeared in 1591, a century after the events.

King John II (1481–1493), wanting to discover the East Indies, sent several ships along the coasts of Africa to explore this route . . . They arrived at the river Zaire . . . Some Portuguese remained there to learn the language and trade with the inhabitants. There was a priest among them. The Portuguese were in contact with the governor of Sogno, an uncle of the king . . . The priest and his companions began to talk about the Christian faith with this prince, to show him the errors of pagan beliefs, and to teach him our religion little by little. What the Portuguese said pleased him, and he was converted.

In this good spirit of faith, the governor of Sogno went to court to make known to the king the true doctrine of the Portuguese Christians and to exhort them to receive the Christian faith, which so clearly brings salvation . . . The king was converted and declared that he wanted to be Christian . . . The king of Congo asked King John II of Portugal to send him priests and all that was necessary for the Christian life.

The ships arrived with the awaited objects; this was in the year 1491 of our redemption . . . The prince of Sogno built a church of trunks and branches, and there he was baptized, receiving the name of Manuel . . . After this office, the Portuguese travelled towards the residence of the court, which they reached after a journey of three days.

The king waited for them at the entrance to his palace, on a throne set on a dais, and received them publicly . . . He saw the presents which the king of Portugal had sent him, the priestly vestments, the ornaments for the altar, the crucifixes, pictures representing the saints, the banners, the gonfalon and the rest. All these objects were explained to him one by one, and he paid incredible attention to them . . . It was agreed first to build a church in order to give the utmost solemnity to the baptism and the ceremonies of worship; in the meantime, the king and the members of his court were instructed in the Christian religion . . . An uprising put an end to the building of the stone church, so one was quickly built in wood . . . It was in this church that the king received the water of holy baptism: he was given the name Joao (John) and his wife that of Lionor (Eleanor), in honour of the king and queen of Portugal. The church was dedicated to the Saviour. That same day some other lords, following the example of the king, were baptized after receiving some principles of Christian doctrine . . .

The second son of the king was opposed to the gospel that began to be preached, which prohibited more than one wife, something that to these people accustomed to take as many wives as they wanted seemed the most arduous of all the commandments and the most difficult to accept . . . The first son, Don Afonso, served Christianity with the utmost fervour, burning the idols throughout his province.

(Filippo Pigafetta and Duarte Lopes,
*Description of the Kingdom of Congo and
the Surrounding Countries*, 1591)

created schools, and sent nobles including his son Henry to study in Portugal. Henry became the first black bishop (1521). But Portugal did not grant its benefits freely; it required a monopoly in trade and wanted to be paid in copper, ivory and above all slaves. The king wanted autonomy for his church, but the Congo was a dependency of the diocese of the Isle of Sao Tomé (1534), a pivot for the traffic in Negroes. The king noted that trade, and particularly the slave trade, completely falsified evangelization. The missionaries themselves took part in the trade: as they were paid in shells, coinage without value outside the kingdom, they converted this into slaves, whom they sold at Sao Tomé.

Missionary followed missionary, Jesuits in 1547, Franciscans in 1557. The latter composed a catechism in Kikongo, the first known work to be published in a Bantu language. From 1575 the Portuguese established themselves in Angola and were less interested in the Congo. The Congolese kings pursued a policy of independence; in 1596 the capital of the Congo, Sao Salvador, became an episcopal city. King Alvaro II succeeded in sending a delegation to the Holy See (1608–1612), but the ambassador died on arrival in Rome. Conflicts between the Congolese rulers and the Portuguese multiplied. Because they had been refused a mining concession, the Portuguese declared war on King Antonio I; the two armies met at Ambuila in 1665, each bearing flags marked with the cross. Antonio was defeated and beheaded. This was the end of the great kingdom of the Congo, which collapsed into anarchy. The evangelization continued in earnest. Periodically the Propaganda sent some Capuchins in the seventeenth and eighteenth centuries; some of them have left accounts. During often brief stays they travelled ceaselessly, baptizing indiscriminately. But the evangelization was not followed up. The country remained without priests for decades. The traditional religions resurfaced, and syncretisms flourished.

When they saw the Europeans disembarking, the Congolese thought that their ancestors were coming up from the subterranean kingdom of the waters to divulge to them the secrets of true life and power. They accepted Christianity to the degree that they could relate it to the tradition of the ancestors. Christian objects, crucifixes and rosaries could be regarded as more powerful 'fetishes' than the old ones, which they were prepared to destroy. Furthermore, the crumbling of the old Congo gave rise to a nostalgia for unity: visionaries emerged who, drawing on the old religious basis and on

Christianity, wanted to revive their people. In 1704, a young Congolese, aged twenty-two, Dona Beatrice, the priestess of a local cult, sought to restore the unity of the Congo. She performed miracles; she suggested an Africanized Christianity; she claimed to be sent by God and St Antony of Padua (the missionaries were Franciscans) to go to Sao Salvador to restore the kingdom. The Congo was the Holy Land and Christ was black; he was born in Sao Salvador. She restored polygamy and threatened the missionaries. She gave new life to the destroyed capital and restored the royal insignia. She imitated the death of Christ and his resurrection. But when she bore a son whom she attributed to the Holy Spirit and who was to be the saviour, she provoked her own downfall. Under pressure from the Capuchins the king had her arrested and pronounced a death sentence against her: on 2 July 1706 she perished at the stake 'with the name of Jesus on her lips'.

The causes and lessons of a failure

In addition to internal difficulties in the Congolese state – there was no rule of succession – evangelization suffered grave deficiencies: a lack of continuity in the apostolate, mediocre clergy, ignorance of the language, baptism without catechesis, the thoughtless destruction of paganism. Just as serious was the collusion between the colonial enterprise and mission: there was total contradiction between a Christianity which was adapted and to some degree nationalized, and the establishment of a missionary church dependent on a foreign ruler which contributed to the expansion of trade.

Some other missions in Africa

Angola apart, the other missions in Africa were even more ephemeral. The mission of the Jesuits sent by Ignatius Loyola to Ethiopia with a hierarchy failed completely (1555). After a first abortive attempt in the sixteenth century, Monomotapa (Mozambique) was evangelized in the seventeenth century and its king was baptized (1652), but the

Portuguese did not have the means to maintain the church. The Lazarists had to give up their settlement on Madagascar (1648–1654; 1660–1675). On Reunion and Mauritius, various religious concerned themselves with those who had been transplanted, colonists and slaves.

Spanish and Portuguese America

The setting up of a church

It cannot be denied that the Spanish power took seriously the duty of evangelization imposed on it in the bulls of donation and patronage. In a century, thirty-four dioceses were created, from San Domingo (1511) to Buenos Aires. Religious houses multiplied. Universities and the indispensable Inquisition were set up. The rulers chose the bishops carefully. Four-fifths were Spaniards from the capital and two-thirds were religious. Several were remarkable figures: the Franciscan Juan de Zumarraga, Bishop of Mexico (1528–1548); Juan del Valle, Bishop of Popayan (1548–1560), who died on his way to the Council of Trent; and Toribio de Mogrevejo, Bishop of Lima (1581–1606), who visited his immense diocese three times and was canonized.

However, the failings of the system were evident. This church did not man itself, and the delays in nominations, which were centralized in Europe, often led to vacancies of more than four years each time a bishop died. Councils and synods organized the provincial and local churches. Mention should be made especially of the councils of Mexico and Lima and the synods of Popayan and Santiago of Chile. The Third Council of Lima (1582–1583) laid down a charter for the whole of the Spanish domain of South America: it adapted the Council of Trent for this mission country. All aspects of Christian life were touched on: priests were obliged to learn the Indian languages and to use them in their preaching.

Councils and synods of Spanish America (sixteenth-seventeenth centuries)

It must not be forgotten that often the civil authorities refused to confirm and publish these decisions.

First Council of Lima (1551)

In conformity with the traditions of the primitive church . . . the infidels who convert to our Catholic faith must in the first place understand what they receive (baptism) and what they commit themselves to . . . We ordain that henceforth no priest shall baptize an adult Indian aged eight or more without his having been taught our faith for at least thirty days, being made to understand that there is a creator and master of all things whom he must worship . . .

We ordain to priests who baptize the Indians that the catechisms and questions that they put shall be made in the language of the Indians, so that these can understand, and that they shall reply in the same language.

First Council of Mexico (1555)

The Indians shall be gathered together in villages, where they shall live as citizens. There are serious obstacles in the way of their living separately, divided from one another by field and mountains, where their way of life resembles more that of animals than of rational and political men, hence the great difficulties in instructing them. For all this it is necessary to gather them, to assemble them, to 'reduce' them in villages, in commodious and convenient places . . . so that they are not deprived of all spiritual and temporal benefits . . . And bishops are to be duly diligent in implementing what has just been said, ensuring that the Indians are brought together, since their evangelization will be far easier if in the first place work is done to make them political, humane men, to lead them away from their bestial customs as a basis for the faith, which needs the ambience of a political life, a Christian and humane culture.

First Synod of Popayan (Columbia) (1555)

Those who refuse to restore to the Indians all that has been unjustly taken from them, in tribute or services, including in this category of those who inflict punishments both the judges who allow them and the persons who take part in them, those who offer their help or advice or who profit from the situation, and finally all those who prohibit marriage among the Indians, shall be excommunicated.

Third Synod of Santiago de Chile (1626)

They must be banned from taking Indians from the province of Cuyo and forcing them to work in the mines (*mita*) in this city of Santiago and its environs, going through the Cordillera, with its heavy snows, which have been the death of large numbers of men, women and children, through hunger and the rigour of storms, winds and excessive cold, and because they come on foot, like slaves, with chains, so that they cannot escape or return to their lands.

A rapid Christianization

The conquerors sought to show that the proclamation of the true religion was the motive behind the conquest. It was primarily a matter of demonstrating faith and power: crosses were set up, solemn liturgies were held, and idols were destroyed. The results were inconclusive. But hardly had the conquest been achieved than a systematic evangelization was undertaken. The most remarkable was that by the Franciscans of Mexico. Cortes had appealed to them, thinking that their poverty would make them more zealous preachers than the secular priests, who were too greedy. The mission of the Twelve landed in Mexico in 1524. It set to work with enthusiasm, and seven years later the first bishop of Mexico, Zumarraga, sketched out a triumphalist stocktaking: 'We are giving ourselves totally to the immense task of the conversion of the infidels. Through the grace of God and by the hands of the religious of the order of our seraphic father St Francis of regular observance, more than a million persons have been baptized, five hundred temples of idols have been razed to the ground, and more than twenty thousand figures of demons whom they worshipped have been broken into pieces and burned . . . and what is a matter for admiration is that of old, in their infidelity, the people of this city of Mexico had the custom of sacrificing to their idols each year more than twenty thousand human hearts, while today it is not to the demons but to God that innumerable sacrifices of praise are offered, thanks to the teaching and good example of our religious.' After fifteen years of preaching, the most famous of the Franciscans, Toribio de Bentavente, known as Motolinia, i.e. 'the poor one', a surname given him by the Indians, put forward the figure of six million baptized Indians. In the evening the religious returned to their house with 'baptismal cramp'. Of course we need to be cautious about the old statistics, yet these religious, rather too zealous for our taste, showed themselves full of concern and love for the Indians, whom they defended against the rapacity of the conquerors.

If we keep to Zumarraga's description, the first evangelizers followed the method of the 'clean sheet': Christianity was built up on the ruins of the indigenous religions and, in consequence, of the indigenous cultures. Beyond question there was some degree of adaptation. Baptism was administered at the start and without delay. Religious teaching, essentially that of children, came afterwards. The catechism was a translation of that for young Spaniards, but it was combined with original audio-visual means: pictures modelled on Mexican paintings, religious theatre and symbolic gestures. The cries of dogs and cats thrown into a fire alive were meant to evoke the cry of the damned in the fire of hell. God's commandments were put in Mexican verse and sung. The splendour of worship and the architectural exuberance of the churches seduced the crowds: there was dancing for the processions of Corpus Christi. However, the eucharist was administered parsimoniously: Indians often waited long years after baptism. The missionaries thought that two sacraments were indispensable for the baptized: marriage and penitence. To begin with, polygamy posed several problems. Which wife should the newly baptized keep? The first or the one who pleased him most? With the aim of training an indigenous clergy, Zumarraga had founded a college for the elite of Indian scholars at Tlaltelolco. However, the priesthood was refused to Indians.

The knowledge of cultures and religions

Unlike the conquerors, the religious did not try to Hispanize the Indians. Grouping them in villages, they sought to take them away from their ancient places of worship, avoid contacts with the depraved colonists and give them Christian habits. In both Mexico and Peru the evangelists made a great effort to learn the Indian languages, for which they made grammars and dictionaries. In Mexico, they were particularly, but not exclusively, interested in Nahuatl; in Peru in Quechua. It was not just a matter of translation. The missionaries wanted to understand in depth the peoples whom they were evangelizing. Many made themselves admirable chroniclers of the civilizations and religions of the American continent. The greater part of our knowledge in this area depends on them. The best known – who is neither the first nor the only one – is the Franciscan Bernardino de Sahagun, who arrived in Mexico in 1529 and remained there until his death in 1590. In 1569 he completed his *General History of the Things of the New Spain (Mexico)*, but was unable to publish it. His aim was not directly ethnographic. He wanted to know the ancient customs and religions so as to be able to root out idolatry: the physician has to know his patient's disease. But throughout his enquiries Sahagun

Why be interested in the ancient civilization of Mexico?

We know about the ancient Aztec civilization from the work of Bernardino de Sahagun (1500–1590). For the Franciscan, this knowledge was a prelude to a good evangelization. The Spanish authorities rejected his motivation and had a number of ethnological works destroyed. Bernardino de Sahagun justifies his enterprise.

The physician cannot apply a remedy for the disease unless he first knows the humour and the causes from which it proceeds; and just as the physician should have a perfect knowledge of remedies and diseases in order to apply to each of them correctly that which combats them, so it is necessary for preacher and confessors, who are the true physicians of souls in their spiritual suffering, to acquire the experience of the spiritual maladies and the medicines that they need . . . It is important for ministers involved in conversion not to limit themselves to saying, among the Indians, that there are no other sins than drunkenness, theft and carnal pleasures; for among them there are other more serious faults which require their remedies The sins of idolatry, the rites of paganism, the auguries and superstitions which they practise, have not totally disappeared. To preach against these practices and to know whether they still exist, it is necessary to know how the natives engaged in them in the time of their idolatry. For unless we have this knowledge, we shall let them do many idolatrous things in our presence without understanding them; indeed some of us pretend to excuse them, claiming that they are childish and inane things. They do not know the true source of them, and although it is idolatry, the confessors never call it to account with their penitents: they know nothing of the language they might use to enquire, and they understand none of the statements made to them in this respect. So in order that the ministers of the gospel who succeed the firstcomers in the culture of this new vineyard of the Lord may have no cause to complain that nothing has been done to dissipate the darkness surrounding the affairs of the natives of New Spain, I, Fr Bernardino de Sahagun . . ., have written twelve books on the divine, or better idolatrous, human and natural things of this New Spain.

(Bernardino de Sahagun, *General History of the Things of New Spain*)

shows an evident sympathy for the peoples whom he is describing; some of their customs were remarkable, and Sahagun regrets them and deplores the lamentable effect of colonization: 'As all the practices (idolatries) ceased with the arrival of the Spanish, who set to work trampling under foot all the customs and all the modes of government of the natives, on the pretext of reducing them to living as in Spain, as much in divine as in human matters, considering them only idolatrous and barbarous, they lost the whole of their ancient government . . . But we can now see that this new organization makes men vicious, produces the most evil thoughts in them and, even worse, works which make them hateful to God and men, not to mention the serious diseases and their shortened life.' Sahagun and the first Franciscans dreamed of a Christian and Mexican state which escaped colonization. At the end of the sixteenth century, such sympathy seemed suspect to the authorities, and Philip II ordered the destruction of these chronicles. Sahagun's work appeared only in the nineteenth century.

This knowledge of Indian languages allowed the publication of a large number of religious works in local dialects: catechisms and pious works. The missionaries tried to 'capture the sacredness' of the ancient culture to put it at the service of Christianity. They avoided speaking of the Trinity so as not to give a new foothold for polytheism. They did not put too much emphasis on the death of Christ so as not to evoke the prohibited human sacrifices. They

Quebec(1608)1674
Baltimore 1793
New Orleans 1793
Mexico 1530
Santiago 1517
Santo Domingo 1511
San Juan 1511
Chiapas 1538
Managua 1531
Caracas 1531
Panama 1513
Cartagena 1534
Quito 1546
Sao Luis 1677
Belem 1719
Lima 1541
Cuzco 1537
Recife 1676
Bahia 1551 (S.Salvador)
Charcas 1552
Asuncion 1547
Rio de Janeiro 1676
Sao Paulo 1745
Santiago 1561
Cordoba 1570
La Imperial 1564 (Concepcion)
Buenos Aires 1620

North Atlantic Ocean

Pacific Ocean

World Expansion of Christianity from the Fifteenth to the Eighteenth Centuries

Moscow ● ● Tobolsk

Irkutsk(Orthodox 1724) ●

Azores
1534 ●

Funchal
1514 ●

Ceuta
(1415) ●

Canaries
1404 ●

Peking(1601)1690 ●

Nanking 1690 ●

Kagoshima(1549) ●

Cape Verde
1534 ●

SENEGAL
(1716)

GUINEA
(1601)

Goa 1533 ●

S.Thomas 1606 ●

TONGKING
(1615)

Macao 1576 ●

Manila 1579 ●

Cochin 1558 ● Tranquebar
(Protestants, 1706)

Sao Tome 1534 ●

S.Salvador(1491)1596 ●

Masuanda Angano 1596 ●

Malacca 1558 ●

MOZAMBIQUE
(1560)

MADAGASCAR
(c17)

Mauritius(1720) ●

Timor(1562) ●

Reunion(1665) ●

South Atlantic Ocean

Indian Ocean

Pacific Ocean

Cape(Protestants, c17) ●

Southern Ocean

1511	Date of the foundation of dioceses
(1415)	Date of the first Christian settlement

Not all the dioceses are indicated and dates
may differ depending on the sources
(foundation or nomination of first bishop)

built Christian buildings on the sites of the ancient pagan temples. They set Christian festivals on the days of ancient Indian feasts. Thanks to the mendicant orders, not only were the Indians of Mexico converted, but they also remained Indians.

To begin with, the first missionaries to the New World had not envisaged the syncretism which still marks Indian Christianity deeply. The majority of Indians accepted the new religion easily. Sometimes there were signs of recalcitrance, but these were usually treated indulgently by the missionaries. However, the chief Don Carlos of Texcoco, who claimed the right to differ for the Indians, was condemned to death by the Inquisition and executed in Mexico in 1539 as a heretic and one who lived with a concubine. The Indians accepted a Christianity which allowed them, without the knowledge of the missionaries – at least for a while – to keep their ancestral heritage. In the old Christianized sanctuaries the Indians celebrated both the Christian festivals and their ancient gods. Where the missionaries had thought in terms of substitution, the Indians were practising cohabitation. In venerating Our Lady of Guadelupe in Mexico, they were continuing the cult of Tonantzin, the mother of the gods, whose temple had been replaced by that of Mary. Sahagun noted this, as did the civil authorities.

This struggle against idolatry was particularly active in Peru, where it had two great moments. The first was the time of the viceroy Francisco of Toledo (1568–1580). For him, the liquidation of Peruvian religion was an affair of state. He had grasped the link between religion and culture. It was necessary not only to evangelize but also to promote Spanish civilization. The books which described the Indian past had to be destroyed. A general visitation by churchmen and civilians should drive out idolatry from the whole country. The abjuration, baptism and execution of the last Inca, Tupac Amaru, was to give the *coup de grâce* to the old religions (1572); the cross prevailed over the sun. At the beginning of the seventeenth century the priest Francisco of Avila noted that the Indians

in his parish, who were performing all their Christian duties, continued to practise the religion of their ancestors, thanks to a clandestine network. Under cover of the Assumption, they celebrated the old deities for five days. This was the origin of a new institution: the Visitation of Idolatries or Extirpation (1609). It was for the Indians what the Inquisition was for the Spanish, but the sentences were more lenient; in the end of the day idolatry was less serious than heresy. While the Inquisitors were Dominicans, the Extirpators were Jesuits. A visitation was rather like a parochial mission: it involved confession and pious exercises, to which was added the denunciation of sorcerers and idolaters. There was a solemn destruction of pagan objects of worship. The penitents burned their mummified fathers, mothers and ancestors, whom they had kept to venerate. Efforts were made to concentrate the population so as to be able to evangelize them better and to detach them from the places of their idols. Many fled into inaccessible places. In parallel, model sermons against idolatry were composed for the priests. An apologetic for Christianity developed, which was at the same time the justification of the colonial order: the misfortunes of the Indians were punishment for their idolatry. In an enormous illustrated volume, *Nueva Coronica y buen gubierno*, a Peruvian Indian described the injustices of the conquest and everyday Christian life. Other authors attempted a deeper analysis of the ancient religions, making comparisons with Christianity, proposing systems of interpretation and grids for classification. Las Casas had begun this. Garsilaso de La Vega (1539–1616), the half-breed son of a conquistador and an Inca princess, wrote his *Royal Commentaries* (1609) in Spain. He presented Inca religion as a slow progress towards monotheism and a providential preparation for the gospel.

'The Communist Christian Republic of the Guaranis'

For a century and a half, between 1610 and 1768, about thirty 'reductions' brought together around

The reductions of Paraguay

Fr Florentin, a Capuchin, had left Port-Louis (Lorient) on 20 April 1711 bound for Pondicherry. In the course of a fantastic voyage he landed in America and visited the reductions of Paraguay before reaching his destination after three and a half years of travelling. The Jesuits passed on his account.

I entered the settlement of St Francis Xavier and went straight to the church; it faced on to large square towards which the main streets led; they were all very broad and paved with timber . . . The (Jesuit) community was made up of seven priests full of virtue and merit . . . This is the order observed in the settlement where I was, comprising around thirty thousand souls. The bell is rung at the beginning of the day to summon the people to church; a missionary says morning prayer and then mass is said, after which everyone leaves to attend to his work. Children between the ages of seven or eight and twelve have to go to school, where masters teach them to read and write, to say the catechism and the prayers of the church, and instruct them in the duties of Christianity. Girls up to the age of twelve also have to go to other schools, where mistresses of tested virtue teach them prayers and the catechism, and show them how to read, to spin, to sew, and all the other works proper to their sex . . . At sunset, evening prayer is said, after which the rosary is recited antiphonally. The union and charity which prevail between these faithful is perfect: as possessions are shared, ambition and avarice are vices unknown, and one sees neither division nor litigation among them. They are inspired with so much horror of impurity that faults in this respect are very rare; they are occupied only with prayer, work and the care of their families . . . Many things contribute to the innocent life which these new faithful lead . . . the

examples of those who govern them, in whom they see nothing but what is edifying . . . and the scant communication with the Europeans. As no mines of gold and silver are to be found in Paraguay, nor anything that excites the cupidity of men, no Spaniard thinks to settle there . . . In all these peoples there is a leader who is called the fiscal . . . He watches over the people, principally in connection with their service of God; he has a memorandum on which are written, by name and surname, all the inhabitants of the populace, the heads of families, their wives and the number of their children; he observes who are absent from prayer, the mass and preaching, and he discovers what has prevented them from being present . . . The populace is divided between different areas, and each area has a supervisor chosen from among the most ardent Christians . . . Before the Jesuit fathers had brought the light of the gospel to Paraguay, this country had been inhabited by quite barbarian peoples, without religion, without laws, without society, without habitation or fixed abode . . . It is not easy to conceive of the work that they did to bring these barbarians together and make reasonable men of them, before trying to make them Christians . . . One sees neither poor people nor beggars there, and all have an equal abundance of all the necessities of life.

(Letter of Fr Bouchet, Pondicherry, 14 February 1716, in *Curious and Edifying Letters*, 1831–43)

500,000 Guarani Indians under the wing of the Jesuits. This apparently limited achievement made a great impact which could still be felt two centuries after it had disappeared. It was seen as a 'triumph of humanity which expiated the cruelties of the first conquerors'. Paraguay seemed to be the realization of a utopia based on Christianity. In the region of the three rivers of the Parana, Paraguay and Uru-

guay, the Jesuits pacified and Christianized the nomadic populations. They settled them in 'reductions', Christian villages sheltered from colonial exploitation. This regrouping of the population, which in other places was often odious, seemed quite beneficial in Paraguay. Community life in the reduction was organized on a Christian basis; the church was at its centre and religious exercises gave rhythm to the day. Individual property could not be handed on. Each reduction was governed by a few Jesuits, rarely more than half a dozen of them, helped by subordinate Indian officials; the Spanish colonists had no access to them. However, the Portuguese from Sao Paulo came there to hunt slaves. The Treaty of the Limits (1750) brought a certain number of reductions into the Portuguese sphere. This was the death of them. The Guaranis resisted for some time, helped occasionally by a Jesuit (this is the basis of the film *Mission*), but the reductions barely survived the suppression of the Society of Jesus in Spain (1768). The system was somewhat artificial; keeping everything in their own hands, the Jesuits had not trained any real authorities.

Portuguese America: Brazil

The evangelization of Brazil began in 1549 with the arrival in Bahia of half a dozen Jesuits with Manuel da Nobrega as their superior; Bahia was the only diocese in Brazil up to the foundation of those of Rio de Janeiro and Recife in 1676. The college at Bahia served as a basis for the apostolate of the Jesuits. They came southwards, took part in the foundation of Sao Paulo (1553) and Rio de Janeiro, and established Christian villages in order to settle the nomads. The Jesuits there in practice had both temporal and spiritual jurisdiction. They set to studying the Tupi language. In the evangelization of Brazil we find many features similar to those we encountered in Spanish America, like the reluctance to give communion to the Indians, the problems posed by polygamy, the emphasis on the splendour of the cult, the refusal of the priesthood to Indians, and so on. The possibilities of evangelization were considerably limited by the small number of missionaries. In 1600 the Jesuits had only sixty-three religious for the whole of Brazil, including priests, students, novices and brothers. This helps us to understand what a catastrophe was represented by the massacre by a Protestant corsair of Fr Inacio de Azevedo and forty Jesuits whom he brought from Europe to Brazil in 1570. Furthermore, slavery presented a formidable obstacle to evangelization; the colonists only thought of capturing slaves in the Indian villages in the region of Bahia or Sao Paulo; hence the flight of the Indians, who saw no advantage in becoming Christians, and the protests of the colonists when the fathers wanted to remove the Indians from slavery.

In the seventeenth and eighteenth centuries, around ten dioceses were added to that of Bahia: Rio de Janeiro and Recife (1676); Saint Louis of Marnhao; Belem (1719), and so on. The great missionary of the seventeenth century was the Jesuit Antonio Vieira (1608–1697), also known as a great preacher. He arrived in Brazil in 1652 and organized about fifty villages along the coast. Like Montesinos on Hispaniola, he told the colonists of Belem and Saint-Louis, 'You are all in a state of mortal sin', and they gave up hunting men. Vieira bore the title of visitor to the Brazilian missions; he tried to obtain just recompense for Indians required to work, but the exploitation continued, and the Christian Indians 'returned to the forest and paganism'. The Jesuit negotiated a peace treaty with the Indian leaders. However, his concern to protect the indigenous populations made the colonists furious and they pillaged the college of Belem and expelled the fathers. The Inquisition condemned Vieira to two years in prison. Recalled to Rome, he was further pursued by Roman tribunals. At the age of sixty-three he set out for Brazil again. He died in Amazonia at the age of eighty-nine. But the abuses began again whenever a new source of profit was discovered – gold, diamonds, coffee. The Jesuits had to show moderation in their struggle against injustices, accepting the importation of the blacks to safeguard the freedom of the Indians.

French and English America

Canada

As in all overseas countries, in Canada, too, the missionaries could only follow the merchants.

The preaching of Fr Isaac Jogues to the Iroquois

After being taken prisoner by the Iroquois, the Jesuit Fr Jogues suffered numerous tortures. He took advantage of this captivity to evangelize them. He was martyred in 1646.

When I was given as a companion to some savages, they began to look at me with curiosity, then they mocked me and ended up by hating me. I did not lose sight of the charge which God had given me to fulfil, and that is why I began to teach them, but with the utmost prudence that I could muster, the worship of one God, obedience to his commandments, paradise, hell and the other mysteries of our faith. At first they listened to me, but when they saw that I returned there frequently, and above all when the game began to run out, they said that I was a demon and the cause of their bad hunting . . . I suffered greatly from hunger, since almost all the meat they ate (and that is their whole diet when hunting) had been offered to the demon, as I have said. So I spent several days without eating . . .

However, when I saw that I was being left alive, I applied myself to studying their language, and since the assemblies not only of our village but of the whole country were held in our cabin, I could begin to instruct the oldest on the mysteries of our faith. They put a thousand questions to me about the sun, the moon and the figure which its disc represents, about the circumference of the earth, the size of the ocean and the ebb and flow of the seas . . .

I tried to lead them from knowledge of the creatures to that of the Creator. I refuted the fables they told about the creation of the world, which in their view had been formed by a tortoise. I made them see that the sun, which has neither intelligence nor life, could not be a god; but that if its beauty had struck them so much that they took it for a deity, he who had created it must be even more magnificent. I added that Areskoï was not a God but a demon who falsely claimed to be the author and preserver of life, the distributor of the goods which they enjoyed.

If the savages had had no more difficulty in believing than in being convinced, my victory would have been quickly won; but one would say that the prince of this world, banished from almost all the earth by the virtue of the cross, has taken refuge in these regions as in an impregnable place . . . I instructed many other adult natives during their infirmities: some did not understand, others rejected me. Some approved of me, but only with their lips, and with a certain politeness which made them feel it coarse to contradict anyone who was speaking, a politeness capable of deluding anyone who was not on their guard.

(Isaac Jogues, *Letter to the Provincial of France*, 5 August 1643)

However, perhaps because economic interests were less, evangelization there was more disinterested than elsewhere. Like all the discoverers, Jacques Cartier had planted several crosses in his explorations of the St Lawrence (1534 and subsequently). In a first French settlement in Acadia (1606–7) it was a layman, Mark Lescarbot, who made himself preacher and catechist of the expedition and of some savages. On his return he exhorted the prelates to send missionaries. Evangelization began above all with Champlain (1567–1637), the founder of Quebec (1608); he envisaged a colony to populate the area and 'the need to propagate the faith among the infidels by bringing them some religious goods'. In 1615 he introduced some Recollects (the Franciscan branch), who settled at trading posts (fur trading), in Tadoussac, Quebec and Three Rivers, and penetrated the native areas. The Jesuits began a ministry in Acadia and then in Quebec. Lumberjacks and merchants came into conflict with the missionaries, who wanted them to settle 'clans of French' to teach the Indians to cultivate the earth. In 1627 the Society of One Hundred Associates founded by Richelieu proposed the populating and evangelization of Canada; only Catholics would be able to come.

After an interruption because of the English occupation, colonization and evangelization resumed in 1632; Champlain returned with Jesuits whose superior was Fr Le Jeune. They succeeded in creating a surge of enthusiasm about Canada in France by annual reports, which for forty years (1632–1673) described the apostolate of the Jesuits among the 'savages'. The missionaries sometimes followed the Indians as they moved around, but tried to settle them in Christian villages like Sillery (1637). In 1639, the first religious missionaries, Hospitallers from Dieppe and Ursulines from Tours, including Marie of the Incarnation, settled in Quebec. The Jesuits embarked on the evangelization of the Hurons, a semi-nomadic people in permanent conflict with the Iroquois, who were allies of the English. The mission had some success, but was annihilated when the Iroquois exterminated the Hurons; the few who escaped took refuge in Quebec (1649). Several Jesuits were martyred by the Iroquois: Isaac Jogues, Jean de Brébeuf and Charles Garnier. In 1657 the Sulpicians settled in Montreal, which had been founded in 1642, thus forming the second missionary institution in Canada after the Jesuits.

In 1674, Mgr François de Laval, initially vicar apostolic of Canada (1658), received the title of Bishop of Quebec. He was responsible for organizing the Church of New France, which from 1663 had the status of a province; for this purpose Mgr de Laval founded the Seminary of Quebec (1663), bringing together all the secular clergy. Missionary activity continued, and from 1665 shifted westwards in the direction of the Great Lakes. From the post of Michilimakinac, explorers and missionaries set out to discover the valley of the Mississippi

(1673, Jolliet and Marquette) in order to reach its mouth (1682, Cavalier de La Salle); New Orleans was founded in 1718. The small number of missionaries, often in conflict with one another (Jesuits, Foreign Missions, Capuchins), did not allow real evangelizations.

When France abandoned Canada in 1763, there were only a few thousand Indian Christians. However, it must be emphasized that behind these modest results there was some degree of originality in this evangelization. It was less bound up with colonization than in other places. Beyond question the European nations contributed towards exacerbating the fratricidal struggles between Indians, and the missionaries often denounced the evil effect of the alcohol and firearms given to the Indians in exchange for furs. However, at that time the Indians were not exploited as they were in other Spanish or Portuguese colonies, different though these were. The Sulpicians put more emphasis on introducing French customs, while the Jesuits abandoned this after a certain time; eventually they fell in with the Indians' way of life, accepting their nomadism. Rather than follow them, they met them when they passed through trading places. Without being the only ones to do so, the Jesuits made a great effort to learn Indian languages, very soon translating catechisms and various religious books. Fr J.-B. de la Brosse became a legendary figure in his apostolate among the Monatagnais of Tadoussac. He published the first Indian book printed in Canada in 1767; it was a book of prayers and a catechism in which he showed how much he had adapted to the Montagnais mentality.

The French Antilles

France formed colonies in the Spanish domain: Guadeloupe (1635) and San Domingo (Haiti, 1665). The apostolate was directed at colonists and black slaves, whose number was considerable compared to the scant population in French Canada: on the eve of the Revolution there were 80,000 blacks on Martinique, 90,000 on Guadeloupe and 400,000 on

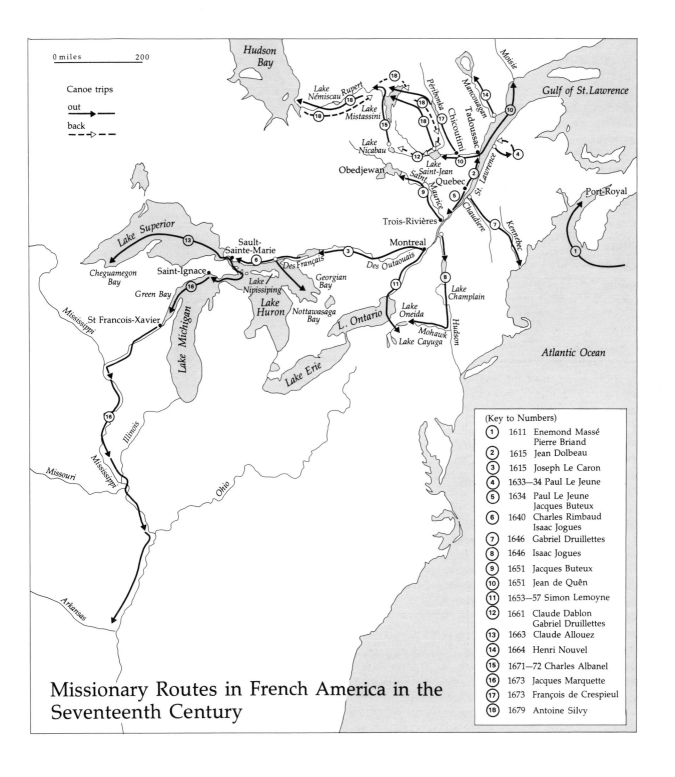

Canoe trips

out ──────▶

back ─ ─ ─▷

Hudson Bay

Lake Némiscau Rupert
Lake Mistassini
Lake Nicabau
Obedjewan
Lake Saint-Jean
Péribonka
Saint-Maurice
Chicoutimi
Tadoussac
Manouagan
Moisie
Gulf of St. Lawrence
Port-Royal
Quebec
St. Lawrence
Chaudière
Kennebec
Trois-Rivières
Montreal
Des Outaouais
Des Français
Lake Superior
Cheguamegon Bay
Sault-Sainte-Marie
Saint-Ignace
Lake Nipissiping
Georgian Bay
Lake Huron
Nottawasaga Bay
Green Bay
St François-Xavier
Lake Michigan
Mississippi
Missouri
Illinois
Ohio
Arkansas
Lake Erie
L. Ontario
Lake Oneida
Lake Cayuga
Mohawk
Lake Champlain
Hudson
Atlantic Ocean

(Key to Numbers)

① 1611 Enemond Massé
       Pierre Briand
② 1615 Jean Dolbeau
③ 1615 Joseph Le Caron
④ 1633–34 Paul Le Jeune
⑤ 1634 Paul Le Jeune
       Jacques Buteux
⑥ 1640 Charles Rimbaud
       Isaac Jogues
⑦ 1646 Gabriel Druillettes
⑧ 1646 Isaac Jogues
⑨ 1651 Jacques Buteux
⑩ 1651 Jean de Quên
⑪ 1653–57 Simon Lemoyne
⑫ 1661 Claude Dablon
       Gabriel Druillettes
⑬ 1663 Claude Allouez
⑭ 1664 Henri Nouvel
⑮ 1671–72 Charles Albanel
⑯ 1673 Jacques Marquette
⑰ 1673 François de Crespieul
⑱ 1679 Antoine Silvy

Missionary Routes in French America in the Seventeenth Century

San Domingo. The royal government still refused to create dioceses and establish recognized schools for fear that the colonists would seek to emancipate themselves. The church was under the control of apostolic prefects, closely dependent on the officials. The ecclesiastical personnel were too small in number and quality, since the religious superiors sent to the islands those they wanted to get rid of; the administrators claimed that they had only the sweepings of the cloisters and the 'scum of the dioceses', or even that 'pious monks do not come to the colonies'. The Jesuits were an exception by virtue of their quality and their concern for an adapted apostolate.

The colonists were often indifferent, if not frankly anti-religious. The Black Code (1685) made it a duty of the owners to evangelize Negro slaves; in general they were uninterested, if they were not actually opposed. The Jesuits, who adopted Creole – some knew African languages – , tried to organize communities of slaves, to train black catechists and to prepare carefully for baptism.

English America

Here it was not so much a matter of evangelizing pagans as setting up European colonists. The English colonies of America welcomed a certain number of Anglicans in Virginia, for example (1607), but above all a host of religious dissidents who found there the freedom they did not have in England. The earliest and most famous were the Pilgrim Fathers of the Mayflower, Puritans who landed in Massachusetts in 1620. It is said that they fell to their knees in thanksgiving and then attacked the Indians, whom they thought an inferior race which God had not chosen. In the first years they showed an extraordinary intolerance (the Witches of Salem, 1692). However, the preacher John Elliott (1603–1690) heard the call of the Indians. He claimed that the twelve tribes of Israel were in America and that Christ would return in New England; he wanted to establish a theocracy. He learned the language, founded a missionary society, translated the Bible and brought together several thousand Indians. This effort was not properly followed up. William Penn, a Quaker disciple of George Fox, settled on the banks of the Delaware in 1682, founding the colony of Pennsylvania, in which freedom of conscience was guaranteed to all. John Wesley was disappointed by his missionary experience in Georgia (1735–1738). However, it was there that he encountered the Moravian Brothers, those dissident Pietists who were intensely missionary. Their organizer, Zinzendorf, himself spent two years in this colonial America (1741–1743). Later, with George Whitefield, Methodism aroused the enthusiasm of the colonists. At the time when the English colonies proclaimed their independence (1776), the new state seemed to be a land of religious freedom. The first Catholic diocese was founded in Baltimore in 1789, and there were Jews in the cities.

Francis Xavier and the evangelization of Japan

Francis Xavier is the type of missionary in modern times which hagiography has immeasurably exaggerated. In his letters, which overflow with evangelical enthusiasm, he comes over as a mystic of mission. These letters were largely edited, but Frs Schurhammer and Wicki have restored the authentic text (1944–1945). This does not diminish the person of Francis; however, it invites us not to make him an isolated meteor, but to put him in his political and religious context.

Francis Xavier's sphere of action was the Portuguese patronage. Arriving on the coast of Malabar in 1498, Vasco da Gama laid the foundations of a Portuguese maritime empire, of which Albuquerque (died 1515) was the first architect. This empire consisted of trading posts in a line from the Persian Gulf to Japan: Ormuz (1507), Goa (1510), Malacca (1511), the Sunda Islands, Macao (1557). Goa became the diocese (1533) and then the archdiocese (1557) of all eastern Asia, the pivot of evangelization. Macao in turn was elevated to a diocese in 1576. The Portuguese patronage linked up with the

The Christian instruction of the Paravars on the Fisher Coast

The first mission that Francis Xavier received was to give Christian instructions to the Paravars, inhabitants of the Fisher Coast, who had been baptized without any catechesis. This letter of 1545 aroused great enthusiasm: it is a good example of the 'first mode' of evangelizing, the 'clean sheet', pure and harsh.

To my companions living in Rome, Cochin, 15 January 1544.

We are among the Christians of Cape Comorin . . . They are numerous, and their number is added to every day. As soon as I arrived on the coast where they live, I tried to discover from them what knowledge they have of Christ our Saviour . . . The only reply I received from them was that they are Christians and that, since they do not understand our language, they know neither our law nor what they are to believe. Since they did not understand me, nor I them, because their mother tongue is Malabar (Tamil) and mine is Basque, I gathered together the most educated among them and sought out people who understood our language (Portuguese) and theirs. After meeting with great difficulty over long days, we have translated the prayers, first of all the way of making the sign of the cross, confessing that the three Persons are one God; then the Creed, the commandments, the Pater Noster, the Ave Maria, the Salve Regina and the general confession, in Latin and Malabar. After translating them into their languages and teaching them so that they are known by heart, I went all round the village with a bell in my hand, to gather together all the men and children that I could find. Once they were assembled, I instructed them twice a day. For a month I taught them prayers, having commanded the children to teach their fathers and mothers and all those in their homes and in their neighbourhood what they had learned at school . . . The children felt great horror at the idolatries of the Gentiles (pagans), to the point that they often fought with the Gentiles and reprimanded their fathers and mothers when they saw them worshipping idols; they came to me and denounced them. I brought together all the young people of the village and went with them to the place where they made idols. The children seized the idols and broke them into pieces as fine as ash; then they spat on them, trampled them under foot and did other things to them. Although it is not seemly to call them by their name, it is to the honour of these children that they did that to one (the devil) who had the great audacity to have himself worshipped by their parents.

Spanish patronage in the Philippines, whose colonists and missionaries came from Mexico (Manila became a diocese in 1579).

The 'two modes' of Francis Xavier

Born in Navarre in 1506, Francis Xavier was part of a group of seven companions who, around Ignatius of Loyola, took a vow in Montmartre on 15 August 1534. In 1540, Ignatius designated him missionary for the East Indies. He left from Lisbon with the title of apostolic nuncio for the domains of the *padroado*, and arrived in Goa in 1542. After some months of a 'European' ministry (college), he left for South India, for the Fisher Coast. Apart from a few translated phrases, he did not know the Indian language or anything about Indian culture. He baptized thousands of people after an ultra-rapid catechesis. He wrote ardent letters to Europe. His method was that of the 'blank sheet'; it was necessary to destroy the signs of idolatry to become a Christian. It was enough for a missionary to be strong and independent. In 1545 Francis was in Malacca and in 1546 on the Sunda Islands. An encounter with a converted Japanese pirate gave him the idea of going to Japan. With several companions he landed at Kagoshima in the south of the island of Kyushu on 15 August 1549. They were well received by the Japanese, who were avid for novelties: spices, materials, arquebuses. Con-

The qualities required of missionaries, depending on the mission field

Circumstances did not allow Francis Xavier to make contact with the culture of India. He was preoccupied with the urgency of baptism. In Japan he came to understand the need for a conversion of the understanding.

To Ignatius of Loyola, in Rome. Cochin, 27 January 1545 . . .
Persons who do not have the necessary talent for confessing, preaching and performing functions connected with the Society, after completing their *Exercises* and having served for some months in humble tasks, would do great service in this country, provided that they had physical as well as spiritual strength. In fact in these countries of the infidels, science is not necessary; it is enough to teach prayers and visit the villages in order to baptize the children there.

To Ignatius of Loyola, in Rome. Goa, 9 April 1552 . . .
It is necessary for them [the fathers who are to go to Japan] to have sufficient knowledge to be able to reply to the numerous questions posed by the Japanese. It would be good for them to be masters of arts, and nothing would be lost if they were dialecticians who could lead the Japanese to contradict themselves in discussions. They should know something of the heavenly sphere, since the Japanese take great pleasure in noting the movements of the sky, the eclipses of the sun, the waxing and waning of the moon, and knowing how rain, storms and hail, thunder and lightning, are produced . . .

(*Letters* 47, 110)

fronted with the complexity of Japanese life, Francis reconsidered his missionary method: a knowledge of the language was indispensable to avoid any confusion; it was necessary to adopt the customs of the country in matters of dress and politeness; the missionary must have done solid philosophical study in Europe and then have attended the Japanese universities. This has been called the 'second mode' of Francis Xavier. In two years he converted rather less than one thousand Japanese, but he understood that evangelism was a long-term work and not a spiritual conquest. As he was told that China was the source of the wisdom of Japan and that from China one could travel to Jerusalem, he decided to go there, but died before he arrived, on 3 December 1552.

The Christian century in Japan

In feudal Japan, mission experienced great success until the end of the sixteenth century: the daimyos, local rulers, showed their independence by becoming Christians, and Christianity arrived at a time when Buddhism was decadent. The Japanese did not separate science and religion; the civilization of Europe seemed to them one gigantic structure, the sole foundation of which was Christianity; and Christianity benefited from the enthusiasm aroused by cannons! Around 1590, the number of Christians may have reached 300,000 in a Japan whose population was one fifth that of today; they were concentrated above all in the south, on the island of Kyushu, and in the regions of Kyoto and Edo (Tokyo). The main organizer of this first church, the Jesuit Alessandro Valignano, arrived at Macao in 1578 as a visitor to the eastern missions. He remained there until 1606. He opted for Francis Xavier's 'second mode', adapting his mode of dress and preferring silk to cotton. The Jesuits destined for Japan were obliged to pass through Lisbon, Goa and Macao to avoid any discussion with the missionaries who practised the 'clean sheet' approach in Mexico and Manila. Valignano had four young Japanese noblemen sent to Europe. Their trip, which took eight years (1582–1590), was a great and exotic success in the Catholic courts of Europe and in Rome.

The damnation of the infidels, a stimulus towards evangelization

Francis Xavier here is only bearing witness to a majority opinion of his time. Adults who die outside the Catholic Church are damned. Certain theologians allowed children the possibility of limbo. This opinion explains the mass baptisms and baptisms of dying infants.

29 January 1552

A great desolation is felt by the Christians of Japan, an enormous regret: that we say that hell is eternal for those who go there. If they feel this, it is out of love of their fathers, mothers, wives, children and others who have already died, towards whom they feel pity. Many bewail the dead and ask me if they can benefit in any way from alms or prayers. I say that there is no remedy for them.

They feel this desolation, but that does not displease me at all; in this way they will not neglect themselves and will not go to damnation with their ancestors. They ask me if God can remove them from hell. I have spoken to them fully on all that. They do not stop crying when they see that there is no remedy for their ancestors. And I too am seized by some grief, seeing such beloved and dear friends weeping over things which are irremediable.

(*Letter* 96)

Few in number – there were never more than one hundred of them – the missionaries made a remarkable effort to understand Japanese culture: there was symbiosis rather than conflict between the two cultures. The missionaries assimilated Japan and transmitted Europe; they introduced printing. The Portuguese Luis Frois, who was in Japan from 1563 to 1597, composed grammars and dictionaries, translated works in both directions and acquired a great concrete knowledge of Japanese religions. Organtino, another Jesuit, said at the end of a long stay: 'I am more Japanese than Italian, since by his grace, God has transformed me in this people.'

Valignano wanted the establishment of a Japanese clergy to include priests and bishops, but it proved difficult to train them: parents would not let their children go to the colleges; learning Latin posed enormous problems to the people of the Far East; and celibacy was not accepted. Japan, which was initially a dependency of Macao, had a Jesuit bishop, Cerqueira, from 1598 to 1614, living at Nagasaki. On his death there were fourteen Japanese priests: seven Jesuit priests and seven secular priests. But in addition to priests there were other ministers, who made it possible for communities to flourish, the dojukus, religious of an inferior category, and the cambos, heads of communities, catechists and many authoritative figures in brotherhoods.

In the sphere of liturgy, the missionaries based themselves on the taste of the Japanese for ceremonies: processions and funerals were solemn; songs, poetry and religious theatre were used to teach the faith. The ministry to the poor, the sick and the lepers was guaranteed in hospitals, but the fathers had to entrust these charitable activities to the brotherhood, since by performing them in person they incurred the scorn of the Japanese, who saw this as the task of slaves. The missionaries of other orders also complained of treachery to the cross of Christ!

The destruction of Japanese Christianity

The political changes within Japan and commercial rivalries between Europeans lie at the beginning of the persecution and almost complete destruction of the church of Japan. At the end of the sixteenth century, several political figures tried to restore the unity of Japan. The Jesuits supported the Christian daimyos, who were thought of as separatists. In 1587, General Hideyoshi, who had the title of regent, promulgated a decree which proscribed Christianity: the missionaries were to leave Japan within twenty days. In fact the decree was not put

Evangelization in Japan is not the same as evangelization in Mexico

The missionaries grasped the difference between the 'clean sheet' method practised in the Spanish colonies and the 'adaptation' recommended in Asia in certain spheres of the Portuguese patronage.

It can easily be observed how little the conversion of Japan resembles other conversions in the world. In fact throughout the Indies of New Spain, in Peru and the Philippines, the Indians do not ask questions. They are content to listen and believe what they are told: to this kind of Indians one can apply the gospel saying 'compel them to come in', for it is necessary to constrain them at least to hear the preaching, so that they can arrive at the knowledge of God. However, in Japan conditions are amazingly different: all the inhabitants there are free individuals and it is as free individuals that they use their liberty; they ask very difficult questions with a truly surprising ingenuity.

Here at Kyoto, in baptism we use the sacred oil that we brought from Manila; the Jesuits did not use oil because they did not have any . . . At the request of ten Jesuits we gave up our way of baptizing so as not so suggest that other forms of baptism were invalid . . . It would be dangerous to want to introduce all the customs of the Roman church abruptly. So all this must be looked upon piously; it is necessary to take the pulse of the Japanese nation in order to know how to grant dispensations and let things go, accommodating greatly to the fathers, among whom there are certainly truly learned and holy men.

(Jerome of Jesus, a Portuguese Franciscan, 1595)

into force. The Spaniards who had come from the Philippines also wanted to have their place in Japan for trade and preaching, and some Franciscans began to evangelize with the clean sheet methods that they practised in Mexico. In 1597, when one of their galleons, laden with silver, was confiscated by the Japanese, the Spaniards threatened Japan with the wrath of Philip II. Then, in the name of the 1587 edict, Hideyoshu had six Franciscans, three Japanese Jesuit brothers and seventy Christians condemned to death. They were crucified at Nagasaki on 5 February 1597. The event did not have any immediate repercussions, but the divisions between Europeans became obvious. The Spaniards wanted to compete with the Portuguese trade in which the Jesuits took part to keep their missions alive. While the Portuguese were content with trade, the Spanish had conquest in mind. Furthermore, Dutch and English Protestants discredited the Catholic powers with the Japanese, who concluded that technology was not tied to Catholicism.

In 1600, Tokugawa Ieyasu became shogun (prime minister); he restored central government, fighting against the Christian daimyos, many of whom apostasized. The missionaries were accused of wanting to change the government of the country, of trying to become masters of the land, and of being opposed to Shinto, the cultural and religious tradition of Japan. On 27 January 1614 an edict which proscribed Christianity throughout Japan unleashed a general persecution, which became increasingly bloody under three successive shoguns; it took on unimaginable forms of cruelty and sadism. In 1622 there were forty-five executions at the great stake of Nagasaki. After the insurrection of Shimbara in 1628, 35,000 Christians were massacred. Japan was definitively closed to Europeans until 1858. Some attempts at clandestine entry by missionaries were paid for by new martyrdoms. However, groups of Christians surveyed, and were rediscovered in the nineteenth century.

India

The impact of the letters of Francis Xavier and the presence of his tomb in Goa brought him the reputation of being the apostle of India. However, we have seen that his stay there was very brief. The evangelization of India had begun in antiquity; several Western religious had spent some time there in the fourteenth century and evangelization assumed original forms above all in the seventeenth century.

The Christians of St Thomas

Traditionally, in South India a Christian community claimed to have been founded by the apostle St Thomas, whose tomb was venerated on the east coast at Mylapore. We know that in the fifth century this church was in communication with the communities of Syria; later, it received its hierarchy from Mesopotamia (Seleucia-Ctesiphon). The Syro-Malabars were considered Nestorians by the Christians of the West. They had been integrated into the caste system. When the Portuguese settled in India, the Christians of St Thomas had no difficulty in regarding themselves as in communion with Rome. But when the Portuguese, in the name of the *padroado*, installed bishops at Goa (1533) and at Cochin (1558), they considered that these Christians were their preserve. In 1559, the Synod of Diamper imposed the wishes of the archbishop of Goa. The Syro-Malabars were cut off from Mesopotamia. Their bishop was to be designated by the *padroado*. They were to follow Latin usage in the liturgy and in priestly celibacy. Dogmatic formulations would be closely controlled. After an apparent submission, a conflict broke out in the seventeenth century. In 1653, part of the community went into schism, having a bishop, Thomas, ordained by a Jacobite bishop of Antioch. Thus came into being the Jacobite church of India, which is regarded as Monophysite.

From clean sheet to adaptation

The Portuguese tried to establish a Christianity of a Western type in accordance with the principle of the clean sheet. Francis Xavier is a good example this. They understood nothing of Hinduism, did not know the languages and preached through interpreters. The bad translations produced ridiculous renderings – *misei*, which was used for 'mass', means 'moustache' in Tamil. The castes seemed to them to be an enormity: the high castes scorned Christianity and the few converts belonged to the low castes. The question 'Do you want to be a Christian?' was translated 'Do you want to be Parangi', which amounted to saying 'Do you want to become Portuguese or European?'. In the trading posts where the Portuguese directly exercised political power, they demolished the pagan temples, put Muslims to death, and established the Inquisition and its auto da fés.

From Goa, in three stages, the Jesuits entered into relations with the great Mogul Akbar (1556–1605), a syncretistic ruler who wanted to establish a universal religion based on Islam, Hinduism and Christianity. The Jesuits could preach at Lahore. The affair had no sequel, since Akbar's successors changed the policy.

The arrival of the Jesuit Roberto Nobili (1577–1656) in South India (1605) profoundly changed the perspective of evangelization. Born in Tuscany of an aristocratic family, he was sent to Madurai in South India, where he lived for more than half a century. He very quickly became aware of the difficulties arising from a lack of knowledge of Tamil and the confusion between Christianity and the European way of life. He knew the experience of Ricci in China (cf. the end of this chapter), but the problems in India were even more complex than those in China. To distinguish political and social behaviour from a religious attitude was difficult in Madurai, an intellectual centre of Brahmanism. Nobili refused to be regarded as 'Parangi'. He presented himself as a Roman rajah (nobleman) and *sannyasi*, i.e. a penitent who has renounced the world. He assimilated to the Brahmin caste and adopted the garb of the *sannyasi*: yellow robe, clogs, Brahminic thread. He learned Tamil and Sanskrit; he initiated himself into Indian philosophy, trying to discover parallels between this wisdom and

Father Robert Nobili portrayed by his provincial

A letter from Fr Alberto Laerzio, Provincial of Malabar, to the General Claudio Acquaviva, Cochin, 20 November 1609.

Like St Paul who, following the example of the eternal Word, made himself all things to all men, Fr Nobili said, 'I too shall become an Indian to save the Indians . . .' He introduced himself to the Brahmins, protesting that he was neither Prangui nor Portuguese but a Roman rajah, i.e. a nobleman, and a *sannyasi*, i.e. a penitent who has renounced the world and all its pleasures . . . From that moment Fr Robert Nobili accepted only Brahmins in his service. Rice, milk, herbs and water taken once a day were his sole nourishment; his costume a long robe of saffron cloth covered with a kind of rochet of the same colour, a white or red veil on his shoulders, a hat on his head in the form of a turban, a wooden sole fixed on a support two inches high and attached to each foot by a peg which went between the toes. He added to it the thread, the distinctive sign of the caste of Brahmins and rajahs, but instead of the three strands which usually formed this thread he used five, three of gold and two of silver, with a cross suspended in the middle. He said that the three golden strands represented the Holy Trinity, the two silver strands the body and soul of the humanity we worship, and the cross recalled the passion and death of the Lord.

Christianity; he composed numerous works in Tamil. He did not preach in public, but waited to be asked for an interview. The converts were not forced to abandon the practice of their caste: they could keep the *kuomi* (tuft of hair at the top of the skull) and the thread, and even celebrate certain festivals. In baptism Nobili suppressed the secondary rites of breathing on the candidate and the imposition of saliva (the *ephphata*), which were repugnant to Indians. These methods, which had some success, provoked the opposition of the

Hindus and several missionaries. Nobili was denounced to Goa and then to Rome. Cardinal Bellarmine thought that he had become a pagan. The Jesuit bishop of Cranganore, Roz, defended him. This gave Nobili an opportunity to specify his thought and expound his missionary method. Pope Gregory XV accepted the adaptations in 1623.

Nobili was able to continue his ministry. However, by reason of his choice, his action was limited to members of the high castes. He could only meet people of low caste secretly at night, hence he was criticized: people chuckled when he offered the host to the untouchables on the end of a stick. So Nobili had the idea of forming a new category of missionaries who would adopt the life-style of other Hindu penitents, the pandaras: these could dedicate themselves to the low castes. Thus there were two categories of missionary, and the Jesuit pandaras became far more numerous than the Jesuit *sannyasis*. At Nobili's death, the Madurai mission numbered 4,000 Christians, 26 of whom were Brahmins.

New problems

The decline of the Portuguese empire, which began at the end of the sixteenth century, became irreme-diable in the seventeenth century. The Dutch, the English, the French and even the Danes established themselves all over India, while the Portuguese clung to Goa without wanting to renounce any prerogatives of the *padroado*. In particular they rejected the nominations of vicars apostolic by the Propaganda. Tense conflicts ensued; diplomatic relations were broken off between Rome and Portu-gal for thirty years (1640–1670); for lack of pontifical confirmation, the bishops of the *padroado* were not replaced. At the end of the century there was a war of oaths: Goa required of all missionaries an oath of obedience to the king of Portugal, and the Prop-aganda required an oath from the vicars apostolic. The French king required French missionaries not to take an oath on either side. The 'Propagandists' began to insist on a repetition of the confessions

of the 'padroadists', validated their marriages and vice versa.

To this must be added the tensions with the St Thomas Christians mentioned earlier and the hub-bub over the Rites Dispute. Nevertheless, there were some very fine missionaries in this period. Juan de Britto, a Portuguese Jesuit, had chosen to become a pandara at Madurai at a time when local wars were bringing many sufferings to Christians. He was condemned to death, but was pardoned and expelled in 1688. Despite threats, he returned to India, refused a bishopric and made numerous conversions. That of a prince brought down on him the wrath of the king of Morava, who had him assassinated. He was not canonized until 1941, since he had been a supporter of the adaptation of rites. The Austrian Jesuit Johann-Ernest Hanxleden was the first to produce a Sanskrit grammar as well as poems and hymns. Constancio Beschi, an Italian Jesuit, who arrived in Madurai in 1711, is regarded as one of the great figures of Tamil literature. Among other things he composed a Tamil gram-mar, epic poems and stories which have become classics. It is said that he baptized on average 300 adults a year; in his day the Christian population of Madurai rose to 150,000, as compared to about a dozen missionaries. However, the mission had its ups and downs, depending on the attitude of the local rulers. Furthermore, Beschi had competition from the Lutheran mission which had become established at Tranquebar.

The Lutheran mission at Tranquebar

The Reformers were not very inclined to preach to pagans. This seemed to them to go against the sovereignty of God, who gives faith to whom he wills, and to be part of the sphere of works. Apart from some isolated cases, it was first in German Pietist circles at the end of the seventeenth century and the beginning of the eighteenth that Protestant-ism became interested in mission, in particular in the framework of the University of Halle. This interpretation was focussed on the person of

The Lutheran missionaries in India seen by a Jesuit

A Catholic missionary can only denigrate a Pro-testant missionary! The purchase of conversions is a topic which constantly recurred until quite recently.

Letter from Fr de Bouzes
Madurai mission, 25 November 1718

It seems to me that the Lutherans plan to imitate the zeal which true Catholics have always had to extend the knowledge of the true God among the idolatrous nations. The king of Denmark is spend-ing a great deal to support some preachers at Tranquebar: this is a Danish place situated on the cost of Cholamandalam or, as they say in Europe, Coromandel. He gives them enough money to support them and several catechists, to buy a printing house and have books printed in Tamil, and to purchase small children and make Lutherans of them. We are told that through money they have won over five hundred persons to their sect. As for us, we are not allowed to assist our neophytes openly, even if we had the means: I have been given very serious advice on this, to the effect that the maniacarem (which is the title of the ruler of one or more peoples) should not imagine that I am rich. This one feature should give some idea of the country in which we live. It is not the same for the Lutheran preachers; they are in a Danish town, where they have nothing to fear from the avarice of the Gentiles.

(Edifying Letters)

August Hermann Francke (1663–1712): 'He who loves Christ must make him known.' Frederick IV, king of Denmark, asked Francke for two of his pupils to go as missionaries to the Danish colony of Tranquebar on the eastern coast of South India (1706). The German Bartholomew Ziegenbalg was the initiator of this mission. The Lutheran mis-sionaries translated into Tamil the Bible, Luther's Lesser Catechism and some Pietist hymns, which they printed from 1713 onwards. An indigenous preacher, Aaron, who was baptized in 1718, was ordained pastor in 1733. To counter the Protestant preaching, Beschi published in Tamil an account of Catholic doctrine in eighteen chapters and founded a catechetical school. However, since he was respected for his knowledge of the language, the Lutherans allowed his Tamil grammar to be printed on their presses (1737). The Protestant mission, after reaching around 18,000 faithful, declined at the end of the eighteenth century.

China

Macao, the port of China

When the Europeans resumed links with China at the beginning of the sixteenth century, they did not immediately make the same connections with Cathay as the travellers and missionaries of the Middle Ages. The Portuguese came into contact with China in 1514, but they did not gain a solid foothold. Macao, at the mouth of the Canton river, until 1557. A wall separated the little peninsula from the interior of China, which the Portuguese could penetrate only twice or three times a year. A Jesuit community was founded in 1565; it served as a staging post with Japan. An episcopal see was created in 1576, and a Christianity grew up on the Western model: the Chinese who became Christ-ians took a Portuguese name, cut their hair, and adopted Portuguese customs like games of chance. It seemed impossible for missionaries to penetrate this continent.

The man of letters from the Great West

In 1578, the Jesuit visitor, Valignano, selected Fr Michele Ruggieri to study the Chinese language. In 1582 he added a new arrival, Fr Matteo Ricci, who had much more facility in this apprenticeship. On 10 September 1583, the two Jesuits went on to the continent. Apart from two brief stays at Macao,

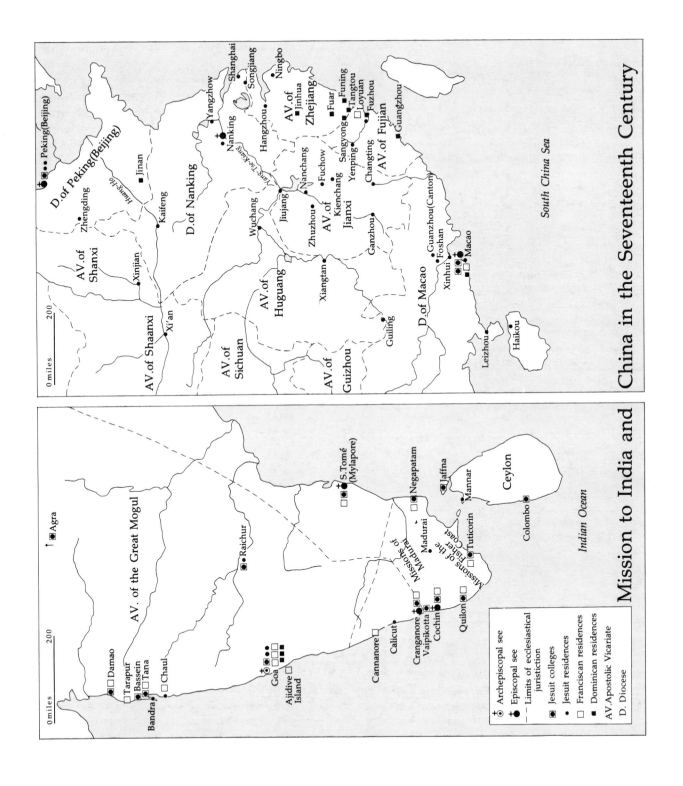

China in the Seventeenth Century

D. of Peking(Beijing)

Peking(Beijing)

Zhengding

AV. of
Shanxi

Xinjian

AV. of Shaanxi

Xi'an

Jinan

Kaifeng

D. of Nanking

Wuchang

AV. of
Sichuan

AV. of
Huguang

Xiangtan

Guiling

AV. of
Guizhou

Yangzhou

Nanking

Hangzhou

Jiujiang

Nanchang

AV. of
Kienchang
Jianxi

Zhuzhou

Ganzhou

Shanghai

Songjiang

Ningbo

AV. of
Zhejiang

Jinhua

Fuar

Funing

Tangtou

Loyuan

Sangyong

Yenping

Changting

Fuzhou

AV. of Fujian

Guangzhou

D. of Macao

Guanzhou(Canton)

Foshan

Xinhui

Macao

Leizhou

Haikou

South China Sea

0 miles   200

Yang-Tsé-Kiang

Huang-Ho

Fuchow

Mission to India and

Agra

AV. of the Great Mogul

Damao

Tarapur

Bassein

Tana

Bandra

Chaul

Goa

Ajidive
Island

Raichur

Cannanore

Calicut

Cranganore

Vaipikotta

Cochin

Quilon

Missions of
Madurai

Madurai

Missions of the
Fisher Coast

Tuticorin

S. Tomé
(Mylapore)

Negapatam

Jaffna

Mannar

Colombo

Ceylon

Indian Ocean

0 miles   200

+ Archepiscopal see
+ Episcopal see
- Limits of ecclesiastical
  jurisdiction
◉ Jesuit colleges
• Jesuit residences
□ Franciscan residences
■ Dominican residences
AV. Apostolic Vicariate
D. Diocese

Fr Matteo Ricci in China: an adapted form of preaching

These texts contain the broad outlines of Ricci's apologetics. Christianity is a religion in conformity with nature and reason. Confucianism, considered solely as a morality and a discipline for life, can be a way towards the true religion.

Fr Matteo (Ricci) adopted the dress of the men of letters, but mainly of those who call themselves preachers of the law. This dress is truly modest and the hat is quite like ours, also made in the form of a cross. And he presented himself as a man of letters not only in his dress but even more in his discourse, claiming to be a preacher of the divine law. For he devoted himself entirely to reproving the two sects of idolaters (Buddhists and Taoists) and convicting them of error. However, when it came to the sect of the men of letters, not only did he not censure them, but he also took them seriously and lavished high praise on Confucius their prince, who preferred to keep silence over what he did not know touching the other life rather than mention it, and appropriated the precepts of his law to shape the life of each individual and govern his family and the kingdom well with right and equity. This form of dress by a foreigner seemed quite new, but it was very much approved of by the men of letters . . . They called the Father a true man of letters, who, worshipping one God, did not want to soil true worship by paying homage to false gods, as several men of letters do in China today.

Father Matthew first began this study of Chinese letters, and after that, being more assured of what he had learned, gained the admiration of the Chinese men of letters who had never read any foreigner from whom they could learn something . . . Fr Matthew began with cosmographical and astrological precepts. After that he wrote twenty-five very brief treatises on different moral questions and on moderating the depraved affections of the soul, which the Chinese have called sentences . . . Fr Matthew laid out his treatise on Christian doctrine in such a way as to commend it chiefly to the pagans . . . The whole discipline of this work consisted in arguments drawn more from the light of nature than from the authority of holy scripture. For by this means the way was smoothed towards arriving easily at the mysteries which depend on faith and divinely revealed knowledge. Nor was there any lack of testimonies drawn from the ancient volumes of the Chinese themselves; these served our purpose, and the whole of the work was not only adorned with them but also confirmed by readers who readily added faith to the opinion of their authors. Moreover in this volume all the sects published among the Chinese were refuted except that which took its origin from the law of nature and which Prince Confucius had chiefly declared; this is the sect of those who are called men of letters . . . So our Fathers used the authority of the sect and simply said that what had happened since Confucius needed to be added to it.

(Matteo Ricci and Nicolas Trigault, *History of the Christian Expedition to the Kingdom of China, 1582–1610*)

Ricci never left the Chinese empire until his death; Ruggieri soon abandoned China. From his first abode at Chao-ch'ing, not far from Canton, Ricci planned to go by stages to Peking: Shaozhu (1589), Nan-ch'ing (1595), Nanking (1599) and finally Peking (1601). At first Ricci modelled himself on the Buddhist bonze. He then saw that the bonzes were not very highly esteemed by the Chinese and in particular by the men of letters, disciples of Confucius, whose importance he came to understand through his knowledge of Chinese language and culture. So he exchanged the bonze's rough robe for the silk robe of the men of letters and took a Chinese name, Li-ma-tu; from then on he presented himself as a man of letters from the Great West, and adopted all the Chinese courtesies.

Ricci had grasped Chinese perfectly and wrote works which brought him the esteem and friendship of the men of letters, like his *Treatise on Friendship* (1595). At the same time, he made Christian civilization and Western techniques known, putting to good use his former study of mathematics and astronomy at the College of Rome with the Jesuit Clavius. He made maps of the world and clocks, and translated mathematical treatises like Euclid's *Elements of Geometry* into Chinese; of course all this was a way of interesting the Chinese in Christianity. He established connections between Christianity and Chinese morality, especially Confucianism. In fact, seeking to convert the men of letters and knowing their opposition to the two currents of popular Chinese religion, Taoism and Buddhism, Ricci made use of Confucius, whom he emphasized at the expense of the two 'idolatrous sects'; for him, since Confucianism was not a religion but a rule of life, it could easily accommodate itself with Christianity, which came five centuries later. From this perspective Ricci wrote in Chinese a presentation of Catholic dogma: *The True Meaning of the Doctrine of the Master of Heaven*. Ricci did not make many converts, but several mandarins adopted Christianity after long scientific conversations with the Jesuit. The best known of them is Hsu Kuang-ch'i, who took the name of Paul on his baptism. At the time of Ricci's death in 1610, the community numbered around 2,000 Christians, spread along the road from Canton to Peking. 'I am leaving you in front of an open door', he remarked to his Christian friends before his death. The Christian mission was tolerated, since the emperor had given land for the tomb of the Jesuit scholar.

Problems to be resolved

If Ricci's successors could regard the future of Christianity in China with some optimism, at the same time they knew that they would have to overcome three great difficulties glimpsed by Ricci. First of all there was the problem of terms: what Chinese words should be used to designate Christian realities, and particularly the name of God? Ricci had thought that he could use Confucian terms:

God could be designated as Heaven (*T'ien*) or the Lord on High (*Shang T'i*). However, certain Jesuits did not agree, particularly those who had lived in Japan; they thought that these terms did not refer to a personal God. Ricci's successor Longebardo wanted to keep to 'Lord of Heaven' (*T'ien-chu*). Finally, after a discussion which was referred back to Rome, Ricci's formulations were accepted. Another question: could Chinese Christians be allowed to continue to pay homage to the dead and to Confucius? Ricci thought so. For him, it was necessary to regard this homage as a social custom. To reject it was to expel Christians from Chinese society. Moreover, even if there might be some superstitious aspects in these rites, in the long term Ricci hoped to laicize them and even Christianize them. Finally, a Chinese church had to have clergy. Ricci and Valignano had accepted Chinese into the Society. But the General of the Jesuits did not want them to be ordained priests. There was a plan to found a seminary to train secular priests, but an educational establishment governed by Europeans was unthinkable to the educated Chinese; to set it up in Macao would be to disqualify it from the start, and Chinese parents would never allow a young person to be torn away from his family. Longebardo thought that for lack of young people it would be possible to ordain widowers. However, these were too old to learn Latin. This was the germ of the idea of a Chinese liturgy.

Hopes and crises

Bringing the questions and enthusiasms of the Chinese mission, Fr Nicolas Trigault came to Europe. With Ricci's notes, in 1615 he published the *History of the Christian Expedition to the Kingdom of China*. Trigault, who obtained from Pope Paul V a brief authorizing a liturgy in Chinese, returned to China with books, scientific material, and a wise Jesuit, Terrentius. Since liturgical authorization had been given, it only remained to create the mass.

The mission experienced the vicissitudes of politics: the fall of the Ming dynasty and the advent of the Manchu dynasty, with the long reign of the emperor K'ang-Hsi (1662–1722). The rulers appreciated the services of Jesuit scholars (Adam Schall and Fernand Verbiest): the regulation of the calendar, the manufacture of cannons, diplomacy, etc. In turn Louis XIV sent French Jesuit mathematicians to Peking (1687). When K'ang-Hsi officially authorized Christianity in 1692, there were good reasons for hope. However, the figures remained modest: there were three dioceses in China depending on the *padroado*, Macao, Nanking and Peking, and five vicariates apostolic dependent on the Propaganda; 117 missionaries, of whom 59 were Jesuits, the others being Franciscans, Dominicans, seculars and Augustinians. The number of Christians can be reckoned as 200,000; they came above all from popular milieu, since in the end little impression was made on the educated.

Quite apart from the small number of workers in a vast territory, the great problems of the beginnings of mission had not been resolved. The idea of a Chinese liturgy was revived in the 1670s and 1680s. Translations were made. However, missionaries were divided on the subject. It was thought sufficient to ordain some Chinese priests who could read Latin without necessarily understanding it. A Chinese Dominican, Gregory Lo Wen-tsao, received episcopal consecration as vicar apostolic of Nanking (1685–1691). Unfortunately, however, this experiment had no sequel.

The missionaries of the other religious orders who landed in China from 1631 usually came from the Spanish Philippines and found the Jesuit permission for ancestor worship and veneration of Confucius among Christians difficult to take. This was the beginning of the Rites Dispute, which was to continue growing until the end of the century. In the end, the vicars apostolic and their priests who were under the Propaganda were in almost permanent conflict with the missionaries of the Portuguese *padroado*, essentially the Jesuits.

The setbacks in the eighteenth century

The Rites Dispute, which will be discussed later, took an important turn after 1693. Mgr Maigrot, vicar apostolic of Fukien, rejected any form of tolerance. On this occasion the emperor discovered the hierarchical structure of the church, which had been hidden from him; he could not accept that his Christian subjects were under a foreign leader who allowed himself to forbid their acts of filial piety and civic fidelity. In 1707 K'ang-Hsi banned all missionaries from China unless provided with a special form of permission (*piao*), which was granted only to those followed Ricci's practice. As a result, in 1717 there were only forty-seven priests in China. In 1724 Christianity was proscribed; the application of the edict depended on the mood of the local governors. The persecution became more severe in 1745. A bishop and numerous priests and catechists were martyred. The Jesuits remained in Peking, but only their scientific work was accepted. In constant hope of a change of government, they wanted to ensure a presence. Several missionaries continued their preaching secretly, leading an itinerant life through vast regions. Some Chinese priests stand out among them, the most remarkable of whom is Andrew Ly (1692–1774). The missionaries tried to gather Christians into villages, to train men and women as catechists and to organize congregations of Christian virgins. In 1784–1785 the persecution became systematic, but the sporadic communities survived until China was forced to open up in 1842.

Korea

It was in this critical period of the church of China that the first Christian community in Korea was born, through the missionaries of Peking. It is possible that Korean prisoners taken off to Japan during a war at the end of the sixteenth century were converted and that they made Christianity known in Korea in turn. Furthermore, since Korea was a vassal kingdom of China, a delegation went to Peking each year to pay tribute and to receive the

The Beginnings of Christianity in Korea

Yi Seng Hun (Peter Ly) relates with remorse to the missionaries of Peking in a letter of 1789 how he organized the first Christian community in Korea. The Chinese original of the letter is lost and it has come down in a contemporary French translation which poses some questions.

When I was baptized (by the fathers in Peking), I had only a superficial knowledge of what I should know. Is my baptism valid? Does it have to be repeated? I await your orders on that.

My intention was to enter the holy religion. However, along with this intention went a desire to know about mathematics . . .

Arriving in my native land, I felt nothing more urgent than to study my religion in the books which I had brought and to preach it to my parents and friends. In doing this I encountered a sage who had found a book of our religion which he had been studying for several years. He instructed me and encouraged me. We helped each other mutually to serve God and win others to his service. Numbering one thousand, and obedient to the faith, these ardently asked to be baptized. At their universal request I baptized several with the ceremonies observed at the baptism which I had received in Peking. At this point persecution broke out; my family suffered from it more than any other and this obliged me to leave the company of my brothers in Jesus Christ. However, in order not to stop the course of baptisms, I appointed two others in my place. One was the sage whom I mentioned earlier, and the other was a man who suffered much in the persecution and who died in the autumn of 1785, a year after he was imprisoned.

In 1786 the Christians gathered to discuss how to confess to one another. It was agreed that Kia should confess to Y and to Pin, but Kia and Y, or Y and Pin, could not confess to one another. In the autumn of the same year the Christians assembled again; in this assembly it was agreed that I should say the holy mass and that I should give confirmation. Not only did I yield to their requests, but I gave the same power to say the mass to ten others. As for the ceremonies, I observed them as they are marked in different books and prayers of the hours, removing some and adding others. I chose the prayers in our formulas of prayers.

I only recognized my crimes of sacrilege in the spring of 1786, from one of these ten, who, seeing himself given the dignity of priesthood, applied himself to reading a book in which he discovered all the crimes into which I have fallen . . . I diligently had the administration of all the sacraments stopped in all the different places in which it was taking part, and warned all the Christians of my sacrileges.

(Archives of the Propaganda, 1791–1792)

calendar. On a visit to Peking the Koreans became interested in the Jesuits' science and their works. Thus a group of Europeanizing men of letters formed in Korea who were sympathetic to Christianity, which they regarded as a science of Europe and a philosophy comparable to Confucianism rather than as a religion. Some abandoned the ancestor cult, and the Korean government became uneasy.

In 1783, a young educated Korean, Yi Seng Hun, a member of the annual delegation, visited the missionaries in Peking and was given books of mathematics and religious works. He was baptized under the name of Peter (1785). On his return to Korea, he baptized one of his educated friends, Yi Pik, who read Christian books and composed works with a Christian inspiration. The two of them organized a community. Peter Ly (Yi Seng Hun) performed numerous baptisms. However, persecution loomed: Peter Ly, under threat, wanted to assure the continuity of the community and introduced it to all the sacraments which he knew through liturgical works. Some members were made responsible for baptism; the community asked him to say the mass and give confirmation. He himself gave power to say the mass to ten others; a system of confession was also put in place. Soon, though, reading a book showed Peter Ly that his mode of procedure was not in conformity with the Catholic tradition. Disturbed, he wrote to the fathers in Peking to confess his sin and ask what should be done. The Christians, numbering around 1,000, had no sacraments, and persecution had already claimed victims (1789). Mgr de Gouvea, the bishop of Peking, replied to certain questions, but made no allusion to the organization that had been set up. After an abortive attempt, a Chinese priest arrived in Korea in 1794. From 1791 to 1802 persecution was continuous. There were many martyrs. The priest was beheaded. Yi Seng Hun, who at one point seems to have denied his faith, was executed in 1801. The church of Korea disappeared until 1831.

The countries of Indo-China

The Portuguese had contact with Siam shortly after they became established at Malacca in 1511. Some of them came to Ayuthia, the capital, and tried in vain to convert the ruler.

Tongking and Cochin-China

An edict proscribing Christianity in 1533 indicates that Tongking was evangelized very early. The persecution of Christians in Japan prompted the Jesuits and other missionaries to become interested in Vietnam. Japanese Christians had been exiled there. This was the starting point for a Jesuit mission which began at Tourane in Cochin-China in 1615: it numbered almost 2,000 Christians. In 1626, the Jesuits entered into relations with the kingdom of Tongking; there too it was thought that baptism made people reborn as Portuguese. The missionary presence was discontinued, since it depended on the Portuguese boat which came from Macao each year to bring goods and presents to the rulers of Tongking and Cochin-China. The missionaries arrived by ship and stayed on. They often lived clandestinely and were periodically expelled; they would then return to Macao and come back to

Vietnam at the first opportunity. The Jesuits began a transcription of the sounds of the Vietnamese language with the aid of the Latin alphabet. This was Quôc-ngu.

Alexander de Rhodes (1593–1660)

Alexander de Rhodes is regarded as the greatest of the evangelizers of Vietnam. He has gained this reputation, at which some take umbrage, by his numerous writings and a certain Mediterranean volubility. He came from Avignon, where he studied mathematics, the key to the apostolate in the Far East, and joined the Society of Jesus, which destined him for Japan. However, he could not get in (1623). For twenty years, from 1625 to 1645, he evangelized Vietnam from Macao in a discontinous way, since he was expelled several times. Between 1625 and 1630 he lived in Cochin-China (in the capital, Hué), where he learned the language, then in Tongking, where he opened a church in Hanoi. His baptism of dying people brought upon him the accusation that he had a water of death which would depopulate the kingdom. He was expelled, and spent ten years at Macao teaching theology. However, he remained in contact with Vietnam through missionaries who were able to go there and by a correspondence with the catechists whom he had appointed. Between 1640 and 1645 he had three stays in Cochin China. Growing opposition to Christianity became evident: a catechist, Andrew, was beheaded, and in July 1645 Rhodes was banished on pain of death. He never returned to Vietnam. Sent as a procurator to Rome in 1649, he asked for help for the 300,000 (?) Christians of the country. He made missionary work known throughout Italy and France, and published a number of works. He was not sent back to Vietnam but to Persia, where he died in 1660.

Some important points in Rhodes's missionary method are worth noting. A good knowledge of the language seemed to him to be indispensable for knowing and understanding the Vietnamese milieu which was to be evangelized; Rhodes contributed to the spread of Vietnamese literature. In catechesis he used elements of local culture: poetry and religious spectacles. He wrote: 'As for the ceremonies which are performed in this country to assuage trespasses . . . the majority are very innocent and we have judged that they could be retained without affecting the holiness of the religion.' In his catechism he tried to present the Christian message rationally, so that it did not seem a foreign doctrine: 'Above all do not say that this law is that of the Portuguese. For the holy law of God is a greater and more ancient light than the sun itself . . . Although it has appeared first to certain kingdoms, it must not be taken as a law of these kingdoms. It is the holy law of God.' To associate Christians with the apostolate he founded the Congregation of Catechists, who were trained as in a seminary. They exercised all the functions in church which did not require a priest. With priests and other ministers they lived in the 'house of God', a characteristic institution of the Vietnamese church. Obligated to celibacy, in practice they were religious. In times of persecution, the catechists looked after the church of Vietnam by themselves. This did not prevent Alexander de Rhodes from ardently wishing for the formation of a local clergy. This was the main objective of his voyage to Europe.

The vicars apostolic

In a memorandum to the Propaganda (1649), Alexander de Rhodes expressed the view that Tongking and Cochin-China needed three or four hundred priests taken from the population, since European priests could not stay there permanently. In times of persecution the priests of the country could hide more easily. The catechists were the designated candidates, but bishops were needed to ordain them. One could no longer count on the *padroado*; it was for the Pope to nominate bishops directly as vicars apostolic to evangelize pagan countries. However, things dragged on.

In the end, in 1658 the Propaganda designated three vicars apostolic for the Far East, and 1663 saw the foundation of the seminary of the Society of Foreign Missions in Paris, which trained secular priests destined for distant missions. The Propaganda had produced an *Instruction for the Use of Vicars Apostolic Departing for the Chinese Kingdoms of Tongking and Cochin-China* (1659). It asked them to dissociate themselves from the 'human means' often used in evangelization hitherto. It stressed the appointment of a local clergy, but reserved the appointment of bishops to itself. In 1664 two vicars apostolic arrived at Ayuthia in Siam, Pierre Lambert de la Motte and François Pallu. The latter never succeeded in setting foot in Tongking. The hazards of navigation took him round the world against his will, and when he arrived in China it was to die there (1684). Lambert de la Motte was only able to make brief stays in Tongking and Cochin-China, but he organized the church, in particular during the first synod of Tongking (1670). He instituted the 'house of God', bringing together all those who worked at the mission: missionaries, seminarians and catechists. He ordained the first Vietnamese priests, laid down religious rules, created a female congregation, and in Siam founded a seminary for training priests in the Far East. Louis Laneau, the vicar apostolic of Siam (1673–1696), hoped to convert the king to Christianity, and organized an exchange of ambassadors between the king of Siam and Louis XIV (1684). A change of monarch produced an anti-Christian and anti-French faction. Relations between the Jesuits of the *padroado* and the vicars apostolic were tense: the war of oaths raged on until 1690, the date when an agreement shared out territories between the *padroado* and the Propaganda.

The end of the eighteenth century is marked by the apostolate of Pigneau de Béhain, vicar apostolic of Cochin-China (1765–1799). He negotiated a treaty of alliance between Gialong, the crown prince of Cochin-China, and France (1787). He claimed several times that the question of rites had poisoned his ministry.

Yet elsewhere

As it progressively conquered Siberia, Russia, too, became missionary. From the sixteenth century, the Tartars of the empire were converted. The metropolitan of Tobolsk, Philaret, sent missionaries to Kamchatka (1705) and to Iakutsk (1724). He even sent a mission to China (1714); Russian prisoners had founded an Orthodox community in Peking in 1689. At the end of the eighteenth century monks from Lake Ladoga settled in Alaska and founded an Aleutian-speaking community.

6

Christian Opinion about Missions and the Crises of the Eighteenth Century

For three centuries, the church of Europe made a considerable effort to evangelize the world: the missionaries spread to all the shores of the planet, though the interior of the continents had to wait for the nineteenth century to be explored. The courage of the preachers of the gospel who launched out on interminable voyages and risked shipwrecks, wars and martyrdom continues to impress us in the twentieth century. At the same time we are struck by the small number of them in immense territories. At the heyday of the mission in Japan there were about 100; of the mission to China, around 120; of the Madurai mission, a dozen. The Spanish colonies beyond question had more numerous effective missionaries. Granted, the priest-missionary was not the whole of the mission. A distribution of responsibilities was effected through responsible local people like catechists. But what did these missionaries represent in the countries which they evangelized? How many Chinese, for example, knew of the existence of Christianity? Or Tamils?

On the other hand, while we should not think that all the Christians in Europe were passionate about missions to distant lands, it is certain that educated opinion about them became increasingly attentive in the three centuries of modern times. It is true that a taste for exoticism mixed voyages and missions indiscriminately. However, a strictly missionary literature had an ever-increasing readership. Not only did it arouse curiosity, but it gradually changed the views held by Europeans about humankind and religions. Furthermore, this literature led them to ask questions about their own Christianity. The methods and objects of evangelization became an object of debate in the church of Europe, and eventually it was first in Europe that the crisis for missions arose and their future was played out.

An abundant missionary literature

Since the Acts of the Apostles, the preachers of the gospel and those around them have left traces of their action. This is what makes it possible to produce a book like this one! The novelty of the sixteenth century and the centuries which followed is that missionary literature gained some status, in particular among the Jesuits, but also among other religious.

The duty to correspond

In the very first Constitutions of the Society of Jesus, Ignatius Loyola gave an important place to correspondence: 'Correspondence between inferiors and superiors will be a help, as will the frequent exchange of news from all quarters' (VIII, 3,3). 'What helps to unite members of the Society with one another and with their head will also be very helpful in keeping the Society in a good state. Thus especially the bond of wills, that is, of charity and mutual love, will be served if everyone is kept informed, receiving news from one another and writing frequently, professing the same doctrine and as far as possible practising unity in all things. But what will serve this in the first place will be the bond of obedience which unites subjects with their superiors' (X, 9).

In the particular case of missions, the superiors wanted to know the climate and the customs of the countries to which they sent missionaries; they also wanted to take stock of the fruits of mission, to show the glory of God, to produce vocations, to arouse the generosity of benefactors and to defend the Society against attacks. From 1565, once a year, the provincial superiors had to send a report to the General in Rome; from these reports an annual history of the Society was extracted, which remained in manuscript form. In principle, these documents were intended for internal use, but for the edification of Christians, some letters could be published. This is how the famous letter of Francis Xavier, which is often cited, appeared in Paris in 1545. From 1583 the annual letters were printed, still for internal use, but passages were passed on to pupils at the colleges and to a wider public. Between 1578 and 1609 around sixty 'Indian letters' were published in France. Many were in keeping with the extraordinary fascination for Japan experienced in the sixteenth century. From missionary letters and notes, several Jesuits planned histories of evangelization which were so many treatises on geography. In addition to the works by José de Acosta and Trigault mentioned in the previous chapter, mention could be made of the *History of the Indies* by P. Maffei, which described the Portuguese empire. This work, published in Latin in Florence (1588), went through many Latin editions and translations. These works contributed to the education of Europeans in geography. Unlike passing travellers who only noted extraordinary things or invented then, the missionary writers were interested in the general case, the 'typical'.

The seventeenth-century *Relations*

Some annual letters to the superiors were published under the name of *Relations*. The *Relations of New France*, which formed a continuous series of forty-one small volumes (1632–1673), became very famous. They were made up of the annual letters sent by the Jesuit superior of Quebec to the provincial superior in Paris. When Fr Le Jeune wrote in April 1632 'from the middle of a forest extending over 800 leagues', he did not envisage a wide audience. In the name of obedience, he was giving an account to his superior of events of the past year. His superior in Paris decided to publish the letter, and the volume found favour. The next volume was even more impressive. Then chapters were introduced. From that time on, even in Quebec, the annual letter was composed with the public in view. However, Fr Le Jeune emphasized its character as testimony.

The *Relations* give valuable geographical and ethnographic information about Canada, and above all reading them led to numerous missionary vocations among both men and women. Reading the *Relations* was one of the factors which decided Marie of the Incarnation, the Ursuline, to embark for Canada in 1639. Her own correspondence, published at the end of the century by her son, can be put in parallel with the *Relations*. In the context of the polemic on the Chinese rites, in 1673 Pope Clement X banned the publication of any work on mission without the express permission of the Propaganda. The *Relations* then ceased to appear.

The *Edifying and Curious Letters* of the eighteenth century

At the end of the eighteenth century, there was great interest in France in the Levant and China.

The royal government gave help to the missions to these countries. The king received a delegation from Siam (1686) which returned to China with Jesuit mathematicians. Works on the country multiplied. In 1702, Fr Charles Le Gobien, procurer of missions to China, published a small volume of around 100 pages entitled *Letters of Some Missionaries of the Society of Jesus, written in China and the East Indies*. Its success prompted the priest to publish a second volume in 1703 with a different title: *Edifying Letters and Curious Writings from Foreign Missions by Some Missionaries of the Society of Jesus*. This title made the collection famous. Fr Le Gobien and his successors continued the series to the point of a thirty-fourth volume in 1776. After the suppression of the Society, an old Jesuit, Querbeuf, undertook a new edition of the *Edifying Letters and Curious Writings* between 1780 and 1783 in twenty-six volumes. Querbeuf arranged the letters by continent, including the *Memoirs of the Levant*. Throughout the eighteenth century there were new editions of the first collections, translations into half a dozen languages, selections, counterfeits and plagiarisms. The success continued in the nineteenth century, during which there were six complete editions of the letters and numerous selections.

The published letters represent only a minute proportion of those which arrived in Europe. Many of them were used to compose great works on China. Some, which were thought too difficult and too scientific, were only published later, like those of Fr Gaubil (1688–1759), who is regarded as the founder of scientific Sinology. In short, the Jesuits were not the only missionary authors. The Dominicans Labat and Du Tertre and the Minim Plumier wrote travel and mission accounts which achieved some fame. The interest of the *Edifying and Curious Letters* lies as much in the intention of the Parisian publishers as in the missionaries on the spot. The association of the two adjectives 'edifying' and 'curious' is important. The Jesuits who made the selections kept to these two aspects. The letters were to edify, to prompt readers to give glory to God and to open their purses to save souls. But they were all also curious, since they provided information which was both entertaining and useful to science. This second aspect helped their success: people were interested to read how porcelain was made in China or about the secrets of ginseng, about the workings of Chinese government or of chicken ovens (artificial incubators) in Egypt. Moreover collections which were too pious sold less well.

Like all missionary literature, even today, the works contained a degree of apologetic for the institution which provided them, and the sincerity of the Jesuits over the *Edifying and Curious Letters* has come under suspicion. Certainly there were cuts, transpositions and improvements in style. Edifying gestures in China are not necessarily edifying in Europe. However, the truth and sincerity of the letters should not be systematically doubted. Whatever else, they are among that literature which contributed towards changing the views European Christians had about the wider world, and at the same time towards changing their views of themselves.

With travel and missionary accounts, the Europeans discovered the existence of other worlds. These could be very ancient and refined civilizations which knew certain techniques like gunpowder and printing before Europe: 'The history of China teaches me how the world is wider and more diverse than either the ancients or we ever conceived', wrote Montaigne in his *Essays*. As for the 'savage', he could prompt two very different attitudes. For some, his 'barbarity' brought out the superiority of the European Christian. But many people also praised the primitive, the 'good savage'. As Mircea Eliade commented: 'They discovered a happy humanity which had escaped the misdeeds of civilization, and models for utopian societies.' This theme sometimes emerges in Las Casas: Bernadin Saint de Pierre exalts such a return to the simple life of the islands in *Paul and Virginie*. In the religious sphere which interests us here, the development of conceptions is no less important.

An attempt to understand non-Christian religions

I mentioned earlier the high esteem in which the ancient religions of America were held by the first chroniclers of Mexico and Peru. Francis Xavier readily consigned all pagans to hell. But many missionaries began to develop the notion of primitive revelation in their apologetic. Diametrically opposed conclusions could be drawn from this: the people who had forgotten this revelation deserved a just condemnation, and the conquerors were God's instrument for punishing their sins. But equally, and this was the argument of the Jesuits in China, this faithfulness to the primitive revelation which they found in Confucius should lead Chinese to the Christian revelation. The pagan religions were a preparation for Christianity. Through the writings of the Jesuits, the Christians of Europe learned that 'among teachings, no doctrine approaches the truth as much as that of Confucius', or that 'the Chinese have always worshipped a supreme deity whom they call "the king of heaven" or "heaven and earth" . . .; the sect of the men of letters does not worship idols, but reveres only heaven and earth' (1615). And Fr Le Comte was ecstatic: 'The people of this country have preserved for almost two thousand years the knowledge of the true God, and honour him in a way which can serve as an example and as instruction even for Christians' (1696). So one could not damn the Chinese to hell like the Moors and the Turks; they were Christians without knowing it!

The fear of relativism

This optimistic view of Chinese religion met with opposition from a certain number of theologians, since it did not seem to fit the facts of the Bible and the traditional theology of salvation. For Christian Europe, the world had been created in 4004 BCE. Now if one was to believe the Chinese chronology, the Chinese arrived before God created light. Pascal was disturbed: 'Which is the more credible, Moses or China?' (*Pensées*, 593). Had the Chinese influenced Moses, or did Moses inspire the Chinese? That is why Bossuet would not accept that the Chinese had kept the primitive revelation. That singled them out unduly at the expense of the Jews. Now apart from the Jews, all the peoples were idolaters and could not be saved in their idolatry. In 1700, five opinions of Le Comte on China were condemned by the Sorbonne as being opposed to a correct theology of revelation and the salvation of infidels. The discovery of so many religions across the world raised question after question about their relationship with Israel and Christianity. There was a need to safeguard the chronological priority of biblical revelation, but also to explain certain parallels. All kinds of migrations of peoples from the earthly paradise or from Palestine were imagined. Hindu mythologies were seen as distortions of biblical texts. In China, figurism had some success. The Chinese character had two senses: the apparent one, that of the Chinese, was imprecise, since it was merely the figure of the profound reality, which was revealed only by the Bible and by Christianity. These wild imaginings and laborious attempts at comparison may make us smile. But such systems of interpretation and grids for classification were the beginnings of a science of religions. In seeking to define the religious, people were attempting to distinguish it from the civil or the profane realm, a move which was essential in the discussions on rites.

Missionary literature, a weapon against Christianity

La Bruyère saw nothing good in these distant voyages: 'Some succeed in corrupting themselves by long voyages, and lose the little religion they had: day by day they see a new cult, different customs, different ceremonies.' The opposition of Bossuet or the theologians of the Sorbonne to Le Comte's statements on Chinese religion in part arose out of a fear that the Jesuit's arguments would be used against true religion. Indeed, what the

A somewhat direct comparativism

The encounter with the great religions of Asia raised questions for the missionaries. How could their chronology, their mythical accounts, be reconciled with the biblical facts? Adopting an apologetic approach from the first centuries, the missionaries tried to discover distortions of the Bible in the Eastern traditions.

Letter from Fr Bouchet, missionary in Madurai, to the aged Bishop of Avranches (Huet, 1630–1721).

As you see, Monsignor, the matter is clear, and one does not need to be very perceptive to observe in this Indian account, full of fables and the most bizarre fantasies, what the sacred books teach us about the flood, the ark and the preservation of Noah and his family.

Our Indians did not stop at that, and after disfiguring Noah under the name of Satiavarti, they were able to credit Brahma with the most remarkable adventures from the story of Abraham. Here, Monsignor, are some features which seem to me to be very similar.

First, the similarity of the names might seem to support my conjectures. It is evident that Brahma is not very far removed from Abraham, and it is desirable that in the matter of etymologies our sages had adopted more reasonable and less forced means.

This Brahma, whose name is so similar to that of Abraham, was married to a wife whom all the Indians call Sarasvadi . . . Vadi corresponds closely to our word madam, and it is quite clear that the first two syllables of the word Sarasvadi, which strictly speaking are the entire name of Brahma's wife, can be reduced to Sara, the name of Abraham's wife.

However, there is something even more singular. Brahma among the Indians, like Abraham among the Jews, was the leader of several different castes or tribes . . . In Tichirapali, which is now the site of the most famous temple in India, every year a festival is celebrated in which a venerable old man guides before him twelve children representing, according to the Indians, the twelve leaders of the main castes . . . The Indians honour the memory of one of their penitents who, like the patriarch Abraham, was dutifully prepared to sacrifice his son to one of the gods of the country.

Nothing seems to me more similar to Moses than the Vishnu of the Indians metamorphosed into Krishna . . . One of the close relatives of Krishna was exposed, in his infancy, in a little cradle on a great river . . . He was taken from it and, as he was a fine child, brought to a princess who had him carefully nurtured and then saw to his education . . .

Among these customs, which the Indians can only have derived from the Jews and which still persist in the country, I include, Monsignor, the frequent baths, the purifications, the extreme horror of corpses, the very contact with which they believe to be polluting, the different order and the distinction of castes, and the inviolable law which prohibits marriage outside one's own particular tribe or caste.

(Edifying and Curious Letters)

Jesuits were proposing as apologetic was sometimes turned against Catholicism: the bold spirits of Europe were less preoccupied with the religious future of China than with the problems of their continent. Bayle contrasted an intolerant Christian France in which the king revoked the Edict of Nantes (1685) with a tolerant China in which the emperor granted freedom to the Christian religion which would never be his own. The 'philosophes' of the eighteenth century, like the authors of the *Encyclopédie*, who had read the *Edifying Letters*, could not agree on the religion of the Chinese: were they atheists or deists? Whatever the reply, Chinese religions could serve as an argument against the universal pretensions of Catholicism. If the Chinese were atheists, the universality of the idea of God affirmed in the catechisms was without foundation. If they were atheists or deists and one could also praise their morality, that meant that God was not necessary as the basis for a morality, far less the Christian revelation. Thus religion was detached from morality, and Christianity reduced to just a particular form of belief. The *philosophes* also enjoyed reading the words of a Chinese ruler reported by Fr de Mailla in one of the *Letters* (1724): 'What would you say if our people went to Europe and there wanted to change the laws and customs established by your ancient sages? . . . What would you say if I sent a host of bonzes and lamas to your country to preach their law there? How would you receive them?' By using China often in his anti-Christian campaigns, Voltaire found a disguised way of touching on the religious problems of Europe.

The Rites Dispute

All these discussions on the religions, and particularly on Chinese religions, came to a head at the end of the seventeenth and beginning of the eighteenth century in the contexts of the Rites Dispute, which some have thought to be the most important controversy in the history of the church after the trinitarian and christological controversies which found their solution in the first four ecumenical councils. The Rites Dispute in effect began during the seventeenth century, and did not officially come to an end until 1939. Independently of the pettinesses and after-thoughts which marked it, this conflict was over a crucial problem, that of the attitude of Christianity to the civilizations it encountered. The evangelizers of America could only think to justify the destruction of the ancient religions in order to establish Christianity: as we have seen, the results were mixed. For thoughtful people like the Jesuits, it was unthinkable to ask the new Christians of India and China to renounce their civilizations, which were thousands of years old and as estimable as those of Christian Europe. Furthermore, in this sphere the missionaries did not have the support of public opinion as they did in Latin America. Beyond question distinctions had

to be made between what was acceptable for Christians and what was not. But could Christians definitively marginalize themselves in society through faithfulness to their faith? These questions remain topical, given the recent concept of inculturation.

The birth of a problem in Asia

From the moment when they gave up trying to Europeanize the Indians and the Chinese who became Christians, the missionaries encountered a series of problems which have already been mentioned. These revolved around three points:

1. *Terms*. Can one use terms drawn from local languages in religious vocabulary, in particular to denote God? Is there not a risk of contamination with pagan religions? The problem was particularly acute in China.

2. *Liturgy*. Can one take take account of the repulsion felt by Indians and Chinese towards certain secondary Christian rites? In India the missionaries gave up insufflation and the *ephphata* in the administration of baptism. In China it was unthinkable to touch a woman in the rites of unction.

3. *Traditional customs*. These were social rites rooted in religion. In China they included reverence paid to Confucius and to ancestors by offerings and tablets. In India there were the caste-system, marriage customs or fertility rites which were thought obscene, and ritual baths. All this was understood under the expressions 'Chinese rites' and 'Malabar rites'.

With Ricci and Nobili, the Jesuits of China and Madurai largely accepted a certain number of accommodations. They emphasized the civil significance of the rites, thinking that little by little, under Christian influence, these rites would be purged of their superstitious elements. The Jesuits were not all of the same opinion, but in Rome their General and the Pope had accepted the practice of Ricci and Nobili. While the Jesuits were the only ones involved, things did not go too far. But in 1631 a Dominican arrived in China and in 1633 a Franciscan; they both came from Manila in the Philippines, in the Spanish sphere. Taking part in a ceremony at which Christians were present, the two missionaries were scandalized that these Christians performed rites in honour of Confucius and the ancestors, and above all that the Jesuits accepted this. The two religious alerted their local superiors in Macao and Manila. However, the matter did not remain local: an appeal to Rome turned it into a European theological dispute.

A European theological dispute

The Dominican, Moralez, expressed his doubts to the Pope in questions which could be summed as as 'Do Christians have the right to honour idols?', by implication Confucius and the ancestors. Obviously Pope Innocent X could only reply to such a question in the negative (1645), and so the Chinese rites were condemned. Ten years later, the Jesuit Martini raised the question in Rome, 'Can one pay purely civil homage to Confucius?'. Pope Alexander VII replied in the affirmative. The supporters and opponents of the rites could appeal to two contradictory responses.

In 1668, twenty-three missionaries – nineteen Jesuits, three Dominicans and a Franciscan – forced to live together by the imperial power which put them under surveillance in Canton, signed an agreement on a common approach. Shortly afterwards the Jesuit visitor from Macao modified it unilaterally. The Dominican Navarette, who was furious, went to Europe to put forward his point of view. From then on his works were to form an arsenal for the opponents of the Jesuits. Navarrete shared his objections to the rites and the Jesuits with the vicar apostolic Pallu, whom he met. The Foreign Missions of Paris forthwith took a firm stand on a dispute which was interfering with other theological conflicts of the time.

In a church of France which was being renewed from top to bottom, bishops, preachers and pious lay people like those of the Society of the Blessed Sacrament were trying to purify Christianity from the 'pagan' elements which were appearing in popular piety. By a misguided comparison, some argued that what they were attempting to suppress in Europe could not be tolerated in China or in India. Furthermore, in moral theology, spiritual directors and casuists were emphasizing the training of the conscience. How did one determine to act in cases of doubt? Was it necessary to look for a probable opinion (probabilism)? Or a more probable opinion (probabiliorism)? Some opted for the most accommodating solution (laxism) and some for the most rigorous (rigorism). Theologians wanted to resolve the Rites Dispute by these categories. The Jansenists, with their rigorist morality, used all this as ammunition against their Jesuit adversaries, whom they termed laxists. The *Provincials* of Pascal and other Jansenist works accused the Jesuits of having removed the cross from their preaching to the Chinese, and of having authorized the cult of idols. At the end of the century, the controversy over Quietism was to meet up with the Rites Dispute in the persons of many of the protagonists. Fénelon had been condemned (1699) on the prompting of Bossuet and indirectly Madame de Maintenon, the mistress of Louis XIV. Now Fénelon had the sympathy of the Jesuits, particularly Fr Le Comte, against whom Bossuet wrote polemic in connection with the salvation of the Chinese. Madame de Maintenon's spiritual director was Brisacier, superior of the Foreign Missions and an opponent of rites.

The dispute comes to a head

At the end of a long study, Mgr Maigrot, of the Foreign Missions, vicar apostolic of Fukien in China, concluded that the Chinese rites were stained by superstition. As a result, in a mandate of 1693, he forbade Christians to practise them; at the same time he rejected the Jesuit vocabulary for designating God in Chinese. The mandate caused a stir in the China missions; Maigrot sent it to Rome to be examined, but Rome could not deal with it

Decree of Clement XI condemning the Chinese rites (1704)

This decree confirms the conclusions of the Congregation of the Holy Office after its examination of Maigrot's mandate in 1693.

1. It is absolutely forbidden to use the Chinese terms *T'ien*, which signifies heaven, and *Shang-ti*, which means sovereign emperor, to denote the true God.
2. The table on which is written *King-T'ien*, which means 'Worship Heaven', may never be put in Christian churches, even with an explanation.
3. In no way nor for any reason whatsoever can Christians be allowed to preside as ministers or to be present at the solemn sacrifices or oblations which are customarily made at the time of each equinox to Confucius and to other departed ancestors, since these are ceremonies steeped in superstition . . .
7. It is forbidden to Christians to keep in their homes, in honour of the ancestors, according to the custom of the Chinese, tablets or scrolls on which is written 'The Throne of the Spirit', or 'The Seat of the Spirit', or 'The Soul of So and So', by which it is signified that the spirit or the soul of some departed person sometimes comes to stop or to repose there, not even with the abbreviated inscription 'The Seat' or 'The Throne', which amounts to the same thing.

The emperor K'ang-Hsi reacts to the condemnation of rites

The emperor received the papal legate Monsignor de Tournon. The legate sent him Monsignor Maigrot to get to the bottom of the problem. During an audience (2 August 1706), the emperor accused Maigrot of ignorance and gave his own interpretation of the rites.

The Europeans cannot grasp the meaning of our books; so it is to be feared that the Pope may make some ruling which, based on false information, will inevitably lead to the ruin of Christianity in my empire.

When I asked you to explain to me an inscription which had only four characters and which you had in front of you, you could not either understand it or interpret it; and even two of the characters were unknown to you . . . Those who have embraced your law (Christianity) use the characters *king T'ien* in honour of Confucius, lowering their heads to the ground before the tablets of the ancestors, and perform the ceremony of *tsi* (offering) at their tombs, and out of ignorance you say that this is worthless. I, the emperor, have declared to you that *king T'ien* is the same thing as when you say in your law *king T'ien-shu*, 'Honour the Lord of Heaven'. And when we bow our heads to the ground before the tablets and make *tsi* at the tombs of the ancestors, this is not to ask for blessing. All this is practised solely to recall the memory of the departed, and to obey the law, which requires marks of respect and filial obedience.

until 1699, after the condemnation of Quietism. 1700 saw the condemnation by the Sorbonne, already mentioned, of Le Comte's five propositions on the religion of the Chinese. During this period, in China, the Peking fathers asked Emperor K'ang-Hsi to declare that the rites had only a 'civic and political' sense. The resultant document was published throughout the empire. However, the Roman theologians thought that they were better placed over dogma than the emperor of China. The more probable opinion had to be chosen.

On 10 November 1704, Pope Clement VI approved a decree of the Congregation of the Inquisition (the Holy Office), which confirmed Maigrot's man-date: it was not permissible to use *T'ien* (heaven) to denote God; Christians must not take part in ceremonies in honour of Confucius and the ancestors. The decree was not published until a pontifical legate, Mgr Charles Maillard de Tournon, settled things locally. Hardly a skilled envoy for the Propaganda, Tournon encountered the opposition of the *padroado*, and the voyage made him sick. At Pondicherry, in a decree in sixteen points (23 June

1704), Tournon banned a host of Indian customs which were tolerated among the Christians. The missionaries might no longer live as *sannyasis*. The Jesuits nevertheless obtained a suspension of the application of the decree for three years, the time needed to refer it to Rome. In December 1705, Tournon presented himself to the Peking court as the Pope's ambassador: the emperor was furious that a foreign ruler could pass judgment on what went on in China by contesting the imperial interpretation of the rites. Maigrot made an equally bad impression on the emperor when he was received because he stumbled over his Chinese; he was expelled from China. Tournon, who was sent to Nanking, communicated the decisions of the Holy Office to the missionaries in a mandate of 7 February 1707. The emperor had Tournon interned at Macao while waiting for the two Jesuits sent to Rome to return with approval of the imperial interpretation and Ricci's practices. But the Jesuits perished in a shipwreck, and Tournon died at Macao on 8 June 1710.

In 1715, by the Constitution *Ex illa die*, Clement XI solemnly published the decisions of 1704, combining them with sanctions and an obligatory oath for missionaries. Calm never returned. The Pope sent a new legate, Mezzabarba, to try to find a compromise with the Jesuits of Peking, who had ceased all their ministry. He was able to grant discreet permissions. On his arrival at Macao in September 1720, Mezzabarba was not received well by the Jesuits. The emperor maintained his former positions. The legate, who wanted to die in Italy rather than in China, wanted to leave as soon as possible. Before embarking, taking with him the body of his unfortunate predecessor, he published a mandate in which he simultaneously affirmed that the Constitution *Ex illa die* remained in force and granted eight permissions which tolerated certain prohibited rites: Confucious could be honoured in a purely civil way. The use of the permissions was optional. Confusion was at its height, since the missionaries were divided between those who accepted the permissions and those who

The permissions of Mezzabarba (4 November 1721)

These embarrassed permissions, which in fact annul the condemnations of Clement XI, leave open the question whether the ceremonies in honour of the ancestors of Confucius are or are not superstitious. For a century there were opposed views on this point.

1. The Christians of China are authorized to have in their houses the tablets of their ancestors, provided that only the name of the departed is mentioned on them, that the agreed declaration is put alongside the tablet, and that there is abstention from all superstition . . .
2. All the ceremonies of the Chinese concerning the departed which are neither superstitious nor suspect but civil, are authorized.
3. That part of the cult of Confucius which is civil is authorized, as are the tablets with his name, provided that every superstitious character and inscription is removed from them and that the agreed declaration is added.
6. It is permissible to prepare tables with sweetmeats, fruits, meat and traditional food, either before the shroud, or around it, in the presence of the tablet thus defined, and in connection with the agreed declaration, omitting all superstitious practices, and provided that there is regard only to custom and piety towards the departed.

rejected them. Endless discussions went on until Benedict XIV annulled the permissions in the bull *Ex quo* (1742) and reaffirmed the decisions of 1704 and 1715. 'The Chinese rites are banned because they are bad.' As for the Malabar rites, the controversies over Tournon's decrees ended with definitive condemnation by Benedict XIV in 1744. Rome never went back on these decisions until 1939, but the malaise persisted in all the Far Eastern missions until the end of the eighteenth century, and again in the nineteenth.

The consequences of the condemnation of the rites: the proscription of Christianity in China

In 1724, the emperor Yuong-chêng proscribed Christianity throughout China. The Jesuits of Peking, who were accepted because of their scientific services, made approaches to the emperor to revoke the decision. In a letter, Fr de Mailla describes the edicts of proscription and the audiences of the Jesuits at court. Involuntarily, Fr de Mailla presents arguments in the spirit of the Enlightenment.

Peking, 16 October 1724
Pronouncement of the Tribunal of Rites
'The Europeans who are at court are of use there for the calendar, and perform other services. However, those who are in the provinces are of no use: they attract ignorant people, men and women, to their law; they build churches or come together without distinction of sex, on the pretext of praying; the empire does not derive the slightest advantage from this . . . Those who are useful must be left at court; as for those who are spread out in Pe-tcheli and in the other provinces of the empire, if they can be useful, they must be brought to court; the others are to be taken to Macao . . . The temples which they have built are all to be changed into public buildings; this religion is to be prohibited rigorously . . .'

Visit to the prince in charge of the matter, who says to the Jesuits: '. . . Over the duration of your disputes, you can see the direction that your affairs are taking; think of the trouble and weariness which they have caused my father the emperor. What would you say if our people went to Europe and wanted to change there the laws and customs established by your ancient sages?'

Our interview with the prince the next day: 'I know,' he told us, 'that your affairs are very difficult; the other day I saw the accusation of the *tsong-tu* of Fukien, and your arguments over our customs (Rites Dispute) have hurt you infinitely. What would you say if, on your taking us to Europe, we behaved there as you behave here? Would you allow it? Over time I will inform myself over this affair, but I tell you that nothing will be lacking in China when you cease to be there, and that your absence will not cause any loss. No one is kept there by force, and no one will allow violations of the laws or tolerate those who work to annihilate customs.'

The Jesuits were received in an audience with the emperor, who took up the same arguments: '. . . What would you say if I sent a troop of bonzes and lamas to your country to preach their law there? How would you receive them? You want all Chinese to become Christians. I am well aware that your law requires it, but in that case what would we become? The subjects of your kings. The Christians that you make recognize only you; in times of trouble they would hear no voice but yours. I know that at present there is nothing to fear; but when the vassals come by the thousands and the ten thousands, then there could be disorder.'

(Edifying Letters)

The decline of missions in the eighteenth century

To the Rites Dispute, which profoundly disturbed evangelization in Asia, were added many other events in the eighteenth century which led to an overall slow-down in evangelization.

The weakening of Catholic power on the seas

The decline of Portugal had begun at the end of the sixteenth century. The Spanish supremacy was ended in 1660. The French supremacy was of short duration. The Treaty of Utrecht in 1713 removed the mastery of the seas from the Catholic powers, and the 'Protestant' maritime powers took their place. The English, Dutch and even Danish seized the Portuguese and French trading posts, guaranteeing them a supremacy in trading. After the treaty of Paris in 1763, English superiority was affirmed everywhere, in America as in India. Far more English emigrated to America than French. The Protestant missions began timidly, but the

Protestant states limited the action of Catholic missionaries. The decline in colonial trade led to a decline in the resources of the Catholic countries and thus of those devoted to missions.

The theological disputes

The Rites Dispute had brought overseas evangelization into disrepute. Jansenist reflections on the small number of the elect did not encourage missionary vocations; the desire to present a pure and hard Christianity without any concessions did not make conversions easy. At the end of the eighteenth century the prists of the Foreign Missions had little admiration for the cultures they encountered: 'The majority of pagan books are no more than a monstrous collection of absurdities, superstitions, fables and some great principles of natural law mixed up in a heap of dung', remarked the missionaries of the coast of Coromandel (India) in 1787. This was far removed from Le Comte's enthusiasm for China. The theological dispute had set the religious orders against one another. 'Enlightened' opinion only noted the difference of method in missionary work (cf. Voltaire). The anti-Catholicism of a number of authors of the *Encyclopédie* played off the writings of the missionaries against them.

The suppression of the Society of Jesus

The joint attacks of the 'philosophes', Gallicans, Jansenists and other religious orders resulted in the suppression of the Society of Jesus. Portugal began in 1759, and all the Catholic countries followed suit. Pope Clement drew a line under the operation by suppressing the Society throughout the church in 1773. Quite apart from the losses in other spheres, the church was depriving itself of 3,000 missionaries who had to leave their posts. By comparison, the other orders and societies of priests had very modest means. During the eighteenth century the Foreign Missions of Paris provided 200 missionaries. In 1780 there were 35 of them between India

---

The end of the Rites Dispute (1939)

Officially, the instruction of the Propaganda dated 8 December 1939 put an end to the Rites Dispute. Arguing from historical developments, the Propaganda accepts the old standpoint of the Jesuits: the honours given to Confucius are civic ones.

It is well known that in the Far East certain ceremonies formerly linked to these pagan rites now, as a result of the changes brought over time in customs and ideas, have only a civil significance, one of respect towards ancestors, of love for the fatherland and courtesy in social relationships . . .

Given that on several occasions the Chinese government has expressly declared that it grants freedom to each individual to profess the religion of his choice and that it does not claim to issue laws or ordinance on religious matters, and that consequently the ceremonies prescribed or performed by the public authorities in honour of Confucius are not aimed at offering him religious worship, but the honour due to an illustrious person with the necessary respect for ancestral traditions, Catholics are permitted to take part in ceremonies in honour of Confucius before his image or before the tablet which bears his name in his monuments or in schools.

---

and China. This is an indication of the relative setback to the Propaganda.

The impotence of the Propaganda

The Propaganda originally had the ambition to take responsibility for the whole of evangelization: organization, recruitment of missionary personnel, financial resources. At the end of the eighteenth century it was far from achieving its aim. The patrons never renounced their prerogatives, even if they no longer had the means of taking up their duties. Missions were sometimes sacrificed for reasons of European politics. The Propaganda never had many personnel at its disposal: the Foreign Missions of Paris, the Lazarists, some religious. For the most part the Jesuits depended on the patronages. Despite its desire, the Propaganda trained few indigenous priests. It was difficult to create seminaries in mission countries. It was a burden to have to send the candidates for priesthood to Rome, since the Propaganda had no financial resources. The missionaries were tempted to engage in trade. In short, the survey of missionary activity which his secretary Stephen Borgia presented to Pope Clement XIV in 1773 was not very optimistic. To begin with there had been hopes of mass conversion, but if Latin America had become a Christian continent, 'the West has had to renounce its pretension to convert the East as it is'.

The French Revolution not only caused upheavals in Europe and in maritime traffic, but also dried up resources for quarter of a century.

The missions of the three centuries of modern times are an important part of the life of the church. The gospel had been proclaimed throughout the world. The church had become universal. The papacy had created an original institution for withdrawing evangelization from the fluctuations of politics, in the form of the Congregation of Propaganda. The problem of the encounter of civilizations with Christianity had been posed but had not been properly resolved. Often the view of the men of the sixteenth to eighteenth centuries was far more positive and benevolent than it was to be in the nineteenth century.

7

The Missionary Renewal in the Nineteenth Century (1800–1880)

Even if it is necessary to distinguish different stages in the history of evangelization in the first three quarters of the nineteenth century, there is a certain unity. Within the church of Europe, particularly in France, the idea of mission became an essential element of Christian existence, both in people's minds and in the many institutions which developed in the service of missions. If the states were never completely indifferent to missions in distant places and it was necessary to come to terms with them, the concern for universal evangelization preceded the great colonial enterprises at the end of the century.

A new political and religious situation

The consequences of the French Revolution and the Napoleonic Empire

It is quite often noted that the Revolution and the Empire marked a pause in missionary activities: congregations disappeared or saw their recruitment drop, and with this had less possibility of sending missionaries; the wars of the Revolution and the Empire damaged relations between Europe and countries overseas; the conflict between Napoleon and the Pope prevented any action on the part of the Propaganda between 1808 and 1814.

However, there were always missionaries far away who reminded Europe of their existence and called for reinforcements. Furthermore, the very upheavals that the Revolution caused in the life of Christians contributed to a renewal and a deepening of the missionary idea. It was difficult, if not impossible, to go to distant lands, and in France, persecution and de-Christianization left their mark on Christians. It was then that maintaining the faith seemed to the religious authorities to be a missionary activity. Memories of reading the *Edifying Letters* inspired the vicar general Linsolas to organize the diocese of Lyons into 'missions'. Groups of women and also men which were already structured, but most often informal, formed for mutual support in prayer and charitable works. The possibility of martyrdom again became a dimension of Christian life. It was from these groups that a host of new religious congregations was to arise when peace returned. They referred back to the time of 'persecution' and most often combined inner mission with mission abroad.

Thousands of priests had to leave France for foreign lands. Those who came to England by the hundred found themselves in a country which did not have a Catholic majority. They asked themselves questions about the return of Anglicans and

The birth of missionary romanticism

The way in which Chateaubriand speaks of missionaries has influenced the whole of missionary literature down to our day.

Here is one of those great and new ideas which belong only to the Christian religion. The idolatrous cults have not known the divine enthusiasm which animates the apostle of the gospel. The ancient philosophers themselves never left the avenues of Academe and the delights of Athens on a sublime impulse to humanize the Savage, to instruct the ignorant, to heal the sick, to clothe the poor and to sow concord and peace among hostile nations: this is what the religious Christians have done and still do every day. The seas, the storms, the ice of the pole, the fire of the tropics, nothing stops them: they live with the Eskimos in their sealskins; they feed on whale oil with the Greenlanders; they traverse the wildernesses with the Tartars and the Iroquois; they mount the Arab's dromedary or follow the wandering Kaffir in his blazing deserts; the Chinese, the Japanese and the Indian have become their neophytes; there is no island or reef in the Ocean which has been able to escape their zeal; and just as once there were not enough kingdoms for the ambition of Alexander, now the earth is too small for their charity.

When regenerated Europe had no more to offer the preachers of the faith than a family of brothers, they turned their eyes to the regions where souls were still languishing in the darkness of idolatry. They were touched with compassion at seeing this human degradation; they were urged on by the desire to shed their blood for the salvation of these strangers. They had to penetrate profound forests, cross impassable swamps, ford dangerous rivers, climb inaccessible rocks; they had to face cruel, superstitious and jealous nations; they had to surmount the ignorance of barbarism in some and in others the prejudices of civilization. All these obstacles could not stop them . . .

(The Genius of Christianity [1802], Part IV, Book 4, Chapter 1)

Protestants to unity with Rome; they witnessed the birth of interest in missions to distant lands among English Christians. In fact, in the last decade of the century several English Bible societies and missionary societies were founded; preachers left for Oceania. The system of the weekly contribution made popular financing of missions possible. These discoveries were to be a powerful stimulus to the idea of mission when these priests could return to the continent. One hundred and fifty emigré priests crossed the Atlantic: around fifty went to Canada and one hundred to the United States. The Sulpicians became seminary teachers, but also missionaries. There were even Trappists who devoted themselves to the evangelization of the Indians. Among these priests, several became the first diocesan bishops in the United States and went on to appeal for priests from Europe. A correspondence grew up between the two continents. Sulpicians returned to France to teach in the reconstituted major seminaries and made the Catholic public aware of missions. The Trappist Dom Augustin de Lestrange, who restored the Cistercian order, lived in America. On his return in 1714 he preached on the missions of the New World.

At the very moment when the concordat which restored religious peace in France was being implemented (1802), Chateaubriand published *The Genius of Christianity*. In his reassessment of the Christian past, he gave a major place to missions to distant lands. The work was read and re-read by those who were to be the architects of the missionary renewal. The missionary became a romantic figure, an adventurer for the faith, who was then until quite recently exalted in all the missionary journals. Moreover Chateaubriand rehabilitated the missionary literature on which he based his work, particularly the *Edifying and Curious Letters*, which appeared in partial or complete new editions under the Empire. A large public was interested in accounts of mission.

The missionary climate of the Restoration

From 1815 on, interest in missions in foreign lands increased among French Christian opinion. However, it has to be stressed that this call to mission did not come primarily from the ecclesiastical authorities of the old Europe but from lay people. After twenty-five years of Revolution and Empire, which they regarded as an unfortunate interlude, bishops and superiors of congregations gave priority to mission at home. 'Our Indians are here', replied the French bishops to a request for priests for the colonies (1815).

However, appeals to Europe for missionaries from abroad multiplied. In Italy, but above all in France, many groups responded to them. In 1817 the Foreign Missions of Paris, orientated on Asia, founded a 'prayer association to ask God for the conversion of the infidels, the perseverance of Christians who live in their midst, and the prosperity of establishments aimed at propagating the faith'. In Lyons, Pauline Jaricot took responsibility for the organization; she adopted and developed the idea of the weekly contribution, which had come from England, by organizing a collection in groups of ten, one hundred and one thousand givers. In parallel, the missionaries of the Rue du Bac published *New Edifying Letters of Missions in China and the East Indies*, in which a focus on suffering won out over curiosity. America was more in view at the Seminary of Saint-Sulpice in Paris, in the person of teachers who had returned from the New World.

The convergence of a series of appeals of this kind resulted in the foundation of the Association for the Propagation of the Faith in Lyons in 1822. The organization sought to support all missions with its prayers and gifts, without giving priority to anyone. The founders were laymen, and the form of the weekly collection was used. The same year,

the Society of Protestant Missions was founded in Paris. In the Protestant world, it was more the revival movements than the established churches which were interested in mission; they thought that members of different Protestant denominations could find a place in the same missionary organization.

The Association for the Propagation of the Faith developed rapidly, spreading from France through Europe and America, not least through the publication of *Annals*, which appeared six times a year. Since not all its members could read, it was recommended that the *Annals* should be read aloud in the evening by the fireside: 'Families should gather round the fire, in the evening after work and on Sunday after the offices, to hear the letters of missionaries and follow them in their travels across oceans, forests, snow and ice, through storms and wild animals.' Many missionaries owed their vocation to reading the *Annals*.

Missionary motivations

By comparison with earlier periods, the motives for Christians to evangelize or for missionaries to go out were not radically new, but through the literature mentioned above one can see distinctive emphases in this first half of the nineteenth century.

It must be remembered that, as in the previous period, evangelization depended on means of transport and a knowledge of the mission field. In the first two-thirds of the nineteenth century navigation made considerable progress; the duration of voyages decreased with the progressive replacement of sail by steam; the opening of the Suez Canal in 1869 brought the Far East nearer, since it took half the time to go from London to Bombay. The nineteenth century was the period of the exploration of the interior of Africa, beginning with René Caillé's travel to Timbuktu in 1828. *Journey to Tibet* (1843–1846) by Frs Huc and Gabet was a best-seller; David Livingstone (1813–1873), a doctor and pastor, combined exploration and evangelization.

When the First Vatican Council was about to open in 1869, French bishops emphasized the providential character of this progress and the discoveries: 'Never since the foundation of the church has such a broad and easy way opened up for the conversion of the infidels, or so wide a door, as in our time. This is not without a great and evident design of providence.'

Obviously the urgency of salvation was the first motivation of missionary activity. There was constant reference to the *Benedictus*, 'to give light to those who sit in darkness and in the shadow of death' (Luke 1.79, quoting Isaiah 9.1). At the end of the Revolution it seems that this urgency was becoming more acute: Satan had shown himself in the great day, and if the church had come through the test, the danger remained. Several preachers and founders of congregations in the Restoration thought that Christians were living in the 'last days', in which the final battle between God and Satan was taking place. Every Christian had to work for his salvation; interest in the salvation of the pagans was a means for the faithful and even more for the missionaries to achieve their own salvation. For missionaries the perspective of martyrdom offered a virtual certainty of salvation. As one of them remarked in 1824: 'As for me, the longer I live, the more I relax and let myself go. If the Chinese to whom I am going in a few days time could cut off my head and hang me, it would suit me very well.' Since baptism was the condition for salvation, we can understand how missionaries could baptize very rapidly, but that did not mean that mission did not have the aim of establishing the church.

Salvation could be obtained only in the one true church, the church of Rome. Of course this was no novelty, but two elements reinforced the conviction in the nineteenth century. The trials of the Revolution had brought the Catholics nearer to Rome. Ultramontanism made continuous progress; the architects of the missionary renewal referred constantly to the Pope: there was the Association for the Propagation of the Faith and there were new congregations. More than ever the church appeared primarily as a hierarchy with Rome at its head; it was on the Pope that this universal concern for the salvation of the human race focussed. The second element was the development of missionary activity among the Protestants; the Catholics, who were afraid of having a march stolen on them, made anti-Protestantism a key motivation in help for mission: 'The biblical societies are sowing error all over the globe . . . We have come to understand everywhere the need to oppose to the gigantic efforts of the Protestant Bible society something as well organized on behalf of the faith' (*Annals*, 1823).

Furthermore, some saw the missions in foreign lands as compensation for the losses suffered in Europe. There were virgin lands, 'the Far West of the church', where a pure church could be built.

However, this strictly legalistic, hierarchical conception of the church is not the whole of nineteenth-century ecclesiology. Another current emerged from Möhler and the Tübingen school which saw the church 'in the line of the mysteries of salvation', and for which Christian expansion was rooted in 'trinitarian missions'.

Missions and civilization

The salvation offered by the missionary was not located solely in the other world. It began in this world, since faith transformed customs, and Christianity brought the only true happiness. Charitable action stemmed from belief in the incarnation and devotion to Christ, God and humankind: Christianity freed people overseas from misfortune. The anti-slavery campaigns of English churchmen like Wilberforce, later taken up by Catholics, were rooted in this conviction. By proclaiming the gospel, the missionary was civilizing the savage and making him abandon his barbarous customs; in the face of the pretensions of the Enlightenment which had thrown Europe into revolutionary chaos, only Christianity could be the basis for a universal civilization. This theme recurred constantly in statements by bishops.

The Protestant missions wanted to civilize just as much, but in the different confessions, civilizing action had its particular features. Coming from working-class and middle-class backgrounds, the Protestant missionaries sought to develop good commerce to check the slave trade in Africa; missions produced cotton which was sold in England. The Catholic missionaries, whose origins were rural, tried to set up Christian villages to develop a sense for work and a taste for Christian community.

The missions and the European states

It is important to emphasize that the zeal for missions precedes colonial expansion in Europe. Certainly, the departure of missionaries was a concern of European governments; for example, the French government wanted religious, both men and women, for its colonies. However, while being obliged to have dealings with the consular authorities, which were not necessarily those of their own nation, the missionaries often set out at their own risk along the African coasts or through China and Vietnam. If martyrs were glorified, Catholics nevertheless regarded as beneficial any political and military action which allowed free trade and religious freedom. Quite often it was religious matters which resulted in the intervention of European governments overseas, as with the Pritchard affair in Tahiti in 1842. France imposed its protectorate on Queen Pomaré, who had expelled Catholic missionaries. To clauses about freedom of trade in China, the Europeans added clauses about religious tolerance (Nanking 1842; Whampoa 1844). Thus the Opium War was providential for the proclamation of the gospel: 'The gospel entered China like the Saviour, the doors being shut. Now that they have been forced, the gospel will bring with it all the temporal benefits which accompany it. The island of Hong Kong is already covered with pious establishments' (*Annals*, 1844). The killing of the missionary Auguste Chapdelaine was one of the reasons for the Anglo-French expedition to China (1858). In addition to religious freedom, the treaty of Tien-Tsin gave France a kind of protectorate of Catholic missions. During the same period, under the pressure of Catholic opinion, which was indignant at the persecutions of Tu Duc, France and Spain intervened in Cochin-China, where French rule became permanently established.

David Livingstone, a doctor and member of the London Missionary Society, has remained a model for explorers and missionaries, fighting against slavery and seeking to promote the Blacks by Christian civilization. Here he expresses his vision of the context of his own work.

As far as I am myself concerned, the opening of the new central country is a matter for congratulation only in so far as it opens up a prospect for the elevation of the inhabitants. As I have elsewhere remarked, I view the end of the geographical feat as the beginning of the missionary enterprise. I take the latter term in its most extended signification, and include every effort made for the amelioration of our race; the promotion of all those means by which God in His providence is working, and bringing all His dealings with man to a glorious consummation. Each man in his sphere, either knowingly or unwittingly, is performing the will of our Father in heaven. Men of science, searching after hidden truths, which when discovered will, like the electric telegraph, bind men more closely together – soldiers battling for the right against tyranny – sailors rescuing the victims of oppression from the grasp of heartless men stealers – merchants teaching the nations lessons of mutual dependence – and many others, as well as missionaries, all work in the same direction, and all efforts are overruled for one glorious end.

(David Livingstone, *Missionary Travels and Researches in Southern Africa*, London 1857, 673f.)

Missionary organization and planning

Though the missionary idea was reborn with the Restoration in Europe, and the Congregation of the Propaganda was reorganized in 1817, the Catholic Church had few means of responding to the demands which came from the four corners of the world; the missions depended on a kind of romantic generosity. American bishops came to Europe to make collections and to recruit priests or seminarians. Isolated preachers took the initiative in evangelizing pagans without any preparation and even without any mission. However, in due course there was a concern to organize in order to find funds and staff and to develop missionary plans.

Recruitment and training of missionary staff

It was during the period when Catholic missions were stagnating that the Protestant missionary societies came into being. While some were connected with a particular confession, many sought to be inter-denominational; they often arose in Pietist milieus or were stamped by revival movements. The earliest of these late eighteenth- and early nineteenth-century missionary societies were the Baptist Mission of London (1792), the London Missionary Society (1795), the Dutch Mission Society (1795), the Church Missionary Society (1799, Anglican), the American Board of Commissioners for Foreign Missions (1810), the Basel Mission (1815) and the Society of Protestant Missions in Paris (1822).

On the Catholic side, the old French missionary societies were re-established and the great old orders restored; Franciscans and Dominicans again provided missionaries. But the major new development in the nineteenth century was the rise of hundreds of congregations of men and women who wanted to respond to the pastoral needs of the time. In a Europe which was still compartmentalized, many of these congregations first worked on a local scale, but gradually, under external pressures, they took on a missionary dimension and sent missionaries to distant places. This period really first saw the rise of the missionary sisters. In 1817 came the beginning of the Marist Fathers and Brothers, in 1835 of the Pallotins in Italy, in 1850 of the Foreign Missions of Milan, in 1856 of the African Missions of Lyons, in 1860 of the Scheut Fathers in Belgium, in 1866 of the Mill Hill Fathers in England and in

1875 of the Society of the Divine Word in Germany.

A missionary doctrine

In 1817, the Congregation of the Propaganda was reorganized. Little by little, despite some resistance from the old patronages, there was no longer any doubt that the direction of evangelization lay with the Holy See. Cardinal Maur Capellari played a key role in developing a missionary doctrine for the nineteenth century, first as prefect of the Propaganda between 1826 and 1831, and then as Pope under the name of Gregory XVI (1831–1846). In the course of his pontificate he created more than seventy missionary circumscriptions, more the sign of a concern for evangelization than an effective achievement.

Gregory set up a system of commissions which was to remain in force until Vatican II: the mission territories were each given exclusively to a missionary institution. While this system facilitated the continuity of missionary action and avoided pernicious competition, it made mission a domain of the institutions rather than an imperative relating to the universal church.

In 1839, when the campaign against the slave trade had already been going on for some decades in England, but was not favoured in Catholic countries, Gregory XVI intervened with the apostolic brief *In supremo*: it stated that the Popes had condemned the slave trade and slavery, and forbade 'all, ecclesiastical or lay, to dare to support this trade in Negroes under any pretext, or to preach or teach in public or in private anything contrary to our apostolic briefs'. This firm declaration was not to the taste of the colonial clergy. 'The poor old man has spoken of slavery like all those who don't know the colonies,' said a priest on Guadeloupe. Several congregations began to educate the Negroes with a view to their emancipation. It has to be added that the Catholics did not want to be overtaken in this matter by the Protestants.

In 1845, the instruction of the Propaganda, *Neminem profecto,* outlined the thought of Gregory XVI on the organization of the new churches. This text, written well before the great colonial and missionary expansion, is extremely important because of its date and content: the mission territories had to become dioceses with bishops as soon as possible; there was a need to train an indigenous clergy and found seminaries for this purpose; indigenous priests must not be thought inferior; one day they would become suitable for the episcopate and for leading their churches. Missionaries had to give all their attention to charitable works and schools: they had to evangelize customs and arts. Finally, the document recommended the holding of synods.

Under the pontificate of Pius IX, Cardinal Barnabo directed the Congregation of Propaganda with a firm hand for twenty years (1854–1874). By canonizing 23 Japanese martyrs of the sixteenth and seventeenth century (1862) and then beatifying 205 others (1867), Pius IX gave a great boost to missionary work in the eyes of Catholic opinion. Moreover it was in the course of this latter beatification that he announced the convening of the Vatican Council for 1869.

This council did not have time to deal with missions, but they were present in several ways. For the first time in a council, the whole world was represented by missionary bishops, vicars apostolic, who were almost all Europeans. 548 bishops represented Europe and 245 the world outside Europe; of these 121 came from America, 41 from Asia (15 each from China and India), 9 from Africa and 18 from Oceania (of whom 10 were Australians). Promises were made about missions. A commission of the Propaganda had prepared a schema on missions which was not very well disposed towards the missionaries, who were offended by it. Legal questions played a major role: the religious had to obey the vicars apostolic. There was once again an emphasis on indigenous clergy, priests and bishops, and there were warnings against nationalism in missions. The hasty ending of the council did not allow discussion of the scheme. The constant emphasis on setting up local churches was not implemented, and this was later

The birth and growth of a church according to Henry Venn

The Secretary of the Church Missionary Society, whose approach underlies the formula 'triple autonomy', clearly affirms in 1851 the stages in the formation of a truly indigenous church, which is to be self-supporting, self-governing and self-extending.

Regarding the ultimate object of a Mission, viewed under its ecclesiastical result, to be the settlement of a Native Church under Native Pastors upon a self-supporting system, it should be borne in mind that the progress of a Mission mainly depends upon the training up and the location of Native Pastors; and that, as it has been happily expressed, the *'euthanasia of a Mission'* takes place when a missionary, surrounded by well-trained Native congregations under Native Pastors, is able to resign all pastoral work into their hands, and gradually relax his superintendency over the pastors themselves, till it insensibly ceases; and so the Mission passes into a settled Christian community. Then the missionary and all missionary agency should be transferred to the 'regions beyond'.

(Memorandum, quoted in E. Stock,
History of the Church Missionary Society,
London 1899, II, 415)

to incur criticism from Benedict XV in the encyclical *Maximum illud* (1919).

Protestant missionary thought

Since it is impossible to deal with the host of figures here, I shall mention simply the name of Henry Venn (1796–1873), one of the fathers of the formula of 'triple autonomy' as a programme for missionary societies to follow with indigenous churches. These had to be led towards financial, administrative and missionary autonomy. An evangelical Anglican,

after a parochial ministry Henry Venn devoted himself to the direction of the Church Missionary Society between 1841 and 1872. In correspondence with numerous missionaries, he shaped missionary thought and method by instructions and notes on service. In 1851 he emphasized the basic principle of 'the distinction between the function of the missionary, who preaches to the pagans and instructs interested and recent converts, and the function of the pastor, who administers the holy things in a congregation of native Christians'. The new Christians had to take up their responsibilities by nominating their catechists or pastors, who had to be in charge of their community to show that they were not 'the agents of a foreign society'. The converts must no longer depend on a church abroad but must become aware that they were members of an indigenous church: 'It is important that the arrangements made in the missions primarily relate to the ultimate establishment of an indigenous church on the ecclesiastical basis of an indigenous episcopate, independent of foreign aid or supervision.' The principle of the three autonomies, which was broadly accepted by the major missionary societies during the lifetime of Henry Venn, was shelved after the death of its author, and only came to the forefront again in the twentieth century. One can establish a certain parallelism between the views of Henry Venn and the content of *Neminem profecto*. The disregard of Venn's thought can certainly be explained by the same factors as those which led to the shelving of the establishment of an indigenous episcopate in Catholic missions.

Methods of evangelization

Preoccupations and methods in part depended on the original background of the missionaries. At the beginning of the nineteenth century, the Protestants, who were recruited from craftsmen, blacksmiths, weavers, shoemakers and carpenters, had an essentially biblical training. As the century progressed, the missionaries came more from the middle class, and set out as couples: in addition to preaching they emphasized the witness of the monogamous missionary family as opposed to the polygamy of the peoples they encountered and the misconduct of certain European colonists. The celibate Catholic missionaries, who most often came from the peasantry, fed anti-Protestant polemic with their indignation that gifts for missions could be used to bring up a family!

The missionaries went to evangelize countries without much reference to the experiences of previous centuries. In general they transposed their experiences in Europe. The starting point was a modest chapel. The Protestants offered the Bible, distributed widely in translations into an increasing number of languages. The Catholics tried rather to impress the populations by the solemnity of worship. They taught prayers, the Our Father, the *Ave Maria*, the Creed, the *Veni Creator*. They fought against superstition and burnt pernicious books, on some occasions even Protestant Bibles!

Both Protestant and Catholic Europeans belonged to a civilization of the written word. They had a fascination with the school, a privileged means of coming to faith and civilization. This emphasis on the written rather than the oral word, combined with the struggle against traditional pagan literature, meant a certain destructuring of local cultures, though this was not necessarily sought. Certainly, many missionaries became ethnologists and made a collection of oral history which is still valuable today. But it is only in the most recent perspective of inculturation that the oral tradition and traditional customs have found a place in Christian expression and liturgy. At all events, missionaries of all confessions made a systematic attempt to get to know the local languages for the needs of evangelization. However, they often still had to preach through the distortions of interpreters.

The human service of the populations held an important place in the preoccupations of the missionaries. Moved by the descriptions of the wretchedness of the pagans presented to them by the journals, the Christians of Europe provided the means for material aid and health care. This aid was the subject of polemic between confessions: each accused the other of buying conversions, speaking, for example in Asia, of 'rice Christians'. Echoing a paternalistic European mentality, missionaries considered themselves as fathers and the needy population as their children; their work seemed a privileged means of sanctification.

The mission fields before 1880

It is impossible to give an exhaustive list of the church circumscriptions which arose in the nineteenth century, so I shall emphasize above all the beginnings of evangelization on the different continents and the specific problems raised by Christian preaching. The use of the 1880s as a cut-off point is not always an absolute; but during these years, in many regions of the world the period of European imperialisms and colonization began, which changed the conditions of evangelization.

European emigration across the world

The nineteenth century was the great time for European emigration overseas. And along with new states, the Europeans were setting up new churches with their particular features. We need not dwell long on the history of these churches here, since this was not a first evangelization. However, on territories where Europeans were establishing themselves there were often also indigenous populations who were soon submerged, if not partially eliminated; evangelizing them remained a preoccupation of these new churches.

Canada and the United States

In Canada, the high birth-rate among French Canadians and the contribution from Irish immigration increased the Catholic community, but this had some difficulty in affirming itself in the face of the official Anglicanism of the English administration. Episcopal sees multiplied during the first part of the nineteenth century; those who were in charge of the North-West Territories, like Saint-Boniface, pursued or undertook the conversion of the indigenous Indians, who had now become very much of a minority.

Although we have to make some qualifications for the initial period, the United States appeared as the land of religious freedom. The Protestant denominations were quite dominant at the birth of the new state. The way westwards was accompanied by revivals, with their characteristic features: camp meetings, trances and so on. The foundation of the diocese of Baltimore in 1789 provided a home for Catholics, who represented barely 1% of the population. Some Frenchmen contributed to the organization of Catholicism in the first decades, but it was the Irish immigrants, arriving in hordes, who put a definitive stamp on the Catholicism of the United States. The plenary council of Baltimore in 1852 brought together all the authorities of a church which had come of age.

Founding new dioceses and building schools were the great preoccupations of the Catholics; like the majority of their fellow-citizens they were not unduly interested in the fate of the Indians. However, several bishops, including the bishop of New Orleans, had Indian missions from the time of the French presence in their heritage. The city of St Louis in Missouri was the centre of an important mission to the Indians entrusted to Belgian Jesuits. The most famous of these missionaries, Fr Pierre-Jean de Smet, devoted himself entirely to the Indians from 1838 until his death in 1873, sometimes acting as negotiator between Indians and the government to settle problems raised by the drive westwards. Unfortunately, the policy of expropriation and the extermination of the Indians carried out by the federal and local authorities reduced to virtually nothing the quite remarkable efforts at evangelization in this area in the first half of the century.

The black slaves who had chosen Christianity were to be found for the most part in the Protestant denominations, most often as Baptists and Methodists. A very few of them were Catholics. In the debates on slavery, the bishops showed themselves prudent in interpreting Gregory XVI's brief *In Supremo* (1893); they did not touch on the question at the Council of Baltimore. During the Civil War there were Catholics in both camps. While vocations to pastorates were numerous among emancipated blacks, there were only a few black priests, and few secular priests devoted themselves to the apostolate to the blacks. From 1871 the members of the congregation of St Joseph at Mill Hill specialized in this ministry.

The other Americas

The Spanish and Portuguese colonies proclaimed their independence in the years 1817–1823. The church, cut off from Europe, experienced the backlash; clergy became fewer, the governments, which were made up of old colonists, often proved anticlerical and several times expelled the religious. The Spanish patronage disappeared, and the Propaganda took over a certain number of mission territories which it entrusted to different orders and congregations: Franciscans, Capuchins, Jesuits, Salesians. The changing whims of the governments often made this evangelization spasmodic.

Australia

Initially a convict prison and then a country of Anglo-Saxon immigrants, Australia welcomed Irish, who formed the beginning of a Catholic community, in a minority among Anglicans and Protestants. However, this minority very soon asserted its personality. Neither Protestants nor Catholics seemed very interested in the Aborigines, who soon disappeared. The Catholic hierarchy was established in 1842.

Oceania

Oceania was the new field of evangelization in the nineteenth century. The exploration of it coincided with the time when the Protestant world began to become interested in missions to distant lands. That is why these thousands of islands were to become the prize in a bitter competition between Catholics and Protestants. The latter, profiting from English maritime supremacy, became established in Tahiti in 1797, in the form of the London Missionary Society. John Williams, a twenty-one-year-old missionary, landed in the Society Islands in 1717. He travelled from island to island in his boat 'The Messenger of Peace', building houses, churches and schools and codifying customs. He was eventually eaten by cannibals in the New Hebrides in 1839.

The Catholics lagged behind. By the vicissitudes of navigation, in 1819 they had baptized two chieftains on Hawaii (Sandwich), and the Fathers of the Sacred Heart of Picpus were sent there by the Propaganda. By the time that they arrived, in 1827, they found Protestant pastors. After four years of competition the Catholic missionaries were expelled, set down on the coast of California with two bottles of water. They returned in 1837. The most famous of the Picpus missionaries was Fr Damien, who devoted his ministry to the lepers on the island of Molokai (1873–1889). On Tahiti, Protestantism was proclaimed the state religion in 1815. The Catholics arrived in 1836, but the queen made them re-embark. They obtained the right to live on the island in 1838. The Pritchard affair brought in France, which imposed its protectorate on Queen Pomaré (1843). The English missionaries had to leave, and were replaced by French Protestants from the Evangelical Missions of Paris, who rapidly trained indigenous pastors.

Western Oceania was assigned to the Marist Fathers of Lyons in 1836. Mgr Pompallier landed in New Zealand in 1838. The Irish colonists formed the basis of the Catholic community, which also approached the indigenous Maoris, in competition with the Protestants (Samuel Marsden). This evangelization also had its martyrs. Protestants and Catholics also competed over New Caledonia from the 1840s on. New Guinea apart, at the end of the century Oceania had been almost completely converted to Christianity of different confessions. In these far-flung islands extending over thousands of miles, the populations were tiny but the cultures very varied. The missionaries, some of whom became ethnologists, tried to Christianize customs, fighting against cannibalism and alcoholism and presenting norms for Christian marriage. But several missionaries thought that not all God's commandments were practicable in Oceania!

India

At the beginning of the nineteenth century the situation of Catholics in India was a difficult one. Almost all the dioceses in the Portuguese patronage were without bishops. While there were still several hundred Goan and Syro-Malabar priests, true missionaries were reduced to a few dozen. In principle the Foreign Missions of Paris had taken over from the Jesuits, who had been suppressed. The number of Christians, which some put at 500,000 at the beginning of the eighteenth century, certainly dropped by one half. For want of priests, many Catholics seem to have returned to the old religion or to have gone over to Protestantism: the Protestant missions, which began in the seventeenth century, increased greatly in the nineteenth century. The earliest Protestant Missionary Society, the London Baptist Mission, had a presence in India in the person of William Carey from 1793 to his death in 1834; he translated the Bible into Bengali and had it printed (1801), edited dictionaries and grammars, founded schools and agricultural and horticultural societies, along with a savings bank, and had infanticide and the burning of widows banned. Other Protestant missionary societies became established in their turn: the Anglicans created a diocese of Madras in 1833; a missionary conference brought together these various societies in 1850. The East India Company, which exploited the country, put obstacles in the way of evangelization. When the British government took over administration of the colony in 1858, greater freedom followed for the missionaries, though the Catholics felt discriminated against. Protestants forced new Christians to renounce the caste system, but by way of compensation offered them varied work in a hierarchy in the mission as assistant catechists, catechists, instructors and pastors.

Faced with the deficiencies of the Portuguese patronage, in 1834 Gregory XVI decided with the Congregation of Propaganda to create five apostolic vicariates. The return of the Jesuits began a renewal of Catholic missions in India. The bull *Multa praeclare* of 1838 reorganized the church, suppressing four of the five dioceses of the patronage in favour of apostolic vicariates. The only one left was Goa, which had Mgr Silva Torrès as its archbishop in 1843. Neither the archbishop nor the Portuguese government accepted the bull, and a conflict over jurisdiction, 'the schism of Goa', followed, lasting until 1886.

The two synods of Pondicherry (1844 and 1849) were the most significant events of the Catholic evangelization of the period. While taking the oath to conform to the condemnation of the Malabar rites in 1744, the priests of the Foreign Missions felt some unease when they were plunged into the Indian world. Some missionaries thought that there would only be an Indian church when it had a framework of an indigenous clergy consisting not only of indigenous priests – of which there already were some – but also of indigenous bishops. Mgr Bonnand, the vicar apostolic of Pondicherry, decided to hold a synod of the twenty priests who worked with him in his enormous vicariate. The synod proposed new methods of training the indigenous clergy: a reorganization of studies to make them more demanding, with the aim of attracting Christians from higher castes who were capable of becoming priests; and an alignment of the indigenous priests with the missionaries in dress and usages. This was a laudable project, but a very clerical one; there was no real definition of intermediary functions like those of catechists, who were very necessary when there were not many priests. These decisions, presented to the Propaganda, inspired

the declaration *Neminem profecto* of 1845. However, the difficulties did not disappear. When one missionary wanted to ignore the prohibitions of the caste system, 2,000 Christians in castes demonstrated vigorously and boycotted the mass and the sacraments for seven months (1847–1848). So the second synod (1849) tried to take account of the local realities in diocesan administration: the creation of local resources, and an extension of the welcome of non-Christians into teaching establishments. In the churches, barriers continued to separate Christians of caste from the out-castes; it was insisted that buildings should be prestigious: Catholic churches had to bear comparison with those of other Christian confessions and the Hindu temples.

A novitiate for indigenous Jesuits opened in 1847. The concern to train an indigenous clergy bore fruit, since by the end of the century the Indian clergy outnumbered clergy from Europe. However, the Indians were not prepared to take responsibility, as Leo XIII emphasized at the founding of a seminary for all India at Kandy, in Ceylon (1893).

China

At the beginning of the nineteenth century, the Christian community was very much smaller than it had been a century earlier. According to the sources, the number of Christians was between 200,000 and 300,000, with between 130 and 200 priests, around half of whom were Chinese. The vast area of China was divided into three dioceses (Peking, Nanking and Macao) and three apostolic vicariates. The Lazarists had replaced the Jesuits in the dioceses; the priests of the Foreign Missions of Paris, Franciscans and Dominicans provided a ministry in the vicariates; Christians lived a semi-clandestine existence.

In September 1803 Mgr Jean Dufresse, the vicar apostolic of Szechuan, held the first diocesan synod in China: thirteen Chinese priests and six Europeans. The decisions of this synod subsequently provided a point of reference for the missions in the

Far East. They related to the training of priests, in which there were hardly any departures from the Tridentine system, and the importance of Latin was emphasized. Young potential clergy were required to spend a year with a European missionary before ordination. There was no question of Chinese bishops. Persecution resumed following the imperial edicts of 1805 and 1811. Mgr Dufresse was beheaded in 1815. Several missionaries and Chinese suffered the same fate in subsequent years. To replace Dufresse, the Propaganda preferred a European over the Chinese who had been presented. On several occasions Chinese priests put forward as candidates for episcopal functions were rejected. Were they thought to be inadequately trained? Or should we see here the consequence of French pressure, since the Europeans had obtained a means of intervention by unfair treaties: Nanking (1842), Whampoa (1844) and Tien-Tsin (1858). In practice this last treaty established a French protectorate over Catholic missions: missionaries had to have a French passport. The religious freedom obtained by the treaties did not prevent the periodic return of violent xenophobic demonstrations, for which missions paid the price along with the other European establishments. The death of missionaries and the massacre of Christians were the occasion for new European interventions like that of 1860, in which the Summer Palace was pillaged and set on fire. One of the rebel movements that the Europeans helped to crush, the T'ai P'ing (The Great Peace) (1850–1864), was in part inspired by Christianity: its leader, Hung Hsiu Chu'an, proclaimed himself the younger brother of Jesus Christ and had the Bible among his sacred books. Despite these difficulties, some dozens of missionary institutions for men and women were formed in China and apostolic vicariates multiplied. Many institutions took up the intellectual tradition of past centuries: in 1873 the Jesuits established an observatory near Shanghai.

In 1807, the London Missionary Society sent Robert Morrison, a shoemaker, to Canton. He had to act in secret and baptized his first Chinese in 1814. He undertook the translation of the Bible. Soon afterwards, a German missionary, Karl Gützlaff (1805–1851), planned to Christianize China in a generation with the help of German missionary societies; he recruited 200 Chinese preachers, who disappointed his hopes. Having worked as a doctor in Shanghai, Hudson Taylor decided to evangelize the interior of China and founded the China Inland Missionary Fellowship (1865), which became one of the most important Protestant missions: he thought that he could evangelize China in five years with around a thousand European missionaries dedicated to live the faith in entire obedience. At the end of the century, forty Protestant missionary societies were sharing China between them.

Korea

The history of the evangelization of Korea in the nineteenth century is the history of a long series of persecutions. After the time of lay Christianity (cf. the previous chapter), the first Chinese priest in the service of Korean Christians was put to death in 1802. Christians numbered around 6,000. Calls to help resulted in the designation of a vicar apostolic in 1831. The persecutions continued. The first Korean priest, Andrew Kim, was executed in 1846 with numerous Christians, and in 1866 two bishops, seven missionaries and several thousand Christians suffered the same fate. Religious freedom was not gained until 1885.

The countries of Indo-China

It was thanks to Mgr Pigneau de Béhain (died 1799), vicar apostolic of Cochin-China, that the ruler of Vietnam (the emperor of Annam), Gia-Long, had been able to ascend the throne. He proved tolerant of Christians. However, on his death in 1820 his son Minh-Mang quickly showed his hostility to Christianity. Proscriptive measures grew more severe and culminated in a bloody persecution which began in 1833. This was to last for half a century, interrupted only by a few calmer periods. Several missionaries, Vietnamese priests and catechists suffered martyr-

Awaiting martyrdom

After a short ministry in Tongking in the reign of Tu Duc, Jean-Louis Bonnard, of the Foreign Missions of Paris, was condemned to death and executed on 1 May 1852 at the age of twenty-eight. A few days before his execution, he wrote to his parents, who were living in the diocese of Lyons.

In chains for the name of Jesus, 25 April 1852 . . .
The Lord has raised his hand to strike me, hell has been let loose, and without sparing the flock has directed its fire principally against the pastor . . . So when you receive this letter, my dearest parents, you may be certain that my head will have fallen under the sword. I shall be a martyr; I shall have died for the faith of Jesus Christ, sacrificed by the infidels, in hatred against this holy religion in which you gave me the first lessons. I still remember those lessons, and they still console me in the depths of my dark cell . . . Yes, my dear parents, sacrificed in this way, like the divine Jesus and all the holy martyrs, by the hand of the evil ones, after all these heroes of faith I hope to rise to the abode of glory . . . Do not weep as you read this letter, which will only be sent to you after my death . . . Rejoice, for my soul has been raised to the abode of the blessed ones . . . I am so happy to die in this way . . . I was still very young when I was with you, but already I desired what is happening to me today . . . My soul is overflowing with joy. Do you all work actively for the salvation of your soul . . . It is up there in the abode of the blessed ones that I shall meet you again . . .

(*La Vie du vénérable Jean-Louis Bonnard*, by a priest of the diocese of Lyons, Lyons 1876, 405–9)

dom. The surviving missionaries had to hide in order to continue their ministry.

Under the emperor Thieu-Tri there was some respite. Mgr Etienne-Théodore Cuénot, vicar apostolic of Cochin-China, chose this time to summon the Synod of Go-Thi, which met in August 1841, in a hut hidden behind thick hedges. In addition to the bishop there were fifteen priests: two Europeans and thirteen Cochin-Chinese; the bishop took advantage of the occasion to consecrate one of the European priests as his coadjutor. The vicariate extended as far as Cambodia, Laos and Siam; among its 8 million inhabitants there were 80,000 Christians; 7 European priests, 32 indigenous priests and 250 religious. Mgr Cuénot wanted to consolidate his church in this difficult period; he was inspired by the Synod of Szechuan held by Mgr Dufresse in 1803. For Cochin-China, the emphasis was on the choice and training of future priests: four stages were planned, from teaching the rudiments of Latin to each potential missionary to the major seminary at Penang in Malaysia. One stage was then to prepare for ordination, which was to be given around the age of thirty-five or forty. The synod also gave priority to catechesis and to the witness of lay people in the evangelization of non-Christians. The synod rejected any borrowing of symbols from the traditional religions and acculturation was limited to an adaptation in the dress of priests. The high number of Cochin-Chinese seminaries in Penang (122 in 1848), the 56 priests ordained during the vicariate of Mgr Cuénot, the mass of settled catechists, fathers of families and itinerant catechists, can all be seen as the fruits of this synod.

During this period Mgr Retord, vicar apostolic of Tongking, took advantage of the calm to resume public worship and make solemn visitations to communities. About half a dozen new apostolic vicariates were created for the whole of Vietnam between 1844 and 1850. With the emperor Tu-Duc (1847–1882), violent persecution resumed and claimed numerous martyrs. Mgr Retord died of exhaustion in his hiding place in 1858 and Mgr Cuénot also died, on the eve of the day on which he was to have been executed. This persecution provoked intervention from France and Spain (1862), which resulted in the French occupation of three

The discovery of the old Christians of Japan in Nagasaki (1865)

In addition to baptism, the criteria of recognition were essentially the cult of Mary, the Pope, and the celibacy of the priests. For the narrator, M. Petitjean of the Foreign Missions of Paris, this was clearly an apologetic argument in favour of Catholicism.

On Friday 17 March, about half an hour after noon, around fifteen people were standing at the door of the church. Prompted without doubt by my good angel, I went to them and opened the door. I had hardly time to recite a *Pater Noster*, than three women between sixty and seventy years of age knelt in front of me and, with hands on their breasts, said in a low voice:

'The heart of all of us who are here does not differ from yours.'

'Truly, but where do you come from?'

'We are all from Urakami. In Urakami almost all have the same heart as we do.'

Then the woman asked, 'Where is the image of the Blessed Mary?' I had to answer all their questions . . . The sight of the statue of Our Lady with the infant Jesus reminded them of the feast of Christmas which they told me they celebrated in the eleventh month. They asked me whether we were not at the seventeenth day of the time of sadness (Lent). St Joseph is not unknown to them either . . .

Only a small number of people know the words of baptism . . . They observe Sunday and the festivals. Now they are observing Lent. In their prayers they often call on God, the most blessed Virgin, their guardian angel and their holy patrons.

Peter the baptizer gave us most valuable information. First it must be said that his formula seemed valid and that he pronounced it distinctly . . . Finally he asked us about the great Head of the Kingdom in Rome, whose name he desired to know. When we told him that the august vicar of Jesus Christ, the Holy Pontiff Pius XI, would be happy to learn the comforting news that he and his Christian compatriots had just given us, Peter burst out with joy. Nevertheless, before leaving us he wanted to be certain that we were truly the successors of their old missionaries.

'You don't have any children?' he asked us timidly.

'Behold, we and all your Christian and pagan brothers of Japan are the children which the good God has given us. As to other children, we may not have them. Like your first missionaries, the priest must be celibate all his life.'

On hearing this reply, Peter and his companions prostrated themselves on the ground, crying out, 'They are virgins, Thank God, Thank God! . . .' Almost everywhere the Christians had an identical organization. There were two main leaders in most of the villages. The first, called the prayer leader, presided over the Sunday prayers and visited the dying . . . The second, the baptizer, administered the sacrament of baptism. He had to have with him a pupil baptizer called to succeed him if he died or when he retired, for he could not exercise his functions for more than ten years.

provinces of Cochin-China; the protection of the missionaries led to colonization. Several congregations of men and women became established.

Japan

Japan had been closed to Europe and Christianity since the seventeenth century. From 1853, the United States and then the countries of Europe put pressure on the ports of Japan: the ports were to be opened, and Westerners were to be given the right to build churches. The building of a chapel dedicated to the Japanese martyrs of Nagasaki in 1865 brought out of the shadows descendants of the seventeenth-century Christians who had maintained the faith and Christian rites in the absence of clergy. Although some refused to join the Roman church, the Japanese church began again; however, Christianity was not authorized for the Japanese, and persecution resumed for five years (1868–1873). With the Meiji era (the era of progress) freedom of worship was granted to all religions; numerous

Church, nation and civilization

Before his departure, in a letter to the Council for the Propagation of the Faith (21 March 1847), Mgr Truffet, appointed vicar apostolic of the Two Guineas in January 1847, explains his missionary programme. Unfortunately he was unable to realize it, since he died in Dakar on 22 November of the same year. His perspectives, which closely resemble ours, were almost completely forgotten at the end of the nineteenth century.

We are not going to establish Italy, France or any other European country in Africa, but solely the Holy Catholic Church, which is above all nationalities and all human systems. With the Grace from on high, we wish to strip ourselves of all that is only European, so as to retain only those thoughts which are the true and only basis for ancient or growing Christianities; the thoughts of the church, which are those of the Spirit of God. And these divine thoughts have a savour which leads them to be tasted by every upright heart, and an intimate power which leads them to take root in any soil trodden by man, provided that these ideas from heaven have not degenerated as the result of an admixture of ideas from earth . . .

(Mgr Truffet says that as a basis for his action he wants to take the instruction Neminem profecto, *which represents the will of Gregory XV.)*

We do not believe that the gospel and the church can establish themselves solidly in a country without bringing civilization to it and without perfecting the customs and institutions that it has already. But civilization, produced or perfected by Catholicism, is not the importation of the social customs of one nation to another; it is the application of social principles, that is, of charity, of order and freedom consecrated by the gospel, to a people whose ideas and customs it corrects and elevates while taking account of its climate, its character and its traditions . . .

The first and perhaps the most difficult duty of the apostle is not the heroism of devotion, but the courage of patience, the denial of all his human being, which brings him down to the level of his neophytes, and to identify humanly with them so that they can identify spiritually with him. If he is to be able to give them the meat of the gospel, he has to receive from them customs which are not contrary to the gospel and to his priesthood.

So we shall be obliged to make ourselves Guineans if we want the Guineans to become Catholics. This reciprocal assimilation is the means of knowing, uniting and making fruitful the religious and social elements which God established wherever he created his children and his images, regardless of the colour of their skin.

The task of foreigners will have been fulfilled worthily when they have succeeded in making it possible for their missions to pass from them without inconvenience, entrusting them to the enlightened piety of an indigenous and canonical clergy . . . If God deigns to give me the strength as he has given me the desire, I shall try to follow this approach in Guinea, so that little by little the mission may become a church governed by the common law and living on its local resources under the paternal supremacy of the Holy See.

---

congregations were established by the end of the century. However, the 'miracle' of the sixteenth century did not take place; the Japanese welcomed the sciences of the West but no longer its religion.

Africa

At the beginning of the nineteenth century, Africa was still for some decades the continent of the trade of Negroes with America. Campaigns for the abolition of the trade were completely successful only when slavery itself was abolished: in 1833 in the English colonies in 1848 in the French colonies; in 1861 in the United States, and elsewhere even later. Having regained a good conscience, Europeans could then launch out on a crusade against the trade in East Africa, which was in the hands of Muslim merchants.

The Europeans, English, Spaniards, French, Dutch and Portuguese were established in some trading posts or small colonies. Within Africa, often ephemeral Muslim empires contributed to the expansion of Islam, which many European authorities regarded as the proper religion for Negroes. However, the greater part of the interior of Africa was unknown to Europeans. The nineteenth century was that of the explorations which made the names of those who undertook them: René Caillé (Timbuktu, 1828); Livingstone (Zambesi, 1856 and afterwards); Stanley (Tanganyika, 1871); Brazza (Congo, 1875).

In the course of the first three-quarters of the century the Christian missions found a place in this context which transformed them into an often murderous adventure: Africa was the grave of missionaries who, in their concern to be faithful to their rules, did not adapt in any way over clothing or food; as yet no protection was known against yellow fever.

The starting point for a systematic evangelization of the West Coast of Africa was the creation in 1842 of the apostolic vicariate of the Two Guineas. Its frontiers were vague. The first vicar apostolic was an American, Mgr Barron, whose flock were the freed slaves who had returned to Africa (Liberia). But he gave up, and his successor died very soon afterwards. Many other deaths followed, yet apostolic vicariates multiplied on the Atlantic coast of Africa up to the end of the century. English missionary societies also became established. Samuel Crowther, a friend of Henry Venn, who came from Sierra Leone, became the first Anglican African bishop (1864). He exercised his ministry in the regions of the Niger, having to cope with misunderstanding from whites, pastors and colonists.

In South Africa, where Dutch Calvinist colonists were established, the English seized the Cape (1806), a factor which gave priority to Protestant missions. In 1799 the London Missionary Society had sent a doctor, John Theodosius Van der Kemp. He evangelized the Kaffirs and the Hottentots, dressed in the style of the country, and married a native woman, causing a great scandal among the segregationist colonists. The Protestant Missionary Society in Paris sent several missionaries to Lesotho (Basutoland) in 1833. The mission began independently of all colonization, and the missionaries dealt with only the ruler of the country. Evangelization progressed to the point that missionary posts could be given to the Basutos in 1863. A local church took shape with the establishment of a Presbyterian synodical regime from 1872. Pastor François Coillard left a legendary memorial in this mission (1861–1880) before continuing it as far as the Zambesi. In 1855 the Oblates of Mary began the black Catholic mission of South Africa in Natal.

The African work of Lavigerie

The missionary vocation of Charles Lavigerie was aroused when he was director of the Work of the East (1857–1861), which supported the Christians of the Middle East. After being Bishop of Nancy, he accepted the diocese of Algiers (1867) as the starting point for a vast project of evangelizing all Africa. His activity and imagination were prodigious. In 1868 he founded the Society of Missionaries of Africa (the White Fathers), and the next year the agricultural brothers and sisters, the latter becoming known as White Sisters. 1879 saw the ephemeral creation of the Armed Brothers of the Sahara, new Templars in the service of the missionaries. For Lavigerie, mission began in Algeria, in opposition to the French government, which did not want the conversion of Muslims: Lavigerie paid particular attention to the Berbers who were the first occupants of the country before the Arab conquest. He founded Christian villages by marrying male and female orphans brought up by the Brothers and Sisters.

As apostolic delegate of the Sahara and the Sudan (1878), he sent missionaries over the Sahara as far as the Great Lakes, where they met Anglicans and Protestants. Several times, White Fathers were massacred in the desert. Lavigerie, who had done his doctoral thesis on the ancient catechumenate,

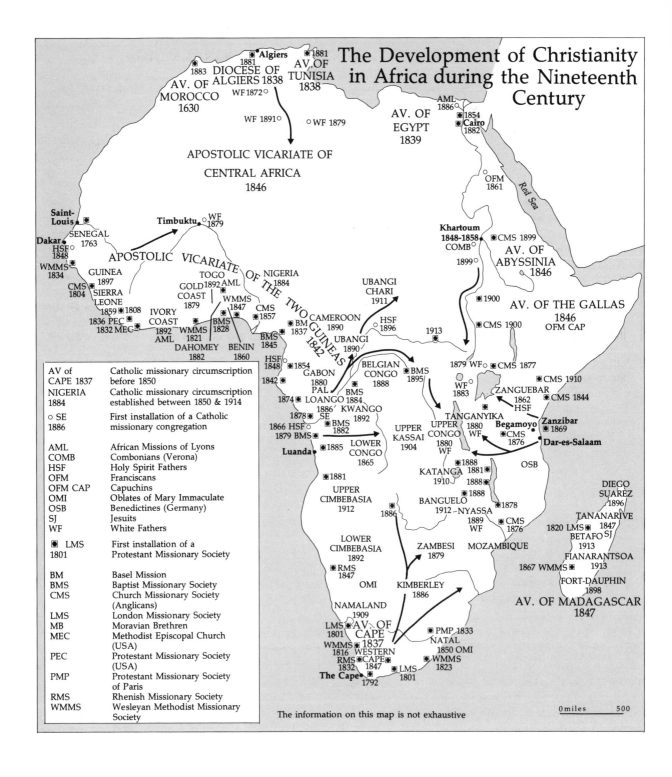

The Development of Christianity in Africa during the Nineteenth Century

Algiers
1881
AV. OF
TUNISIA
1838
1883 DIOCESE OF
AV. OF ALGIERS 1838
MOROCCO
1630
WF 1872 ○

WF 1891 ○   ○ WF 1879

AML
1886 ○
1854
Cairo
1882

AV. OF
EGYPT
1839

○ OFM
1861

Red Sea

APOSTOLIC VICARIATE OF
CENTRAL AFRICA
1846

Saint-
Louis
Dakar
SENEGAL
1763
HSF ○
1848
WMMS
1834
CMS
1804

Timbuktu ○ WF 1879

Khartoum
1848-1858
COMB ○
1899 ○

CMS 1899

AV. OF
ABYSSINIA
1846

APOSTOLIC VICARIATE OF THE TWO GUINEAS 1842

GUINEA
1897
SIERRA
LEONE
1859
1808
1836 PEC
1832 MEC
IVORY
COAST
1892
AML
DAHOMEY
1882
TOGO
GOLD 1892
COAST
1879
WMMS
1821
AML
WMMS
1847
BMS
1828
BENIN
1860

NIGERIA
1884
CMS
1857

BMS
1845

CAMEROON
1890
BM
1837
UBANGI
1890

UBANGI
CHARI
1911

HSF ○
1896

1913

1900

CMS 1900

AV. OF THE GALLAS
1846
OFM CAP

HSF ○
1848
1854
GABON
1842
1880
PAL
1874 LOANGO
1878
1866 HSF ○
1879 BMS
BMS
1884
1886 KWANGO
SE
1892
BMS
1882
LOWER
CONGO
1865

BELGIAN
CONGO
1888
BMS
1895

1879 WF ○ CMS 1877

WF
1883
ZANGUEBAR
1862
HSF
CMS 1910
CMS 1844

Luanda

1885

UPPER
KASSAI
1904

UPPER
CONGO
1880
WF
TANGANYIKA
1880
UPPER
1880
WF

Begamoyo
CMS
1876

Zanzibar
1869

Dar-es-Salaam

1881

UPPER
CIMBEBASIA
1912

1886

KATANGA
1910
1888
1881
1888
1888
BANGUELO
1912
1878
NYASSA
1889
WF
CMS
1876

OSB

DIEGO
SUAREZ
1896
TANANARIVE
1820 LMS
1847
BETAFO SJ
1913
FIANARANTSOA
1867 WMMS
1913
FORT-DAUPHIN
1898

AV. OF MADAGASCAR
1847

LOWER
CIMBEBASIA
1892
RMS
1847
OMI

NAMALAND
1909
LMS
1801
WMMS
1816
RMS
1832
WESTERN
CAPE
1847
The Cape
1792

ZAMBESI
1879

KIMBERLEY
1886

MOZAMBIQUE

PMP 1833
NATAL
1850 OMI
WMMS
1823
LMS
1801

AV. OF
CAPE
1837

AV of CAPE 1837	Catholic missionary circumscription before 1850
NIGERIA 1884	Catholic missionary circumscription established between 1850 & 1914
○ SE 1886	First installation of a Catholic missionary congregation
AML	African Missions of Lyons
COMB	Combonians (Verona)
HSF	Holy Spirit Fathers
OFM	Franciscans
OFM CAP	Capuchins
OMI	Oblates of Mary Immaculate
OSB	Benedictines (Germany)
SJ	Jesuits
WF	White Fathers
◉ LMS 1801	First installation of a Protestant Missionary Society
BM	Basel Mission
BMS	Baptist Missionary Society
CMS	Church Missionary Society (Anglicans)
LMS	London Missionary Society
MB	Moravian Brethren
MEC	Methodist Episcopal Church (USA)
PEC	Protestant Missionary Society (USA)
PMP	Protestant Missionary Society of Paris
RMS	Rhenish Missionary Society
WMMS	Wesleyan Methodist Missionary Society

The information on this map is not exhaustive

0 miles   500

Instructions to the White Fathers of Equatorial Africa (1879)

Cardinal Lavigerie first of all commends a loving approach to the populations who are encountered; he gives advice on hygienic clothing and emphasizes evangelization and education in an African context.

To succeed in the transformation of Africa . . ., the first requirement is to train the Africans chosen by us in conditions which from the material point of view leave them truly Africans. In general that has not been done so far, and I have to say that in Algeria we have fallen into the common error . . . Young Blacks, even those whom one wants to make instructors or catechists, must be in a state which allows them to live the African life at their own expense and, if possible, a state which honours them, gives them influence and is unquestioningly accepted by all, so that they can be a powerful help to missionaries instead of being a burden on them.

Does this state exist? I shall not speak here about the young women, since I believe that it is inappropriate to begin with them. Their turn will come, but only later. But I do not hesitate to say that in the case of the young men, this state exists. It is universal, universally honoured, and fulfils all the conditions that one could desire to assure their existence and their influence, namely medicine . . .

In speaking of the material education of our young Blacks, I have said that they should be African. But on the other hand their religious education must be essentially apostolic. There are in fact two ways of making men like us. The first is to make them like us outwardly. That is the human approach, the approach of the philanthropic civilizers, those who say, as was repeated at the Conference of Brussels, that to change the Africans it is enough to teach them the arts and crafts of Europe. It is to believe that when they are housed, clothed, fed as we are, they will have changed their nature. But they will only have changed their garb. Their heart will be just as barbarian, even more so; for it will also have been corrupted and will apply to its corruption what it has learned of the secrets of our luxury and our softness.

The divine manner is quite different . . . The apostle addresses the soul . . . and to gain the soul he condemns himself, if necessary, to abandoning all the outward customs of life. He becomes a barbarian with the barbarians, as he becomes a Greek with the Greeks. This is what the apostles did, and we do not see any of them trying first to change the material customs of the peoples. They sought to change their hearts, and once these hearts were changed, they renewed the world . . .

In each station, it will be necessary to take the largest possible number of children and begin to train them . . . In order to secure the children, the Fathers can resort to purchase, since unfortunately slavery still exists. They can also gather some abandoned children or children who have been condemned to death as a result of local superstitions.

(Cardinal Lavigerie, *Écrits d'Afrique*, ed. A.Hamman, Paris 1966, 176f.)

restored this period of preparation for baptism. He asked missionaries to adapt to the outward practices of Africa in dress, lodging, food and language, but he thought that there would be a church of Africa only through Africans. Lavigerie, who was made a cardinal in 1882, reached the height of notoriety with the restoration of the title of Archbishop of Carthage and Primate of Africa which he took for himself. However, that happened in another period.

Madagascar

Coming from Mauritius, English missionaries from the London Missionary Society became established in the heart of Madagascar in 1820, called by king Radama I, who dominated the highlands, to be teachers. The missionaries brought the Bible with them. To translate it, a script had to be chosen, one which was simpler than the Arabic characters hitherto used to write Malagasy. The king, who was open to foreign techniques, wanted his people to become literate, but did not authorize baptism. On his death in 1828 his chief wife took power under the name of Ranavalona I. Very attached to ancestral beliefs and jealous of national independence, she was at first favourable to teaching. The missionaries began the translation of the Bible. The queen authorized the first baptism, but gradually saw that Christianity was shaking the sacral basis of her power; the religion of the foreigners was banned to the Malagasys (1835). The missionaries had to go, but they left the Bible as a parting gift to the young community. In order to restore the tradition, the queen launched a violent persecution against the Christians which lasted until her death in 1861. No one could have a printed text except at court. Christianity held up well, despite the most refined tortures which made more than one hundred martyrs. The Bible was read in secret, and a clandestine form of worship was organized. In 1861 the Christians, who numbered 300 when the missionaries left, proved to have grown to more than 6,000. The English missionaries returned. Queen Ranavalona converted to Protestantism in 1869, which gave a greater weight to it; however, it did not become a state religion, since there were also Catholics.

In 1832, the apostolic prefect of Reunion, Mgr de Solages, who had landed at Tamatave, had died of fever and hunger without being able to reach Tananarive and meet the queen. Another French priest, Pierre Dalmond, took up the enterprise. He too left from Reunion and spent two years (1837–1839) evangelizing the island of Sainte-Marie on the coast, which was a French possession; he then worked on the island of Nosy Bé on the north-west coast of Madagascar. Having become apostolic prefect of Madagascar, he left for Europe to look for missionaries for the main island. He obtained support from the Jesuits, but died in 1847. The Jesuits took over. During the time of persecution, from 1855 Fr Finaz was able to spent two years incognito at Tananarive. In 1861 the Jesuits began to preach openly, but since the upper classes were inclined towards Protestantism, the Catholic community comprised mainly small children and slaves.

The Middle East

At the end of this panorama, mention must be made of missions in the Middle East. Here, however, it was more a matter of supporting Christian minorities in the Muslim world of the Ottoman Empire (Maronites were massacred by the Druze in 1860). Because they were unable to convert the Muslims, the Catholic missionaries tried as in the past to attract the other Eastern 'schismatic' Christians to the Roman church. So this was more a matter of changing rite or confession than of evangelization proper. However, we should not neglect the aspect of Christian and Catholic witness in the Muslim world.

8

The Missions of Colonial Imperialism (1880–1940)

The date 1880 does not represent so radical a break in the history of evangelization and the history of the world as, for example, the French Revolution. Many of the features of evangelization described in the previous chapter still apply in this new period, and I shall not go over them again. There was no radical change in the perspectives of Cardinal Lavigerie, whose initiatives I described earlier. In the 1880s it was not so much Christian missions that changed as the political and economic situation. Colonial fever seized most of the countries of Europe. In general, the missions came to regard European colonial expansion as providential for the proclamation of the gospel and the promotion of civilization. So there is a close link between colonial imperialism and the prodigious development of missions at the end of the nineteenth century. However, over and above the polemic against the ambiguity of the link, it is important to reflect on this history, even though there is some backlash against it at present. From the perspective of the Catholic Church, the pontificate of Leo XIII, which began in 1878, also marked a renewal of missionary perspectives which took account of the new context. Though people were not always aware of it at the time, the First World War (1914–1918) was the starting point of a development.

The colonial fever

The colonial imperialism which began to assert itself in the 1880s resulted from the convergence of various movements of thought and opinion, some of which we met as early as the beginning of the century. The geographical societies dreamed of the discovery of the world; sailors, soldiers and traders at the ports were in search of places where they could engage in their activities; utopians sought virgin lands in which to establish their ideal communities; humanitarian and missionary preoccupations found a place here.

Africa above all was the object of fierce competition between the European countries. The accounts of Stanley's exploration aroused the greed of Leopold II, King of the Belgians. In 1876 he convened an international geographical conference in Brussels which decided to found an International African Association; its aims were the exploration to Africa and opposition to the slave trade. In 1878, Leopold II became head of an International Association of the Congo of which Stanley was the executive agent. The French, English and Portuguese did not take well to the conquests of the Association, which encroached upon their territories. The Berlin Conference (1884–1885) met to

Article 6 of the Treaty of Berlin (1885)

All the powers exercising rights of sovereignty or influence in the aforesaid territories commit themselves to supervise the conservation of the indigenous populations and the amelioration of their moral and material living conditions and to contribute to the suppression of slavery and above all the trade in Blacks; they will protect and encourage, without distinction of nationality or creed, all the religious, scientific or charitable initiatives created and organized to these ends or aimed at instructing the natives and helping them to understand and appreciate the advantages of civilization.

Christian missionaries, scholars, explorers, their escorts, possessions and collections will equally be the object of special protection.

Freedom of conscience and religious tolerance are expressly guaranteed just as much to natives as to nationals and foreigners. Free and public exercise of all forms of worship, the right to build religious buildings and to organize missions belonging to all the religions will not be subject to any restriction or constraint.

'arrange the most favourable conditions for the development of trade and civilization in certain regions of Africa'. The Treaty of Berlin (1885) led to a division of Africa: every European power occupying part of the African coast had the right to conquer the hinterland; hence the colonial frontiers perpendicular to the coast which sometimes cut tribes and races in two. King Leopold became the ruler of an 'Independent State of the Congo', which became the Belgian Congo in 1908. Article 6 of the Treaty of Berlin regulated humanitarian and religious problems; in a way it was a charter of missions. The division of Africa was completed during the 1900s: England, France and Germany were its chief beneficiaries; Italy, Portugal and Spain had to be content with more restricted domains. The Europeans put an end to slavery in the territories which they administered, but replaced it with forced labour for works of public utility and portage.

Imperialism and mission

Colonialism certainly opened up an enormous mission field, and one could discuss *ad infinitum* the collusion between imperialism and evangelization. Local missionaries were able to facilitate the conquests, and the colonizers invited missionaries to settle in the conquered territories in order to set up schools and hospitals. The humanitarian arguments put forward by the colonizers coincided with the preoccupation of the missionaries; some shared the same prejudices about the superiority of the white man and the universal value of European civilization. Furthermore, despite certain reservations, the missionaries regarded the conquest as providential for evangelization. However, one feature came to be accentuated at the end of the nineteenth century: the nationalism of the missionaries. In the majority of territories the missionaries belonged to the nation of the colonizers, and they exalted Catholicism and fatherland in the same breath. Missionaries, soldiers and administrators of the time give the impression that they were all working at the same task.

However, we must be careful not to generalize about this convergence of views between missionaries, administrators, soldiers and colonists; the situation varied a great deal among the colonizing states and even from one territory to another. The Belgian Congo supported Catholicism, but the Catholic missionaries accused the French administrators of West Africa of favouring Islam and not fighting enough against pagan customs, in particular those of marriage. While the administrators wanted schools to teach only the language of the colonizing country, missionaries tried to express themselves in the language of those whom they were evangelizing. They were helped by indigenous catechists, on whom the administrators looked with some suspicion, since the catechists were outside their influence. Missionaries protested against the forced labour and the diseases and vices imported from Europe, which led to the extinction of fragile tribes. To keep their independence and protect the new Christians from pernicious influences, the missionary authorities established their stations far from the administrative centres, or created Christian districts in the cities. However, this policy brought with it the risk of marginalizing the converts in their people, from whom they were separated.

The Holy See and the missions

The long pontificate of Leo XIII (1878–1903) corresponds to this time of rising colonial imperialism and in particular to the partition of Africa. Though the Holy See was in a difficult situation in Rome and in Italy, Leo XIII did not shut himself up in a defensive position. Throughout his pontificate he asserted his concern for a restoration of Christianity with the papacy at its heart; in this perspective the universal mission was an integral dimension of his vision of Catholicism. Perhaps he thought that the difficult relations between the European states and the Holy See were compensated for by the world expansion of the church. With his contemporaries he associated colonization, civilization and mission, the church being the source of true civilization. While practising a flexible democracy, Leo XIII thought that Roman centralization was the best guarantee of an evangelization detached from any compromise with the political powers.

The Pope and the Propaganda, which was firmly directed by Cardinal Simeoni (1878–1892) and then by Cardinal Leochowski (1892–1902), had the Instructions of 1659 and 1845 as their essential points of reference: the independence of evangelization from the political powers and the formation of new churches with bishops and dioceses. The anachronistic privileges of the states had to be abolished and an indigenous clergy trained. Certainly Rome had to take account of political resistance and the atmosphere of the cultures in which missions were set. The Propaganda insisted that prefects and vicars apostolic should send in their quinquennial reports regularly, and these had to

---

The European conquest, a providential fact

In an article in Le Correspondant *of 10 June 1902, Mgr Le Roy, Superior General of the Fathers of the Holy Spirit, had judged scandalous the way in which the companies were exploiting Gabon and demoralizing the population. However, some years later, in 1911, he regarded the conquest as providential.*

More discussed – and beyond question more open to discussion – is the timeliness of the European conquest. Is it a good thing? Is it a bad thing? – Gentlemen, it is a fact, a necessary fact and a providential one. Let us try with all our strength to mitigate the inevitable damage that it causes, taking advantage of the evident opportunities it offers to press forward our peaceful conquest. That is the best thing that we can do. No river overflows into the plains which it irrigates without bringing with it a good deal of sand and, often, a good deal of mud. But, whether Europe denies or asserts the fact, whether it wishes it or rejects it, in Africa willy-nilly it remains God's messenger . . . It will break down the ramparts which Islam sets up against it, it will annihilate the bloody despots who create a desert before them, it will ruin the negro traders . . . it will mitigate the horrors of the slave trade, of slavery, of cannibalism, of infanticide and all other barbaric practices; it will open up routes, bring places nearer, make travelling and transport easier, and prolong human life. In spite of the accidents, the imperfections . . . and sometimes the crimes, all these are the foundations of Christianity; this is the largely prepared field over which the workers of the gospel will pass.

(A. Le Roy, *L'Évangelization de l'Afrique (1822–1911)*, Lyons 1911)

---

respond to the questionnaire drafted in 1877. It committed the mission churches to convening synods and sending accounts of them to Rome.

Concerning an indigenous clergy

There is constant reference to the training of an indigenous clergy in official texts from the end of the nineteenth century. These often refer to the Instruction of 1659. However, an ambiguity remains. If there is unanimity over indigenous priests, this is not the case with bishops.

Conclusion of the Instruction Cum postremis *of the Propaganda for the East Indies (19 March 1893)*

Let those who are at the head of missions remember that the Sacred Congregation is giving them not only advice but also orders which they must carry out, particularly in all that concerns the conversion of pagans and the training of indigenous clergy.

They are to submit willingly to these orders of the Sacred Congregation, confirmed by the authority and positive will of the Holy Father. They are to submit as to an order from Jesus Christ himself, for whose glory they work, persuaded that whatever the fruit of their labours, God will always recompense their efforts.

Pope Leo XIII's apostolic letter Ad extremas *on the foundation of seminaries in India (24 June 1893)*

The Catholic faith will not have an assured future among the Indians, and its progress will remain uncertain, as long as there is not an indigenous clergy properly trained for priestly functions, who are capable not only of helping the missionaries but of themselves competently pursuing the interest of religion in their own cities . . .

The zeal of the missionaries who have come from Europe is encountering many obstacles, above all ignorance of the language of the country, which is very difficult to master; likewise the strangeness of its customs and morals, which are not easy to understand even after a long stay. This forces European priests to live there as in a country which is not their own. Moreover, because the population is mistrustful of foreigners, it is clear that the work of indigenous priests will prove far more fruitful. They know perfectly the tastes, the mentality and the customs of their nation; they know when to speak and when to keep silent . . . A time may come in Europe or in Asia when the foreign clergy have to abandon India, out of either force or necessity. In that case, if there is no local clergy, who can save the religion, since there will no longer be a single minister of the sacraments or a single preacher? . . .

The usage and rule which the apostles followed was to begin their task of evangelizing by spreading Christian teaching among the population; they then soon chose some inhabitants of the place to initiate them into the sacred mysteries and even elevate them to the episcopate. Following their example, the Roman pontiffs have always had the custom of ordering those responsible for the apostolate to make every effort to choose a local clergy when the Christian community has become sufficiently important. Thus the propagation and conservation of Christianity in India make it necessary to ordain as priests Indians who can be priests whatever the circumstances, distribute the sacraments normally, and remain at the head of their Christian compatriots.

The opinion of Mgr Lavigne SJ, Bishop of Trincomalee, Ceylon, on the question of indigenous clergy (9 March 1904)

The remedy (to the difficulties raised by the indigenous priests) would be for the European missionaries once and for all to resolve to regard the native priests as their equals in the priesthood, to honour them in public, to love them and make them feel at home . . . The native clergy should be given a real place and influence in the episcopal council . . . If a bishop has rights, so too does the native (indigenous) priest, stated and regulated by canon law . . . The absence of these canonical forms means that the native priest believes or claims to be handed over to the whims of the bishop, and the victim of all who denounce him. It is only a step from this to wanting to shake off the yoke . . .

If the bishops maintained with each of their priests the affectionate relations of a father to his children, I am persuaded that the native priests would love their bishop and support him on every occasion instead of agitating against him.

If the bishop supports his native clergy against muddled minds and professional denouncers, the priests will support their bishops.

If priests feel loved and supported by their bishop they will cease to sigh for native bishops. For it is quite certain that the people prefers the direction of European missionaries to that of natives, and that the good priests have more confidence in the impartiality of a European bishop than in that of the native bishops.

(Letter to Mgr Zaleski, apostolic delegate)

Negotiations with the states were often difficult. While China and the Holy See would have liked to establish direct diplomatic relations, France categorically refused to renounce its role of compulsory intermediary between China and the Catholic missions, the 'protectorate' which had been recognized by the treaty of Tien-Tsin (1858). With regret, Rome had to yield (1887) so as not to risk a break in diplomatic relations between France and the Vatican. In 1886, Portugal renounced its historic patronage, apart from Goa and three dioceses. So the Pope could set up the ordinary organization of the church (dioceses and bishops) in India. At the same time he sent an apostolic delegate (his direct representative for religious affairs) there. In 1891 it was the turn of Japan to have its dioceses and bishops.

The Pope would have liked to centralize the work of the Propagation of the Faith in Rome, since certain Catholics in Spain, Austria and elsewhere balked at having their offerings for mission going through France, all the more so since the distribution was entrusted to lay committees. But a visit of the secretary of the Propaganda to Lyons and Paris in 1887 showed that the time was not ripe for a move.

The Pope endorsed the action of the society against slavery along with that of Cardinal Lavigerie, and this was implemented by the Treaty of Brussels (1890). In the same year, Leo XIII instituted for the whole church a collection at Epiphany which the Propaganda sent to missions concerned with slavery.

On two occasions, in 1893, first the Propaganda and then Leo XIII, addressing the bishops of India, once more emphasized the need to train indigenous clergy. The Pope called for the establishment of a pontifical seminary for all India at Kandy (Ceylon). However, while there was general agreement over the question of indigenous priests, indigenous bishops were another matter, even in Rome.

The pontificate of Pius X (1903–1914) was essentially marked by the reorganization of the Propaganda in 1908. The constitution *Sapienti consilio* limited its territorial domain: a certain number of European countries (England, Ireland, Luxembourg, the Netherlands) were removed from it, as were the United States and Canada, while certain Indian missions in Latin America were entrusted to it. Its competence was also restricted. While the prefect of the Propaganda (the Red Pope) had almost unlimited powers in the mission field, some spheres like dogma, the sacraments and the religious life were transferred to other Roman congregations.

The missionary movement in Germany was particularly dynamic at the turn of the century, among both Protestants and Catholics. The German empire became interested in colonial conquest rather late. However, once it had joined in the race, it called for missionaries and support for its territories of the Cameroons, Togo, South-West and East Africa. Theological reflection on mission also began in Germany, initially among the Protestants; the best known missiologist is Gustav Warneck (1834–1910) of the University of Halle. He stimulated work among the Catholics, and in 1911 an institute was created in Münster and a journal of missionary sciences, edited by Joseph Schmidlin (1876–1944). Robert Streit (1875–1930) devoted himself to the monumental bibliography *Bibliotheca Missionum*.

The Protestant missions

Since Protestantism is not centralized, it is difficult to synthesize any overall missionary thought or directives in it, all the more so since the Protestant missionary societies usually wanted to be independent of the established churches, though they did not refuse to collaborate with them. We keep finding Protestants and Anglicans in the panorama of the countries evangelized. Some of their problems resembled those of the Catholics. Nationalism also weighed heavy on Protestant missions, but in a rather different way. For a Catholic, Protestant often meant English, and that meant a quasi-enemy in colonial conflicts. The French authorities often asked the Society of Protestant Missions in Paris to replace English or German missionaries in territories like Polynesia, Madagascar, Gabon and the Cameroons, which were conquered by France. The Society proved very reluctant to accept this request.

Soon ministries in the Protestant churches and the Anglican church were entrusted to indigenous ministers: the Nigerian Samuel Crowther was consecrated bishop in 1864, the Indian V.S. Azariah in 1912, a Chinese in 1918 and two Japanese in 1922. However, there was often the same reluctance as among Catholics to entrust them with complete responsibility for their churches.

Missionary theological reflection had begun in Britain in Edinburgh in the 1860s, and the first World Conference of Missions was held there in 1910. The new Christians expressed their astonishment at the multiplicity of Christian denominations. A Chinese delegate, Dr Chang, called on the missionaries of Europe and America to bring down their ecclesiastical barriers in the mission field. They might be explicable in terms of the local history of their churches, but they were incomprehensible to pagans who were hearing the message of the eternal gospel. Lutherans, Presbyterians, Wesleyans, Baptists, High Church and Low Church Anglicans, conformists and nonconformists all listened to him. They saw the uselessness of these divisions for their mission fields. It was a deeply emotional moment, and also marked the beginning of the ecumenical movement.

Some mission fields (1880–1914)

I shall not embark on an exhaustive tour of the world here. In many of the countries mentioned in the previous chapter, evangelization ran its course without any extraordinary events. In any case, it has already been possible to touch on the life of some particular churches in the presentation of the general aspects of mission.

Asia

The colonization of Vietnam (French Indo-China) from 1885 allowed a church to flourish. In percentage terms (almost 10% of the population), apart from the Philippines it was one of the most important churches in Asia.

However, it was upon China that the Christians of all confessions pinned their great hopes at the turn of the century. Europeans and Americans devoted considerable personnel and funds to it. Yet the situation was far from easy. Without being a colony, China was under the thumb of European powers which exploited it and humiliated it. After the defeat of China by Japan in 1895, the Europeans obtained new concessions. The missionaries were by no means least to profit from this. In 1899 Mgr Favier, Bishop of Peking, secured the same status for European bishops and priests as Chinese officials, bishops being equivalent to viceroys. 'We have no troops, no arms, no munitions. We have nothing: no railways, trade, customs, banks, nothing!' said the young Chinese emperor Kuang-chu, who wanted to undertake radical reforms, in 1898.

However, he was overthrown by his aunt, the old empress Tseu-hi, who thought that she could rely on the secret societies, in particular the Boxers, 'the fist of concord and justice'. The Boxer Rebellion erupted on 20 June 1900 in Peking; the German minister was assassinated. It was the signal for a massacre of foreigners and Christians: 300 Europeans fell victim, including around 50 missionaries, but there were also more than 30,000 Chinese Christian victims, Catholics and Protestants, including around 100 priests and religious. On 14 August of the same year Peking was recaptured and pillaged by the European troops, who demanded enormous indemnities by way of reparations. The Chinese empire crumbled in 1911–1912, giving way to a republic which had chaotic beginnings.

Paradoxically, these events were a stimulus to Christian missions. It was thought that from every point of view the salvation of China lay in conversion to Christianity. In 1902–1903 England and the United States signed conventions for their missionaries. There was a considerable effort at evangelization in the first fifteen years of the twentieth century. To the numerous congregations already present in 1900, more than twenty congregations of men and thirty of women were to be added. The new Catholic Foreign Missionary Society of America, with its headquarters at Maryknoll, New York, founded in 1911, gave itself China as a mission field. The evangelization campaigns seemed to bear fruit. According to statistics, the number of Catholics doubled in twelve years, from 720,000 and 1,375 priests in 1900 to 1,430,000 and 2,298 priests in 1912. But the Chinese population had already increased to more than 400 million. A similar movement was evident among other Christians, though their statistics are less precise. Dr John R.Mott, an American Methodist who was one of the key figures behind the 1910 Edinburgh Conference, proposed 'the evangelization of the world in this generation'. He made a tour of China in winter 1912, particularly addressing young people: '7,057 signed a promise to study the gospel, and to pray to God each day for light.'

The converts came from a popular level, in towns and in the country. In Inner Mongolia, the Scheut Fathers had taken up the system of reductions again: in the Ordos country they acquired land on which they settled Christian families. However, feeling a demand among the Chinese, who sought development for their country, Catholics and even more Protestants threw themselves into an intellectual ministry; the Jesuits took up the tradition of the seventeenth and eighteenth centuries. In 1879 the Episcopalians had created the first Chinese university in Shanghai. In 1903 the Jesuits laid the foundation for the Aurora University, again at Shanghai, where they already had an observatory. The secondary colleges multiplied. A number of religious were good Sinologists. However, teaching was aimed more at openness to Western languages and sciences than to a deepening of Chinese culture. Modelled on that of Christian Europe, the training of Chinese priests separated them from their milieu, in minor and major seminaries. They learned Latin better than the Chinese of the literate.

Granted, many missionaries thought the link

Hesitations over a completely Chinese church

While recognizing that the main obstacle to Christian preaching is the fact that Christianity is a foreign religion, Fr Japiot finds it hard to see how the church of China can be entrusted entirely to the Chinese.

Tai-ming-fu, 1 March 1896

Confucius is the saint *par excellence*; the men of letters are his disciples . . . To attack this class is not easy. Our religion is a foreign religion which goes against all their ideas and demolishes their Confucianism. The cult of the dead which they practise with many superstitions is also a great obstacle. Our devotion seems to them to be self-interested, and they readily believe that we are working to overturn their institutions . . . There are many Chinese priests; I believe that there are a dozen of them in each mission; there are thirty missions in China and several vicariates. The time has not come to make vicars apostolic of them; that might lead to a schism. The national spirit does not die with clerical education. Our indigenous priests, with a solid faith and enlightened piety, still regard us as foreigners; left to themselves, they might perhaps produce a Chinese Christianity! One of our great concerns is to supervise our catechists so that they do not distort the Christian truths which they teach in their own way . . . However, they have good will and try to do good. But if European missionaries were driven out of China, Christianity there would be seriously compromised. Moreover, if the Propagation of the Faith and alms were to disappear, our ministry would have to be restricted to the old Christians, since we pay all the expenses of the new ones . . .

(E.Japiot SJ, private archives)

between mission and European protection to be beneficial. But several were also aware of the

Chinese humiliation and wanted to de-Europeanize mission. Hudson Taylor, founder of the China Inland Mission, refused the indemnities the English consulate had called for as compensation for the destruction of his missions during the Boxer revolt: 'Missionaries must be prepared to work without any support guaranteed by man, contenting themselves with the promise of the one who said, "Seek first the kingdom of God."' The ministry in China of the Belgian Lazarist Vincent Lebbe began in 1901. He very soon felt ill at ease in a mission which was too closely connected with French power. He wanted to make himself a 'Chinese with the Chinese' and work for the birth of a truly Chinese church.

Africa

Africa was the new field of evangelization at the end of the nineteenth century. Granted, missions were established on the coasts in the middle of the century, as we have seen. But it was the colonial conquest which allowed Christianity to penetrate the interior of the continent. For all that, the task of the missionaries was not always easy. Many still succumbed to tropical diseases, and many were assassinated by those opposing the colonial penetration.

Missions in Africa had a certain number of common features. The populations of Africa were those whom both missionary literature and travel or colonial literature down to the middle of the twentieth century called 'barbarian', emphasizing the duty to bring them civilization. The missionary journals always took some delight in making their readers shudder with colourful accounts, like the scenes of cannibalism recounted by Mgr Auguoard in the Congo, who came to be called 'the bishop of the cannibals'.

Since Europe had divided Africa, the colonizing nations wanted missionaries as far as possible to be of the same nationality as the colonizers, though this was not an absolute rule until 1914. By virtue of the 'right of commission', territories were shared between the congregations: the White Fathers devoted themselves more to the interior of Africa, which was in contact with Islam; the African Missions of Lyons and the Spiritans covered the African coasts and their hinterland, the Africa of animism or fetishism, to use the expression of the time. There was always the inevitable competition between Catholics and other Christian confessions, each seeking the support of administrations or criticizing them for favouring rivals. However,

Not a very flattering portrait

The least that can be said is that the author, a missionary of the Paris Foreign Missions, does not look very favourably on those who are to be evangelized. This is certainly one way of showing the Catholics the difficulty of a task which is aggravated even further by the presence of Protestants.

The black population of southern Africa comprises three distinct races. The Kaffirs (infidels) deserve their name perfectly. Of all the African races, the Kaffirs are the most difficult to convert. They are characterized by a profound religious indifference and an abject materialism. Our freethinkers, always in search of atheistic populations, might perhaps find among them the ideal of which they dream. The Kaffir tribes split into two great branches, the Basutos and the Zulus. The Basutos appear more susceptible to being won over to European civilization; the Zulus, who are treacherous, fierce and untamed, have so far rejected all the approaches of the English. But both are equally enemies of work: dissolute, deceitful, liars and thieves. Any idea of morality would seem to be extinct in the conscience of the Kaffir: when accused he boldly persists in denial until one has been able to convict him; caught out, he shows neither shame nor repentance . . .

The Hottentots used to live in the plains of the Cape. Driven back first by the Dutch and then by the English, they are dragging the débris of their tribes over southern Africa . . . everywhere strangers, everywhere miserable and rejected. Their customs are very dissolute, but they have a more submissive and timid nature than the Kaffirs, and in this respect at least they would be more accessible than the latter to the approaches of Christian civilization.

The Bushmen are the pariahs of southern Africa. Forced back into the deserts and caves in the mountains, they live without clothing and without any other means of subsistence than theft. The other Blacks chase them like wild beasts . . . If Christianity does not come promptly to raise them from their abject state and civilize them, in a century this unfortunate race will have disappeared from African soil.

This is the ungrateful material on which Catholic missionaries in southern Africa have been working for fifty years. That readily explains the slowness of their progress and the complete failure of the Protestant missions. Idleness, and the custom of stealing which goes with it, together with polygamy, are the two main obstacles to the conversion of the Blacks. Unfortunately, the testimonies of Protestant travellers have taught us that these evil natural dispositions have been kept alive by the Protestant missions, jealous of being able to send their subscribers each year a list of their alleged converts.

(Louis-Eugène Louvet, *Les Missions Catholiques au XIXe siècle*, Paris 1895)

often, like the Germans in the Cameroons, the powers were able to be even-handed with the confessions.

Almost all the missions in Africa were in contact with Islam, the great adversary. In fact Christianity and Islam were seeking to convert the same 'animist' populations. Islam fomented revolts, and was thought responsible for the slave trade in the East, which was very substantial. The fight against the slave trade was the major preoccupation of missions in East Africa and especially of the White Fathers: the first converts were often children ransomed from slave traders. It was almost impossible to convert Muslims, but Charles de Foucauld thought that a silent presence (1901–1916) amongst them could be a preparation for their evangelization.

In general the African missions were supported by two basic institutions, the catechists and the schools. The catechists came from the first converts. When the missionary did not yet know the language of the country, the catechists were initially interpreters in preaching, but they quickly became missionary helpers. Their status and training varied

A catechist in Upper Volta

Alfred Simon Diban Ki-Zerbo, who was born around 1875 and died in 1980, the first Christian of Upper Volta, was a catechist for several decades. His son, the historian Joseph Ki-Zerbo, collected his father's life story.

After the revolt (1915–1916), the fathers abandoned the mission . . . All the time the fathers were away, summoned under the protection of the commandants, I took charge of the whole spiritual life of the mission. I led the men's prayers every Sunday. Thursday was the day of prayer for the women, under my direction. Tuesday and Wednesday were devoted to the young, boys and girls. I taught them the catechism. At other times I visited the old and the sick at home. In emergencies I administered baptism. With all the experience I had acquired in the previous missions I had no great difficulty in doing this work.

After the return of the missionaries (1916) . . . I pursued the same activities for decades, more than half a century . . . To the directly religious activities I added many others. In fact, apart from the work of the smith or the weaver there is no activity which I have not mastered or tried to engage in: cultivator, gardener, hunter, cook, mason, tailor, basket-maker, cobbler, cattle-breeder, nurse, choirmaster, carpenter, catechist . . . I have worked at everything and succeeded by dint of work. Thanks to my work, God has filled me with good things.

(Joseph Ki-Zerbo, *Alfred Diban, premier chrétien de Haute-Volta*, Paris 1983)

depending on the confession, the place and the period. There was sometimes a hierarchy amongst them. The role of the catechists was to lead the small communities which the missionary visited from time to time: they helped Christians to pray, prepared the catechumens for baptism, and baptized in urgent cases.

Among the Protestants, to be a catechist was sometimes a stage on the way to the ministry of the pastor; among Catholics the function rarely led to the priesthood. The ordinations of black priests were in single figures until the 1920s. Adult married men were preferred as catechists. There were also some women catechists in East Africa. At all events, the catechists played an important role in the evangelization of Africa.

The mission tried to set up a school as soon as possible, to civilize and evangelize. The schools often had difficult relations with the authorities. What were their professional aims? Were they solely religious? Had only European languages to be taught? What local language was to be chosen when there were many of them? Some countries subsidized the missionary schools generously. In French territories laws against the teaching congregations had repercussions on the mission schools, which no longer had any right to a legal existence.

Every developed mission, Catholic or Protestant, had its dispensary. The best known was that of Albert Schweitzer in Gabon. The Catholic missionaries liked to compare the mission station with a mediaeval monastery.

One can follow the progress of the evangelization of West Africa by the successive divisions of the apostolic vicariate of the Two Guineas, which was created in 1842. It shows the progress of colonial conquest and the increase in the number of missionaries. There were the domains of the French (Senegal, Sudan, Ivory Coast, Dahomey, Gabon, Congo), the English (Gold Coast, Nigeria and so on) and the Germans (Togo, Cameroon). Each territory and each congregation had its heroic and legendary missionaries and bishops.

After the setback to the crossing of the Sahara, Cardinal Lavigerie brought his White Fathers into the Africa of the Great Lakes by Zanzibar and Bagamoyo from 1879 on. Missionaries were still massacred (1881). This was the beginning of the evangelization of Uganda and Tanganyika. In Uganda, King Muang, fearing the invasion of his country by the Europeans, launched a violent persecution of Christians of all confessions, Cath-

A mission programme for Cameroon

The German Pallotins began the evangelization of Cameroon in 1890. Here they set out a mission programme which can be found among many other missionaries: the establishment of a Christian society.

What do we want in Africa? . . .

We other Catholics do not go there to discover treasures and to become rich; we do not go there to till the earth, to spread the doubtful interests of Western civilization and introduce needs hitherto unknown; we do not go there to found a new fatherland, even a far better one . . . The missionary is in search of more there; he is in search of immortal souls . . . It is Jesus Christ, through the church, who sends the missionary . . . He does not see the Negro as an object to exploit or a tool to use, or a servant to do everything or a passive slave, but as a fellow human being, a brother loved by God who has the same rights as the White. In the eyes of the missionary, the soul of the Black has exactly the same value as his own; it has been redeemed at the same price, the incalculable price of the blood of Jesus Christ. He wants to save this soul . . . Let us look at the work more closely . . . The Catholic missionary does not arrive with a wife (as the Protestant missionary does) . . . He comes with the crucifix in one hand, the rosary in the other and the breviary under his arm. His appearance causes the savages no fear; out of curiosity, they flock round him, asking themselves, 'What can this strange white man want of us?' He talks to them in a friendly way and delivers a message that they have never heard before, the Good News. The children of the bush listen to him with curiosity and amazement; to begin with they cannot understand a word and believe nothing that the white man tells them . . . Then they abandon their fetishes and change their lives completely . . . The best among them are baptized . . . Others follow the new converts in their turn; the number of catechumens increases; they all offer their labour, under the direction of the missionary, to build a church . . . Then a school is built where the children are taught, and the missionary has the encouraging experience that these negroes in their natural state are no more stupid than white people; on the contrary, they often reveal quite extraordinary spiritual capacities . . . Two years pass in this way . . . The missionary has received aid from Europe; colleagues have followed and sisters have come to teach the girls. An orphanage has been built; the number of children baptized in their infancy can be counted in hundreds . . . (The time arrives when boys and girls from Christian schools are married.) The young couples have the house which the mission has built for them. Alongside it is the great field which they are to till. They have learned to work at the mission; they will not suffer any lack. In this way, after long and laborious work there arises what constitutes the foundation of every state and every human society: the family . . . Several families then form a village of Christians and numerous Christian villages can form a Christian state; and from numerous black Christian states a new Africa, a Christian Africa, will arise. And this vast country . . . can harbour many hundreds and thousands of flourishing people, making them joyful and peaceful in this world and doubly happy in the next.

olic, Anglican and Protestant: there were eighty martyrs around Charles Lwanga in 1886, their ages ranging from fifteen to thirty. The Catholics have been canonized. In the same years the Germans and their missionaries established themselves in the hinterland of Zanzibar (1885).

While exploiting in a shameful way his Independent State of the Congo, which did not become Belgian until 1908, King Leopold of Belgium organized a mission for which he wanted only Belgian missionaries. The White Fathers penetrated east of the Congo and reached the Great Lakes (1880). Then the Scheutists, a congregation recently founded in Belgium, reached the basin of the Congo and the Kasai; finally the Jesuits penetrated the region of the Kwango. The missionaries gathered the catechumens in farm chapels where they received their Christian education while working for the mission. A campaign developed over what was deemed an exploitation of the converts. A general agreement was then signed between between the Holy See and the independent state, after which the missionaries were supported as such, and not just their schools and hospitals. Without the same freedom of action or even financial support, many Protestant groups also engaged in the evangelization of the Belgian colony.

Madagascar

Following the two French interventions on Madagascar in 1883–1885 and 1895–1896, the large island, initially a protectorate, was soon annexed purely and simply as a colony. Twice, during the military interventions, the Catholic missionaries were expelled. Then the laity took over the direction of their church from the institutions set up by the missionaries. During the first period, the main figure was Victoria Ramasoanarivo, the niece and stepdaughter of the Prime Minister. The young lay people who formed the Catholic Union visited the mission posts regularly and put in place suitable structures, which remained. On the loss of independence, these lay people became auxiliaries. With the encouragement of the colonial power, the London Mission, the main Protestant organization on Madagascar invited the Protestant Missions of Paris to take its place; the acceptance was a reluctant one. Despite the anticlericalism which was manifested with the arrival of Victor Augagneur as Governor General in 1906, the French presence furthered the development of Catholicism. The larger part of the island, which had not had missionaries, saw new congregations arrive.

Orthodox missions

Apart from a Greek and Slavonic emigration to many parts of the world in the nineteenth century, it was above all the Russian Orthodox Church which engaged in truly missionary activity in the form of the progressive colonization of Siberia. Archimandrite Makary evangelized the Altai plateau between 1830 and 1844, translating scripture and the liturgy into the dialects of the region. Beyond question the greatest Russian missionary of the nineteenth century was John Veniaminov, Archbishop of Irkutsk from 1840 to 1868, who first as priest and then as bishop evangelized the Yakuts of Siberia and the Eskimos and Indians of Alaska. He created four dioceses in these regions. When he became Metropolitan of Moscow in 1868 he founded the Orthodox Missionary Society (1870).

Orthodox mission in Siberia

His missions in Siberia (1896–1906) raise many questions for Archimandrite Spiridon.

I once went to a Buryat to lie down in his hut. What did I see in this hut? Among a number of idols hung an image of the Blessed Virgin with the infant Jesus in her arms. 'Are you baptized?' I asked him. 'Yes,' he replied. 'Then why do you have idols in your hut? You should have only Christian images; you should pray to the true God, Jesus Christ.'

'My father,' he replied, 'that is what I used to do, and I prayed only to your Russian God. But then my wife died, and after that my son. I lost many horses. I was told that our old Buryat God was very angry with me, that he had caused the death of my wife and my son and driven away my horses. So now I address my prayers to him and to your Russian God... You know, father, it is very painful and now very sad for me that I changed my God for yours, a new God.' And with these words the Buryat began to weep. I felt very sad for him, to the point of suffering for him myself and at the same time for all those like him. Then all of a sudden I realized what it was to steal someone's soul, to deprive him of what is most precious to him, to snatch him away and ravish his holy of holies, his natural religion and philosophy, giving him nothing in exchange but a new name and a cross on his chest. The Buryat of whom I am speaking seemed to me the most pitiable and unfortunate man in the world, deprived of his ancient religion and cast on the chances of destiny. From then on I promised myself that I would not baptize the natives, but only preach Christ and the gospel to him.

I also encountered great difficulties in preaching the gospel to the Buddhists... I went to their pagoda. The monks, the lamas, were already seated in their places. I began my preaching by relating how God created the world, how he sent his only Son on earth for the salvation of humankind... When I had finished... a lama began to make a speech: 'Mr Missionary, you have explained your Christian religion to us... Now, we ask you to listen to us in turn, although we are pagan and without culture... The Christian religion is certainly the highest and the most universal... The Christ is the incarnate Logos. His doctrine has shown the world new ways of living for humankind... But, Mr Missionary, look at things impartially: does the world live as Christ has taught? Christ preached love of God and neighbour, peace, gentleness, humility, universal forgiveness... Christ was like that, but you Christians are not. You live together like wild animals. You should be ashamed to speak of Christ when your mouths drip with blood... Who steals, engages in debauchery, pillages, lies, makes war and kills more? Christians are the first renegades from their God. You come to preach Christ to us and you bring us horror and grief... [*The building of the Trans-Siberian railway is in process.*] We thought that the Russians would introduce light and the love of Christian doctrine into our barbarian existence... Your workers came into our huts already drunk, made the Buryats drunk, debauched our wives... Until that time we did not know the use of locks, we had no thieves, far less assassins... We fear that your Christianity is making us even worse, and will turn us into complete savages.'

(Archimandrite Spiridon, *Mes Missions en Sibérie*, Paris 1950)

In the middle of the nineteenth century the Academy of Kazan became a centre for missionary study. Nicolas Ilminsky, a linguist and lay theologian, directed the translation of the Bible and a large number of religious books into about twenty Siberrian languages. Beyond the frontiers of the empire, the Russian Church evangelized in China, Korea and Japan. In Japan, two Japanese Orthodox priests were ordained in 1872 and a cathedral was built in Tokyo in 1891.

At the end of the nineteenth century and in the years before the First World War, the expansion of

Instruction and education in the Congo missions (1920)

The quinquennial report to the Propaganda by Mgr Augouard, of the Fathers of the Holy Spirit, vicar apostolic of Brazzaville, could be taken as the stocktaking of a missionary life, since the bishop died the next year (1921). Note the influence of the First World War on his mentality.

... The experience of forty-two years has led me to note that it was not a good thing to raise the Blacks to the European level so soon. It is necessary to rescue them from the degradation and savagery in which they had been sunk for so many centuries; but it is good to guard against forcing them towards too refined a civilization, which for the moment they are incapable of understanding and accepting. As evidence of this I have the example of the Blacks who went to fight in France. They have adopted European habits of comfort and European vices, and when they return home they no longer want either to work or to obey. In the opinion of those who know, these Blacks who are supposed to be civilized present great dangers to our colonies, where the wind of insurrection is growing and we have already been obliged to act ruthlessly.

Another comment which is no less serious: certain clergy from France, Italy or elsewhere, driven by a zeal which is more imaginative than practical, baptized a certain number of soldiers whose language they did not know. These supposed Christians, who cannot say even the most elementary prayers, are unwilling to accept instruction; they demand to be admitted to the sacraments although they live like abominable pagans. These Christians are a slur on religion and they create many difficulties for us.

In my vicariate, my principle has always been to prefer quality to quantity. We insist on three years in the catechumenate, and that is not too much for bringing inveterate pagans to the practices of the Christian life.

Outside religious education we give what I would call civic education. It is rudimentary and the same for all Blacks without distinction. Rather than make them proud sages, we try to make them good workers – in a word, useful to society.

However, that does not prevent us from paying special attention to the most intelligent children, from seeking vocations and forming an elite which is already a credit to the mission. As for the young girls, we seek to give them just as practical an education and to keep what is good in the indigenous customs. Thus they are set to work in the fields, and with rare exceptions it is forbidden to teach them dressmaking, embroidery, laundry or cooking. In the Congo these occupations are reserved for men, and that is excellent, since otherwise the young women or girls would inevitably be lost to the service of Europeans.

(Jehan de Witte, *Monseigneur Augouard*, Paris 1924)

---

the missions was in full flow. Books and journals offered a triumphalist survey for their readers. The Congregation of the Propaganda made around 7,000 priests available for mission, half of them in Asia, and 13,000 religious and brothers.

The First World War and the missions

The 1914–1918 war had important consequences for the life of the missions, but these varied greatly from one territory to another. First of all, it affected missionary personnel, who were conscripted for military service. In China, one third had to leave their posts for the front, and some never returned. It was the same, to a lesser degree, in the English colonies.

The German missionaries were caught up in the war, which was extended to the colonies. English, Belgian and French troops occupied the German colonies: Togo in autumn 1914, Cameroon in January 1916, South-West Africa in July 1915. Only German East Africa around Lake Tanganyika resisted until the end of 1917. The German missionaries were interned and expelled. The break in solidarity among Catholics did not help them much in the eyes of the Africans. French or English missionary societies took the place of the Germans, and black children had to change languages at school. There were similar instances in India and Oceania.

The war also resulted in a drying up of resources in colonies and missions, and even more difficulties for trade and provisions. Areas of Africa suffered famine, and Spanish 'flu was rampant everywhere. Furthermore, the European powers conscripted troops in their colonies either to fight in Europe or to serve as porters in African conflicts. This resulted in a number of revolts in which the church authorities were sometimes involved. An African pastor, John Chilembwe, opposed conscription in Nyasaland in 1915 and stood for African patriotism against the injustice of colonization. He was executed. It is possible that the events of the war led to a number of black prophetic movements, but the link has yet to be proved, in particular in the case of Prophet Harris on the Ivory Coast.

However, in many countries the war did not stop conversions. There were many of them in the Belgian Congo, in Uganda, Nigeria and Rwanda. In China, despite the decline in missionary personnel, the communities grew rapidly, even more among the Protestants than among the Catholics. American missionary societies founded several universities (Yenching in Peking in 1919) and colleges. There was also a marked increase of Christians in India, with massive conversions in the south.

The Holy See had little influence on the drafting of peace treaties. However, by entrusting the German colonies to the victors in the form of mandates, the Versailles Treaty required mission schools to be maintained, and the Convention of Saint-Germain (10 September 1919) guaranteed freedom of conscience, worship and the foundation of institutions in the member states of the League of Nations. The war had contributed towards changing the mentalities of the colonized and the Christians of the young churches. A number signed nationalist manifestos in China, Korea and Nyasaland. A Methodist from

the Gold Coast, Dr Aggrey, took part in the assembly of the first All Black Congress in Africa.

Missionary organization and plans

The Catholics

Despite its setting against the background of the First World War, which relativized all other preoccupations, the pontifical brief of Benedict XV (1914–1922) proved fruitful for the history of missions. From the institutional point of view, by creating the Congregation of Eastern Churches, the Pope relieved the Propaganda of responsibility for the East, to centre it more on evangelization. In 1916, Fr Paolo Manna, from the Foreign Missions of Milan, founded the Clergy Missionary Union to interest all priests and seminarians in mission. It soon became a world-wide institution with its base in Rome. In 1918 the Pope chose Cardinal van Rossum, an energetic Dutchman, as Prefect of the Propaganda. Van Rossum was determined to rid the missions of nationalism.

Provided with briefing from the colonies, on 30 November 1919 Benedict produced the apostolic brief *Maximum illud*. Discarding customary ecclesiastical language, the Pope expressed all that was on his mind, and particularly his anxiety that for Christians, nationalistic passions were much stronger than the community of faith, in war as in missions. Evangelization was an essential element in the life of the church, but the Pope called on those in charge of missions to engage in serious self-criticism. They had regarded their activity as their own preserve, refusing to allow new Christians to take responsibility in the church, and they had confused God's cause with the cause of their country. He went on to reiterate solemnly the call in the Instruction of 1659 to train an entire indigenous clergy and to separate evangelization from nationalistic propaganda. 'The church is Catholic. In every nation it is foreign.' The encyclical was not received very well in China. The Pope was thought to be ill-informed. Despite some hesitations, the Propaganda began to implement the encyclical. In 1920 it asked missionaries to distance themselves from politics and not to forsake the vernacular for their own national language. The dispatch of visitors and apostolic delegates without any diplomatic role to countries in the mission field emphasized the independence of the church.

Pius XI (1922–1939) continued the momentum of Benedict XV. Roman centralization seemed to him to be a guarantee of the freedom of the church. That is why, in May 1922, the Pope decided to transfer the work of the Propagation of the Faith from Lyons to Rome. In the same year there was a solemn celebration of the tercentenary of the Congregation of the Propaganda. Mgr Celso Costantini, apostolic delegate in China, was designated legate for the first Council of China, which brought together around fifty bishops in Shangai in May–June 1924. The council envisaged establishing a church which was Chinese in its framework and its artistic expression. Taking advantage of the Holy Year of 1925, the Pope decided to organize a great missionary exhibition which presented works, objects and photographs from missions to satisfy the curiosity of the more than one million visitors who attended. The exhibition was then transformed into the Lateran missionary and ethnological museum under the direction of the great ethnologist Fr Schmidt.

The encyclical *Rerum Ecclesiae* (1926) took up the themes of *Maximum illud* on the indigenous clergy and the birth of indigenous churches: there was a need to consider the end of the missionary period. The Pope asked the contemplative orders to envisage foundations in the mission countries. This appeal was responded to by the creation of a Chinese Trappist order. A missionary Sunday (the third in October) was instituted in April 1926. Long years of preparation reached their fulfilment when on 18 October of the same year Pius XI consecrated the first six Chinese bishops. It was then the turn of the Japanese and the Vietnamese. In 1927, St Thérèse of the Infant Jesus, canonized two years previously, became patron of missions, while at the same time the Apostolate of Prayer proposed a missionary intention. Between 1935 and 1940 some instructions from the Propaganda brought an end to the Rites Dispute: certain gestures formerly regarded as superstitious were in due course said to have only a civic significance, and from then on missionaries were relieved of their oaths on rites.

In 1933 Cardinal Fumasoni-Biondi became Prefect of the Propaganda, a position which he held until his death in 1960, and from 1935 to 1953 Mgr Constantini was Secretary of the Congregation. The presence of these two men in missionary affairs meant that the pontificate of Pius XII flowed on smoothly from that of his predecessor. On 29 October 1939, the Pope consecrated twelve bishops from missionary countries, including the first African bishop and the first Malagasy bishop.

The Protestants

In the Protestant world, the efforts to achieve ecumenism in mission called for by the 1910 Edinburgh conference attracted the most attention. Two men dedicated themselves especially to this task, John R. Mott (1865–1955) and J. H. Oldham (1874–1969). Both were leading figures in movements of young Christians, the latter a key figure in the Student Christian Movement. An International Missionary Council was set up in New York in October 1921 by 61 delegates from 144 countries: they truly represented missionaries working on the ground. A spiritual organism, the Council was also interested in the social and economic problems of the countries that were being evangelized. In his numerous travels, John R. Mott tried to set up Christian councils. To this end he convened an assembly of 1,000 chosen delegates, half of whom were Chinese, in Shanghai in 1922. In 1928 the council gathered delegates from fifty countries to meet on the Mount of Olives in Jerusalem. The council opposed racism: 'No one part of humanity has a monopoly of the gifts of God'; it called for social justice and the training of indigenous ministers. Fundamentalist movements also developed in opposition to the ecumenical movement.

Generally speaking, the Protestant theology of mission was split between two tendencies. Some, following Karl Barth, emphasized the absoluteness of the Word of God in Jesus Christ, with a consequent rejection of the search for points of contact in non-Christian cultures and of adaptation in the strict sense of the term. The main representative of this tendency was H.Kraemer, with his work *The Christian Message in a Non-Christian World* (1938). But of course this did not mean that the church should not be de-Europeanized and that the message should not be expressed in such a way that those who were being evangelized could understand it. The other tendency was represented by Maurice Leenhardt, the pastor and ethnologist of Oceania, and his journal *The Non-Christian World*. It sought to give an organic role to cultures and religions in the pastoral work of evangelization. In fact the International Missionary Council adopted a perspective more of 'practical Christianity' than of theological speculation.

The development of Catholic thought on mission

Looking through missionary literature of the period between the two wars, one feels a contrast between the missionary journals addressed to a wider public and a theological thought which was becoming deeper and more refined. The former often continued the exotic and chauvinistic genre which had begun in the nineteenth century: there were many accounts of the barbarous or picturesque customs of the peoples who were to be civilized and evangelized; the Catholic missionary always had to struggle not only against Islam and fetishism, manifestations of the devil, but also against the errors of Protestant heretics and schismatics. In 1931, a traveller who was amazed to see many bells in Syria in which he discerned the sign of a Christian presence, was told by a missionary, with a sigh: 'You have to know that many of these bells are schismatic and thus represent souls which have left the true way'.

Ecumenism did not arouse much enthusiasm in Catholics engaged in mission, and it was not encouraged in the encyclical *Mortalium animos* (1928). However, the foundation in London of the Society for the Languages and Civilization of Africa in 1926 led representative Protestant and Catholic missionaries to collaborate. So that they could speak there with one voice, the Catholics founded the Missionary Conference of Africa (1929). More positively, in the Catholic world during these years a real science of mission developed in the spheres of theology, history and the knowledge of non-Christian cultures. The German school in Münster under Schmidlin (who died in 1944) was continued by the Benedictine Thomas Ohm (died 1962). In Rome the German oblates Streit and Didinger continued the publication of the *Bibliotheca Missionum*, while G. Rommerskirchen brought out a *Bibliografia Missionaria* annually after 1933. A faculty of missiology was created at the Gregorian University in Rome in 1932, and in 1933 a scientific missionary institute at the College of the Propaganda. There was also a centre of Catholic missiology in Louvain under the Jesuit Fr Charles (1882–1954). He argued that the aim of mission is 'the planting of the church', rather than the 'conversion' of people as soon as possible. This theory has since been challenged. From 1923, annual missiology weeks were held in Louvain, and an Auxiliary Society of Missions was founded there in 1926.

In France, things were less structured. In Lille, under the stimulus of Abbé Prévost, the movement *Ad Lucem* came into being in 1931: lay students decided to bear witness to their faith by practising their profession as doctors or teachers in mission countries. There were courses on missiology in various Catholic institutes in France, with varying success.

Dozens of missionaries were linguists and ethnologists and founded museums which reflected cultures from all over the world.

So why has China not been converted?

The relative optimism of the end of the nineteenth century disappeared in the 1930s. The results do not correspond to the means utilized. Explanations have to be found.

'What have you been doing in China for 300 years?' people ask in Europe. 'You haven't even converted three million persons; you're at a standstill. So move on! Rome has sent you an army of conquerors. More than thirty male congregations and more than twenty female congregations are following in the wake of the 96 vicariates or apostolic prefectures of the vast republic, not to mention the 1,370 indigenous priests . . . Has so much work, so much sweat, so much blood, had such a meagre result! Have you done all that you can? All that you should? Are you adopting the right method? Are you going about converting souls in the right way?

So why is China not being converted? Because it does not want to be. And it does not want to be because it does not know. Whether its ignorance is deliberate or not, vincible or invincible, it exists; we see it every day. It is maintained, if not supported, by the deleterious atmosphere of a paganism going back over millennia. An immense weight lies on the understanding of our Chinese, crushes them, and prevents them from seeing the truth. Their spirit and their will are confronted with enormous obstacles, the most formidable of which is called original sin, with the marks of its threefold concupiscence: the basic pride of the men of letters, an attachment to the good things of the earth without a concern for the other world, and the place given to the pleasures of the body and the senses . . . China is not being converted. And whose fault is that? The missionaries? No. The Catholics of the world? To some extent: if they had prayed more, if they had complained more that the kingdom of God was not coming, grace would have flowed more abundantly over this vast desert of souls. Whose fault is it? That of the pagans themselves? Yes.

(A. Gaspement SJ, in *Les Missions Catholiques*, January/February 1931)

The mission fields in the 1930s

Many think that the period between the two World Wars were the finest period of Christian and particularly Catholic missions, because of the tremendous number of missionary personnel and their resources, the growth of conversions at least in certain countries, and the abundance of specialist literature. If questions were beginning to arise, the period of great doubt had not yet come.

Asia

China still attracted attention. Catholic statistics are always very precise, though they can vary depending on sources. In 1933 there were 51 foreign missionary societies of women religious, 27 foreign missionary societies of male religious, and two indigenous societies. Several had more than doubled their number since 1914: Jesuits, the Divine Word, Franciscan priests from Maryknoll. The faithful also doubled between 1914 and 1947: at this last date there were 3,251,000 baptized Christians, 2,542 Chinese priests and 3,046 foreign priests. The number of Protestants seems to have grown considerably in the immediate pre-war period to reach perhaps 1,300,000 in 1947. If we add 300,000 Orthodox, the last figure known for all Christians would be around 5 million, hardly 1% of the Chinese population. Christianity was more of a visible reality in the great cities, particularly Shanghai, but it was virtually unknown in the interior of China. In the 1930s some were amazed at the tiny results of such an investment in personnel and institutions. The convening of the first Chinese Council (1924), the first indigenous bishop (1926), and striking personalities who became Christians (the diplomat Dom Celestine Lu became a Benedictine abbot, and General Chiang Kai Shek, president of the republic, and his wife converted to Protestantism), the birth of Catholic Action, an adaptation of Christian art, the end of the Rites Dispute, the interest of intellectuals in Western culture – all this kept up hopes. However, many intellectuals were also turning towards Marxism, and anti-clerical organizations sought to counterbalance confessional groups. The Kuomintang government, for a while associated with the Communists, wanted to put a ban on European imperialisms and limit the Christian proselytism of the schools (1928). The civil war between Communists and Chiang Kai Shek's Nationalists, which lasted from 1926 to 1937, was prejudicial to the missionaries and Christians; missionaries lost their lives in it.

In Japan the number of Catholics slowly grew (100,000 in 1930); the Protestants reached almost the same figure. The Catholics were more numerous in the south (Nagasaki and Hiroshima). The Christians put emphasis on an intellectual apostolate (the Sophia University, founded in Tokyo in 1922). The first Japanese bishops were installed in 1927. In the 1930s, the nationalistic reaction brought Shintoism to the fore. By 1940–1941 all the bishops of Japan were Japanese, and the Archbishop of Tokyo even justified the Japanese war aims.

In many other Asian countries it was still the foreign character of Christianity and its links with colonization which were emphasized by the Communists. A Vietnamese priest and some Christians were massacred by the Communists in a village of Annam in May 1931. There was also criticism of the links between Christianity and nationalism in Catholic ranks.

In India there were more than 6 million Christians in the 1930s, but this was less than 2% of the population. The majority were in the south, and in particular on the west coast, where the ancient Christians of the Syriac rite had settled. There was a small upsurge of conversions to Catholicism in the regions west of Calcutta, among the still 'animistic' population exploited by the great landowners. Catholics, Anglicans and Protestants put the emphasis on the development of scholarly establishments. In Ceylon the proportion of Christians exceeded 8%. However, Buddhism increasingly asserted itself as national religion.

In this panorama of Christianity in Asia we must not forget the Philippines, which strictly does not belong to the missionary world. An old Spanish colony conquered by the United States in 1898, the Philippines had a population which was more than 90% Christian, with a Muslim and 'animist' minority. So it represented almost two-thirds of the Christians in Asia. In 1902 a Filipino priest, Gregorio Aglipay, founded an independent Filipino church because Rome refused to nominate an indigenous bishop. This church, which was based on opposition to the American occupation, attracted a substantial proportion of Catholics. Its position weakened after the Second World War, and in 1961 it was fused with the Episcopalian Church.

Africa

In Africa, too, the missionary framework developed in all confessions, which were in lively competition. Colonization led to an economic development which had repercussions on the traditional religious mentalities. Islam and Christianity tried to attract the African 'animists'. For a long time the European missionaries were still numerically in the majority, but proportionally the number of African pastors grew much more quickly than that of the black priests, who were far fewer. In 1939 there were only 78 African priests out of 1,233 in the Belgian Congo. In the whole of Francophone Africa there were only 27.

Local circumstances and the attitude of the colonial administrations gave each church its particular aspect. But we can find common features throughout Africa. Education was a universal preoccupation; the administrations encouraged it, requiring the language of the colonizing country to be taught. While in the French colonies the mission schools coexisted with the official schools, which were far fewer, in the Belgian Congo the church had a virtual monopoly in public teaching. The development of schools, a heavy burden for the missions, sometimes took place to the detriment of the training of catechists, whose condition was inferior to that of teachers. On the other hand, as the schools and dispensaries welcomed people of all religions indiscriminately, the Christian churches extended their possibilities of influence.

Christian education sought to transmit the values of a universal morality. The missions were particularly vigilant in the struggle against the semi-slavery of forced labour, supporting campaigns against it organized by others. The missions tried to improve the conditions of women in the family sphere by fighting against polygamy and for a free choice of spouse. Some missionaries lost their lives as a result of this campaign.

In the 1930s, there were mass conversions in several regions of Africa. At the time the missionaries spoke of the 'whirlwind of the Spirit'. There was the case of the Dagaris who lived at the frontier of the Gold Coast and Upper Volta: in 1929, during a terrible drought, they prayed in the chapel of the fathers to the God of Christians, who sent them torrential rain; moreover, their leader, who was thought dead, was cured by an injection from a missionary. Lesotho experienced a similar whirlwind. It was even more spectacular in Rwanda-Burundi. At the beginning of the 1930s the annual growth of Rwanda Christians approached 80% and that of catechumens 200%. Between 1932 and 1936, Catholics increased from 81,000 to 233,000. Without necessarily challenging the action of the Spirit, recent studies, some of them by Africans, have shown the importance of the context of these events: the impact of economic crisis and a certain social pressure. Joining the church facilitated education and access to administrative posts. Furthermore, after the vicar apostolic of Rwanda, Mgr Classe, deposed and replaced the local ruler, there was a rumour that the new ruler was requiring his subjects to convert to Catholicism. Some missionaries complained that this excessively rapid rise diminished the quality of the catechumenate and Christian life.

One movement which had begun in the nineteenth century developed in the inter-war period and still has not stopped growing: the multiplication of independent churches and African prophetic or messianic movements. If all these movements indicate a concern of black Christians for identity, they take different forms. In the Protestant context Africans form independent churches, parting company with European churches whose authority they no longer accept, but preserving doctrines, ritual and organization. However, other prophetic movements use Christianity for their own ends and reinterpret it in African categories. They choose what suits them from scripture, in particular from the Old Testament. This is both a political reaction against European elements and a recovery of the symbolism of traditional religion through imagery and transformed Christian rites. These groups call themselves Zionist churches or, in southern Africa, the 'Ethiopian church', with reference to the Ethiopians in the Bible. This last church, which was formed in 1892 in reaction to segregation, retains the cult of the dead and healing by incantation. For these groups, which reject the foreign character of Christianity, Africa becomes the place of revelation: Jerusalem and Bethlehem are in Africa; Jesus himself is black. God has spoken to his African prophet. In 1913, following a vision of the archangel Gabriel, William Wadé Harris, monitor at a Methodist mission in Liberia, preached a religion based on the Decalogue; he fought against fetishes and accepted a moderate polygamy. The movement spread widely on the Ivory Coast. The administrations had difficulty in coping with the multiplication of these groups. In southern Africa there were 76 such churches in 1911, 520 in 1932 and 800 in 1945. The movement which developed most widely is that of Simon Kimbangu in the Belgian Congo. This Baptist catechist attracted crowds for six months (April–September 1921) in his village of Nkamba, healing the sick in the name of the Spirit. In a difficult economic period he gave new hope to his compatriots, but he disturbed the defenders of public and Catholic order, who had him condemned to death.

A Methodist mission on the Ivory Coast

Pastor Roux describes the development of the Methodist mission on the Ivory Coast between the wars. The functioning of the mission depends not only on the pastor and the catechists, but also on other ministers who make it possible for the communities to keep closely together and for worship to be regular.

It is very rare for the first action in a village to be that of the missionary, or even of a catechist. Almost always the witness of neighbouring villages opens up the way. When the leaders of all the communities of the same tribe meet every three months to discuss the affairs of the church, they usually choose a new village on which, in the course of the following months, they focus their testimony. They then take advantage of every possible occasion to meet again as a group in this village: markets, marriages, funerals bring there men and women who quite naturally meet for morning or evening prayer in the courtyard where one of them has been welcomed by kinsfolk. Each time, a few people from the village come to see what is happening. They ask questions, gradually come to take part in the meetings, until one day they ask for regular visits for the people of the village. Then they build a small chapel . . .

But how could a pastor and a dozen catechists, even with the help of a few 'monitors', guarantee Sunday worship, and morning and evening prayer, in so many villages, the number of which is constantly increasing? Here again church members, entrusted with ministries of good-will, play a large part in the work. These are above all the lay preachers, and those elders of the church, men and women, whom Methodism calls 'class leaders'. These class leaders are Christians from each village chosen by the communicant members. Each of them is responsible for a homogeneous group of between ten and twenty-five people . . . He knows them and follows them better than a catechist responsible for a dozen villages could, let alone the pastor, who is such a stranger . . . The lay preachers, and soon these will include women, form an organized body in the church. They, too, are proposed by the Christians of their village. After a period of probation they have to be approved by the assembly of the lay preachers of the circuit for their role to be confirmed . . . The preachers meet once a week at three or four central points of the region for half a day or a day of study under the direction of the pastor or one of the most qualified catechists . . . First they are taught to read and write . . . then come practical exercises in homiletics . . . It is thanks to these people that worship can be celebrated every Sunday in every village.

(André Roux, *L'Evangile dans la forêt*, Paris 1971)

His sentence was commuted to life imprisonment, and the 'passion' of the prophet lasted thirty years until his death in 1951. The repression gave rise to a religious movement which developed from internment camps: disciples translated Scripture, preached and composed hymns. The administration recognized the movement in 1959.

Apart from local insurrections, there were no political upheavals in Africa until the conquest of Ethiopia by Fascist Italy (1935–1936). The majority of Italian Catholics rejoiced at this. Bishops blessed the flags and the regiments sent to Africa. After the expulsion of the missionaries of different nationalities, Italian missionaries surged into Ethiopia. The Fascist government ravaged the Ethiopian Coptic Church, to replace it with one which was more conciliatory.

America

Both in Latin America and in Anglo-Saxon and French America, the end of the nineteenth century and the beginning of the twentieth saw the resumption of an evangelization of the indigenous population. There were missions among the Indians and the Eskimos (Inouits), in the north of Canada by the Oblates of Mary, and in Alaska, also among the Indians and Eskimos, by the Jesuits.

9

The Last Half-Century (1940–1990)

The Second World War was the beginning of the end of colonial imperialism, though not of imperialism. This had major consequences for evangelization associated with the European presence. The independence of the old colonies, attained by almost all of them in the 1960s, changed the status of the churches quite profoundly. Furthermore, the Communist regime subjected the churches to real persecutions. Political events, combined with the acceleration of the phenomenon of secularization, led to often radical questioning of the significance and methods of evangelization. In the Catholic Church, the Second Vatican Council was the starting point for this renewal of the theology of missions, but the other Christian churches experienced similar revisions.

The Second World War and the missions

While the global conflict caused upheaval among many populations in the world, its effect on missions differed, depending on the country. In 1941, the Italian defeat in Ethiopia signified the re-establishment of the independence of that country and its church and the return of the missionaries who had been driven out by the Italians. The concordat signed between the Holy See and Salazar's Portugal in 1940–1941 gave a privileged status and financial support to missionaries in the Portuguese colonies. It was in the Far East that the war

weighed most heavily on the mission countries which fell under Japanese domination. In Japan itself, the government required all Christian officials to be Japanese. In Siam (Thailand), which was allied to the Japanese, Christians were persecuted for four years (1940–44): French bishops and missionaries were arrested, seminarians and women religious dispersed; worship was forbidden and Buddhism imposed on the schools; religious buildings were destroyed and priests, religious and Christians executed. Part of Oceania was the theatre for the war between the Japanese and the allies. In New Guinea and Polynesia, in addition to the destruction, the missions suffered the internment of the missionaries – many of them died. The presence of foreign troops destabilized societies. The artificial prosperity brought by the Americans, which disappeared with the return of peace, reactivated and transformed the myth of 'Cargo', a syncretistic form of religion which associates biblical revelation with the hope that all the inhabitants of the islands will one day share in the riches of the Whites, brought by 'Cargo'. The atomic bomb dropped on Nagasaki in August 1945, which claimed 80,000 victims and put an end to the war, killed 7,000 of the 10,000 Christians in the parish of Urakami. Furthermore, in many of the colonized countries which had borne the brunt of the war, aspirations for independence were affirmed. The Christian churches, which were more or less closely allied with the colonizers, had to clarify the nature of these links if they were not to be swept away along with foreign domination. We shall see later that responses varied depending on local circumstances, but at the highest level the authorities quite quickly defined clear, yet cautious, principles.

A missionary doctrine in a time of decolonization

The Roman positions

Pope Pius XII devoted his Christmas 1945 message to the unity and universality of the church. An essential feature of the church is that it should transcend nationalism: 'In a time as troubled as ours still is, in its own interest and in that of humanity the church must do everything possible to emphasize its indivisible and undivided integrity. Today, more than ever, it must be supra-national. It must be supra-national because it embraces all nations and all peoples with the same love; it is also supra-national because nowhere is it alien . . . Just as Christ assumed a true human nature, so too the church takes into itself the fullness of all that is authentically human.' In 1946 a Chinese, Mgr Tien, was made a cardinal and soon became archbishop of Peking; the ordinary hierarchy was established in China. In 1948, a letter from the Secretariat of State noted the political transformations caused by the war and a desire for independence. 'But this thirst for emancipation, often accompanied by violence, is not without danger if one considers at the same time the present state of weakness of the Western powers, on whom their situation and their vocation as messengers of the gospel had conferred the task of older sisters towards continents "still in darkness and the shadow of death".' While calling for prudence, the letter thought that where overseas peoples were concerned, the Western powers should consider more their ethnic particularities and, rather than engaging in a colonization which was too often inspired by self-interest and materialism, take account of the aspirations of the indigen-

ous peoples towards fair social progress, which in any case was called for by the dignity of the human person. The celebration of the Holy Year of 1950 was accompanied by an exhibition of Christian art in mission countries. The Secretary of the Propaganda, Mgr Celso Costantini, who was behind it, tried to define an art which was expressed in the culture of each people: 'The new Christian art must not simply be an external imitation of pagan art . . . it must provoke a renaissance of local ancient art, like an old stump putting out a new shoot . . . Where the church goes, it creates a new civilization, of which art is simply one of the finest fruits.'

In the encyclical *Evangelii Praecones* (1 June 1951), which commemorated the twenty-fifth anniversary of *Rerum Ecclesiae*, the Pope rejoiced at the statistical progress of Catholicism over the previous twenty-five years, but he deplored the persecutions in China. He recalled the emphases of his predecessor: 'The ultimate aim of missions is for the church to be firmly and definitively established among new peoples, and for it to receive its own hierarchy, chosen by the inhabitants of the place.' Referring to famous examples in the history of the church, the Pope emphasized the role of lay people, catechists and Catholic action in evangelization. Furthermore, Communist threats led Christians in the mission field to devote all their attention to social problems. In his Christmas messages of 1954 and 1955, Pius XII was more specific on the legitimacy of demands for independence: the Europeans had not done their duty, and Communism had profited from it. His concern was that 'a just and progressive political freedom should not be refused to these peoples and that no obstacles should be put in their way'. Furthermore, the Pope was disturbed about the situation of the Catholics of China, to whom he addressed a letter (1952) and an encyclical (1954). In the encyclical *Fidei donum* (1957), Pius XII paid particular attention to Africa. The church there was undergoing a magnificent expansion in countries which were in full political and technological development. Missionary congregations and local clergy could not suffer. Evangelization was not a

Message from the Ibadan Conference to the churches of Africa

The Conference of the Churches of All Africa met for the first time in Ibadan, Nigeria, in 1958. Today it unites 141 Churches and National Christian Councils (Protestant) from thirty-nine countries. Here are some extracts from its message.

We, the delegates of the first Conference of the Churches of All Africa ever to take place on this continent, rejoicing that God has brought us together in his name, send our fraternal greetings from Ibadan, in Nigeria, to all the Christian churches of Africa.

We come from Sierra Leone, Gambia, Ghana, Nigeria, French West Africa, Liberia and Togo, the Cameroons, French Equatorial Africa, the Belgian Congo, Angola, South Africa, Mozambique, the Rhodesias, Nyasaland, Tanganyika, Kenya, Uganda, the Sudan, Egypt, Ethiopia, Madagascar and other parts of the world. Although we speak different languages, the reason which has brought us together is the same: we worship the Lord Jesus Christ and are witnesses to his gospel. In him we are one, whether we speak Ibo, Yoruba, Duala, English, Afrikaans, Zulu, Sesutu, Portuguese, French, Kikuyu or any other language spoken by the peoples who live on the African continent. We are one in him who was born in Bethlehem in Judaea, who had to flee to Egypt under Herod, who died and rose again in Jerusalem, and lives today in Ibadan as he lives in every town and village in the world which his Father has created. In our conference he has given us such a rich experience of this unity in Christ that there is no danger of our ever forgetting it . . .

We believe that God is commanding us to overcome the differences within the church and to work for the suppression of all the injustice due to racial discrimination which we believe to be contrary to the will of God.

We rejoice at the progress made in the African territories towards their emancipation, and we pray God that this liberation of these human talents and energies may be used in the service of the one whom we hail as the Lord of the human race.

From now until the end of this century the African continent will witness unparalleled events and changes, welcome to some and feared by others . . . We humbly recognize our responsibility towards God and this continent, and we devote ourselves to their realization, having faith that we will be guided and supported by our Christian brothers from all over Africa and the world.

In the name of the Father of all men, in the name of his Son who has saved us, and in the name of the Holy Spirit who inspires us, we declare ourselves to be one in Christ. Amen.

---

sphere reserved for a specialized personnel. The bishops of the whole world had collective responsibility for it. They could indicate this responsibility by sending some of their diocesan priests as temporary aid (*'Pretres fidei donum'*). The lay militants of Catholic Action could perform a similar service.

On several occasions Pope John XXIII (1958–1963) emphasized the personality of the new churches and their cultural expression. He remarked to black writers and artists who had met in Rome in April 1959: 'The church is not identified with any culture, not even with the Western culture with which its history is so closely mixed. For its own mission is of another order: that of the religious salvation of humankind. However, the church is always ready to recognize, to welcome and even to inspire anything that is to the honour of the human intelligence and the human heart on other shores of the world than the Mediterranean basin which was the providential cradle of Christianity.' In the encyclical *Princeps pastorum* (November 1959), he addressed all the clergy of the missions, emphasizing the position in them of indigenous priests. While keeping them under the jurisdiction of the Propaganda, in the majority of colonized countries the Holy See had transformed the apostolic vicariates into dioceses, thus in a way anticipating the proclamations of independence.

In the Protestant world

The missionary authorities had an important role in the foundation of the World Council of Churches in Amsterdam in 1948. John R.Mott was made honorary president. A Chinese and then an Indian were also presidents in turn. The General Assembly of the WCC at Evanston in 1954 adopted the following text: 'The legitimate right of people to self-determination must be recognized. The right to independence and an autonomous government must be guaranteed and governments must take the necessary risks to attain this end rapidly.' To limit the inconveniences of multiplying churches, the authorities tried to regroup the churches of the newly independent nations into national or continental conferences. In 1958 a Conference of Churches of All Africa was formed at Ibadan, Nigeria; in 1959 an East Asia Christian Conference was founded at Kuala Lumpur, Malaysia. In 1961, the WCC Assembly in New Delhi, in which a large number of new African and Asian churches took part, decided to integrate the International Missionary Council into itself.

Even if the Christians of Europe largely shared the mentality of their environment, according to some historians the positions taken by church authorities and Christian movements, particularly in the missions, contributed to the acceptance of the independence of the old colonies by public opinion.

The mission field at the time of independence

The war did not interrupt evangelization; at most it got in the way of the renewal of personnel. In the immediate post-war period, the missionary societies set out again confidently, all the more so since the colonial administrations were more favourable to them than before. If in many cases the struggles for independence involved the churches only in limited violence, in countries where Communist regimes had taken power there was widespread persecution.

Asia

In China, the war allowed some clarification of relations with Europe: once the unjust trade treaties had been annulled in 1942, the Holy See and China could at last establish diplomatic relations; dioceses replaced the old apostolic vicariates. However, during this period Mao Tse-tung achieved the conquest of China, defeating the Nationalists, and violently persecuted the Christians in the territories he recaptured: numerous priests, men and women religious and faithful were massacred, and churches burned. The People's Republic was proclaimed in 1949; the regime recognized religious freedom but asked Christians to emancipate themselves from foreign countries by achieving a triple autonomy: of government (no links with foreign powers, in this case the Vatican), of finance (no funds from Europe) and of preaching (no foreign missionaries). The Protestant missionaries left, and a Christian church formed in China which was rigorously controlled by the Communist powers. Mgr Riberi, the interim nuncio, rejected the triple autonomy and was expelled. All the foreign Catholic missionaries were driven out, and persecution broke out of bishops, priests and lay Christians who remained faithful to Rome: many were to spend several years in re-education camps; several died under torture. A Catholic patriotic association was set up to organize a church in accordance with the views of the government; diocesan assemblies elected twenty-five bishops who rejected all links with foreign countries. Pius XII, in the encyclical *Ad Sinarum Gentes* (October 1954), expressed his pain at this separated church and called on Chinese Catholics to resist. Very strict about this 'schismatic' church to begin with, Catholic opinion subsequently proved more comprehensive among those who wanted to save what could still be saved.

In 1954, two-thirds of the Christians and priests of North Vietnam, which had become Communist, left their country to settle in the south, where the Christian community reached the figure of 1,200,000. 400,000 Catholics remained in the north,

Total salvation by the one universal Christ

My stay of twelve years in India and my contacts with Hindu friends have only intensified in me this vision of total salvation by the Christ who is as universal as he is unique.

There are Christians who, more or less consciously identifying the destiny of the world with the destiny of Christianity as it was formulated in the first ten or fifteen centuries of its history, see the accession of new peoples to Christianity as little more than a numerical growth of the church and its wider diffusion in space.

On the level of revelation, the Church has everything from the beginning; on the level of the developments by which it enters the human world – or rather by which the human world is assumed and transformed – no century marks a definitive limit.

In the seventeenth century, Ricci and Nobili saw in the continents which were opening up to evangelization the advent of new forms of civilization into the church. The church will no longer simply say, as in the time of St Augustine, 'The Latin language is mine, Greek is mine, and so too is Syriac'; it will add Sanskrit, Tamil, Chinese and all the ideas and feelings brought by these languages which never penetrated the Mediterranean, Germanic and Slavonic worlds.

Spiritualities which have not yet blossomed, forms of contemplation, new formulations of the mystery, types of worship and the consecrated life doubtless await, and perhaps will await for centuries, the advent of civilizations like those of India and China within the one multiform church. The Christianity of yesterday and today will always be the Christianity which is to come. The eternal spirit will always be in creation the one who brings this to pass.

(Jules Monchanin, *Théologie et spiritualité missionaires*, Paris 1985 – the texts date from 1948–1951)

cut off from all links with the rest of the church.

The Korean War (1950–1953) resulted in a violent persecution of Christians in the north of the country: dozens of priests, including the apostolic delegate, and religious perished – either killed or put in concentration camps. By contrast, in the south the Catholic communities, and even more the Protestants, experienced a remarkable boom.

Christian churches developed structures in connection with the independence of India. In 1944, a National Council of Protestants and a Catholic Episcopal Conference were set up; these organized a Council of India in 1950. The United Church of South India was the most original creation of the time. It is the result of the fusion, in 1947, of the Anglican Church and Congregationalists, Methodists and Presbyterians, bringing together more than one million Christians; it retained the episcopate but bishops were subject to the synod. More than three-quarters of the bishops, priests and religious in the Catholic Church were Indians. Furthermore, the authorities strictly limited the entry of foreign missionaries into the country. Quite apart from the important investment of Catholics in teaching, which was already ancient, two new forms of Christian presence marked the post-war period. In 1948, in Calcutta, a teacher of Albanian origin, Agnes Gonxha Bojaxhiu, who became Mother Teresa, founded the congregation of the Missionaries of Charity who worked among the poorest in the vast city; her fame is now world-wide. In 1950, Abbé Jules Monchanin, a priest of the diocese of Lyons, who had already been in India for eleven years, and Fr Henri Le Saux, a Benedictine monk, founded the ashram of Saccidananda at Kulitalai in South India (for more details see *How to Understand Hinduism* in this series) . The two set out to lead a Christian contemplative life on the model of traditional Indian monasticism. After the death of Monchanin (1957), Le Saux went increasingly far in his doubly ecumenical effort to bring Christians of different confessions into contact with Hindu spiritual figures and to share their mysticism.

In South-East Asia (Ceylon, Burma, Malaysia, Indonesia), where Buddhism and Islam are the dominant religions, depending on the country, the number of Christians grew, but apart from Ceylon they represented only a tiny minority. They encountered the opposition of the Communist guerrillas and the militant Buddhist monks who, on the occasion of the 2500th anniversary of the birth of the Buddha in Rangoon (1956), pressurized the governments into making Buddhism the state religion.

Africa

In the often tense context of the struggles for independence, the fifteen years which followed the war were fruitful for Christianity. It is estimated that the number of Christians doubled between 1950 and 1960 (from 23 to 46 million). The most spectacular progress was still evident in the Belgian colonies, the Congo and Rwanda-Burundi. A missionary journal of the 1950s marvelled: 'The Belgian Congo and Rwanda-Burundi are the most flourishing missions that the history of the church has ever seen.' Almost 30% of the population of the Belgian colonies was Catholic in 1954. There were 3,000 Catholic missionaries, but also 1,700 Protestants, whose schools now had the right to government subsidies. The Catholics did not appreciate the creation of lay establishments by the administration, however benevolent. The apostolic delegates co-ordinated the tasks of evangelization in the name of the Propaganda. Each political zone had its own.

However, the rise in the number of indigenous priests and bishops was slow. In 1950 there were still only 800 black priests as compared to thousands of European missionaries. In the Belgian Congo there were no indigenous Protestants in positions of authority; there were 100 African priests and 3,000 foreign missionaries. When the ordinary hierarchy was set up in the majority of African countries between 1950 and 1960, most of the bishops designated were still European.

Although many of them had been trained in Rome, on the occasion of a congress of Black African intellectuals in Rome in 1955, several African priests expressed a wish for Africanism to be taken into account in the life and liturgy of the church. Their reflections formed a book which attracted some attention: *Black Priests Ask Themselves Questions* (1956). However, the tone adopted towards the authorities was still very deferential.

This excessively European character of Christianity is doubtless the explanation of the continued progress of independent or messianic churches. In 1968, David Barrett, in a survey, noted 6,000 denominations. The Heavenly Christians founded at Porto Novo in 1947 by a Methodist joiner gained a large following from the Ivory Coast to Nigeria. The rise of independence sometimes led to difficulties in the life of the Christian communities, but there were great differences from one country to another, The countries of the Maghreb, which saw Christian communities that were not indigenous disappear almost completely, are no doubt a separate case. In subsequent years the independence of the Sudan in 1956 led to the expulsion of 360 foreign missionaries and forcible Islamicization in a region where there were 400,000 Christians. The Mau-Mau rebellion in Kenya (1952–1954) was based on the traditional religions and sowed terror among Christians. The missions in the Belgian Congo, often presented as a model, suffered greatly from the troubles which followed independence (1960–1967): 215 missionaries were killed, half of them Belgians.

However, many Christians of all confessions took part in the processes leading to independence, some priests accepting political responsibilities, like Fulbert Youlou in Congo-Brazzaville. The religious authorities often published declarations affirming the legitimacy of the claim to independence. In 1953 the archbishop of Dar-es-Salaam (Tanganyika) remarked: 'The era of overseas colonies is rapidly drawing to an end. This had to be. The church will look with satisfaction on the moment when the colonial peoples are capable of guiding their own destinies.'

The bishops of Madagascar, who had been very cautious about the various movements and revolts after 1946, recognize the legitimacy of the aspirations of the Malagasys to independence.

Desiring to respond on every occasion to the real preoccupations of Christians, and knowing that many people are raising the question of the legitimacy of their desire for the independence of their country, we reaffirm the following principles:

The Church is not a political power charged with promoting a form of government or declaring whether or not a people is capable of governing itself, and it does not intend to be commandeered by any current of opinion or any force in power or aspiring to be in power . . .

The ardent desire of the church is that both individuals and peoples shall progress towards greater well-being, always assuming more of their responsibilities . . . The church, like natural law, also recognizes the freedom of peoples to govern themselves . . .

In conclusion, we recognize the legitimacy of the aspiration to independence and every constructive effort to achieve it. But we would warn you against possible deviations, especially against the hatred which cannot find a place in a Christian heart.

Madagascar

The brutality of the French conquest, which suppressed a kingdom, explains why nationalist movements appeared on Madagascar at the time when France took possession of it. Some of them were clearly anti-Christian. At the end of the Second World War the Democratic Movement for Malagasy Renewal was formed and called for independence for the island. The rebellion of 19 March 1947, based on traditional beliefs, proved violently xenophobic and sometimes anti-Christian; missionaries were massacred and churches pillaged, but Protestant parishes and Catholic figures also took part in it. The colonial repression was bloody. The bishops condemned violence and on several occasions reaffirmed the legitimacy of the aspiration to independence, in particular in the declaration of 27 November 1953. The ordinary hierarchy was established in 1955, and in 1958 the Evangelical Church of Madagascar was formed; in 1968 it united with two other Protestant churches to form the Church of Jesus Christ on Madagascar.

The 1960s – a turning point

All the events which shaped the world and the church during the 1960s necessarily had an impact on evangelization. The last colonies became independent. The Second Vatican Council (1962–1965) renewed ecclesiology and reflection on the presence of the church in the world. The upheavals of 1968 and the clash of ideologies put in question the basis of missions. After the development of the Third World, which had been emphasized at the expense of evangelization, had proved disappointing and alienating, in some Christian communities the stress was now placed on liberation. Furthermore, the fall in the recruitment of clergy in the East particularly affected the missionary institutions, while the majority of young churches could not yet provide sufficient personnel.

Evangelization at Vatican II

The very convening of the Council demonstrated the reality of world evangelization, since all the continents were represented by their bishops, who, in contrast to Vatican I, were in part indigenous. One third of the Council was drawn from Europe and one third from the Americas. The last third was divided between the other parts of the world: Asia with 13% of the bishops, Africa with 11% (32 indigenous out of 350), and Oceania 2.5%; the religious superiors made up the rest. The council commission *De missionibus* reflected all parts of the world equally. The constitution on missionary activity, *Ad Gentes,* was definitively drawn up only at the end of the Council, after a very laborious process of redaction; its composition, which is not always coherent, reflects this.

The fathers of the council were divided on how to speak of mission. One tendency did not want to make it a marginal part of the church and therefore sought to integrate it into the constitution on the church, which was done (cf. *Lumen Gentium).* Some challenged the omnipotence of the Congregation of Propaganda and were ready to suppress it. However, the will prevailed to regard mission as a specific activity, hence the composition of quite a substantial decree, *Ad Gentes.* This means that to grasp the council's thought on mission (or missions) it is necessary to read *Ad Gentes* in connection with the other conciliar documents. Mission is constitutive of the church; it has its roots in the divine missions within the Trinity; the bishops have collegiate responsibility for it, i.e. the particular churches regarded as a body with Peter's successor at its head. The aim of mission is to plant the church, but not in a narrowly legal and hierarchical sense: 'The Church never ceases to send heralds of the Gospel until such time as the infant Churches are fully established, and themselves continue the work of evangelization' (*Lumen Gentium,* 17). In the carrying out of missions, *Ad Gentes* gives a special place to the Synod of Bishops, a creation of the Council and the Pope, and maintains all the prerogatives of the Congregation of Propaganda. However, the decree emphasizes the role of the bishop and the place of the diocese in mission; the missionary institutions must be dependent on the bishop. A certain number of statements in *Ad Gentes* can be elucidated by other Council texts. The Decree on Ecumenism, and the Declarations on Religious Liberty and on the Non-Christian Religions, call for some modification in the methods of evangelization; the Constitution on the Liturgy calls for all that had long been said on adaptation of and respect for cultures to be taken seriously. The Christian message is not solely a religious one; the Constitution on 'The Church' in the Modern World'

also relates to mission. In every sphere, the Council, which sought to be an *aggiornamento* of the church, introduced a category unfamiliar in times of certainty, that of dialogue.

The applications of the Council

In 1967, within the framework of the reorganization of the Roman Curia (the central government of the church), happier names were given to several congregations: 'The congregation hitherto called *De propaganda fide* will henceforth bear the name of the Sacred Congregation for the Evangelization of the Peoples or *De propaganda fide* (the Propagation of the Faith).' Its competence remained vast, but from then on in a number of spheres it had to work in collaboration with the Secretariat for Christian Unity and the Secretariat for Relations with Non-Christians, organizations which arose out of the Council. The instruction of 24 February 1969 took further the emphasis on particular churches by suppressing the commission system in the missionary dioceses: the territories were no longer to be granted exclusively to a particular missionary institution, but the local bishop was to seek from the Congregation for the Evangelization of the Peoples a mandate for the religious institution(s) of his choice. The institutions were under the jurisdiction of the bishops, linked with the conferences of bishops. Developing the passage of *Ad Gentes* (35) which emphasizes that the whole church is missionary, in 1970 the Congregation for the Evangelization of the Peoples proposed a document on the missionary role of the laity and another on the catechists.

Disquiet quickly made itself felt in Roman circles and elsewhere. Had the Vatican II texts been badly interpreted? Would not an emphasis on religious freedom, ecumenism, the values of the non-Christian religions, a concern for all the great problems of humankind, chill missionary zeal again and distract Christians towards other tasks? in the encyclical *Populorum progressio* (1967), Paul VI put forward the integral development of every human

Vatican II

Decree on the Church's Missionary Activity,
Ad Gentes

1. Having been divinely sent to the nations that she might be 'the universal sacrament of salvation', the Church, in obedience to the command of her founder and because it is demanded by her own essential universality, strives to preach the gospel to all men . . .
2. The Church on earth is by its very nature missionary since, according to the plan of the Father, it has its origin in the mission of the Son and the Holy Spirit..
6. The missionary task which must be carried out by the order of bishops, under the leadership of Peter's successor and with the prayers and co-operation of the whole church, is one and the same everywhere and in all situations, although, because of circumstances, it may not always be exercised in the same way . . . The special end of this missionary activity is the evangelization and implanting of the Church among peoples or groups in which it has not yet taken root. All over the world indigenous particular churches ought to grow from the seed of the word of God, churches which would be adequately organized and would possess their own proper strength and maturity. With their own hierarchy and faithful, and sufficiently endowed with means adapted to the living of a full Christian life, they should contribute to the good of the whole church.

Dogmatic Constitution on the Church,
Lumen Gentium

23. The task of announcing the Gospel in the whole world belongs to the body of pastors to whom, as a group, Christ gave a general injunction and imposed a general obligation, to which already Pope Celestine called the attention of the Fathers of the Council of Ephesus. Consequently, the bishops,

each for his own part, in so far as the due performance of their own duty permits, are obliged to enter into collaboration with one another and with Peter's successor, to whom, in a special way, the noble task of propagating the Christian name was entrusted. Thus, they should come to the aid of the missions by every means in their power, supplying both harvest workers and also spiritual and material aides, either directly and personally themselves, or by arousing the fervent co-operation of the faithful.

Pastoral Constitution on the Church in the Modern World, Gaudium et Spes

91. The proposals of this Council are intended for all men, whether they believe in God or whether they do not explicitly acknowledge him; they are intended to help them to a keener awareness of their own destiny, to make the world conform better to the surpassing dignity of man, to strive for a more deeply rooted sense of universal brotherhood, and to meet the pressing appeals of our times with a generous and common effort of love.

Constitution on the Sacred Liturgy,
Sacrosanctum Concilium

Provided that the substantial unity of the Roman rite is preserved, provision shall be made, when revising the liturgical books, for legitimate variations and adaptations to different groups, regions and peoples, especially in mission countries.
40. The competent territorial ecclesiastical authority must in this matter carefully and prudently consider which elements from the traditions and cultures of individual peoples might appropriately be admitted into divine worship. Adaptations which are considered useful or necessary should then be submitted to the Holy See, by whose consent they may be introduced.

↓

↓

Decree on Ecumenism, Unitatis Redintegratio

4. Catholics must gladly acknowledge and esteem the truly Christian endowments for our common heritage which are to be found among our separated brethren. It is right and salutary to recognize the riches of Christ and virtuous works in the lives of others who are bearing witness to Christ, sometimes even to the shedding of their blood. For God is always wonderful in his works and worthy of all praise.

12. Since co-operation in social matters is so wide-spread today, all men without exception are called to work together; with much greater reason is this true of all who believe in God, but most of all, it is especially true of all Christians, since they bear the seal of Christ's name. Co-operation among Christians vividly expresses that bond which already unites them.

Declaration on the Relation of the Church to Non-Christian Religions, Nostra Aetate

1. Men look to their different religions for an answer to the unsolved riddles of human existence. The problems that weigh heavily on the hearts of men are the same today as in the ages past. What is man? What is the meaning and purpose of life? What is upright behaviour, and what is sinful? Where does suffering originate, and what end does it serve? How can genuine happiness be found? What happens at death? What is judgment? What reward follows death? And finally, what is the ultimate mystery, beyond human explanation, which embraces our entire existence, from which we take our origin and towards which we tend?

2. Throughout history even to the present day, there is found among different peoples a certain awareness of a hidden power, which lies behind the course of nature and the events of human life. At times there is present even a recognition of a supreme being, or still more of a Father... The Catholic Church rejects nothing of what is true and holy in these religions. She has a high regard for the manner of life, their precepts and doctrines which... often reflect a ray of that truth which enlightens all men. Yet she proclaims and is in duty bound to proclaim without fail, Christ who is the way, the truth and the life. In him, in whom God reconciled all things to himself, men find the fullness of their religious life.

being as an aspect of evangelization. Official statements sought to prevent deviations. In 1968, Cardinal Bea replied to questions on the topics: 'Do missions still have a *raison d'être* today? Should pagans be disturbed in their good faith? Have stomachs to be filled before baptism is given? Is it not enough simply to be Christian? Why do we want everyone to be Catholic?' Cardinal Marella, President of the Secretariat for Non-Christians, spelt out the relationship between dialogue and mission in 1968: 'Dialogue – That's the great, formidable word of our time.' The cardinal appealed to Dr Visser 't Hooft, the former secretary of the WCC: 'The church has no need to make excuses to people for having to preach that they need Christ or for inviting them to follow him. The true vocation of the church is to preach the gospel to the ends of the earth. No restrictions can be put on this mission.' Dialogue is not yet mission, but leads to it: the Secretariat went on to propose guidelines for dialogue with the various religions.

Populorum progressio made Christians sensitive to the problems of the Third World; they were more generous towards economic aid than towards missions. In 1971, the Congregation for the Evangelization of the Peoples warned: 'In a context of secularization it is important not to confuse missionary activity with development and above all to reduce it to this, at the risk of forgetting the specific object of the mission of the church, which is the preaching of the gospel in the expectation of the heavenly Jerusalem.' Disquiet was increased when during the 1960s there was a move in some quarters from development and evangelization to theologies of liberation. In 1973, the centenary of the birth of St Thérèse of the Infant Jesus, Cardinal Rossi invited Carmelites to pray that the next episcopal synod should not be distracted from its aim of the evangelization of the contemporary world 'in favour of social and cultural objectives raised in public opinion by radically atheistic and fundamentally materialistic currents of thought'. The bishops of the 1974 synod touched on evangelization in very different ways, depending on the place from which they came. The bishops of the West were thinking of secularization, indifference and atheism; the bishops of Africa and Asia were preoccupied with finding a language which took account of the cultures of their countries; for the bishops of Latin America, behind evangelization lay the political problems of liberation. Almost everywhere questions were being asked about mission: can one still hope for an extension of Christianity? The synod entrusted to the Pope the creation of a synthesis of its work.

Paul VI did this in a very personal way in the apostolic exhortation *Evangelii nuntiandi*, 'to preach the gospel to men and women of this time'. He took into account the council texts on evangelization, but also the ten years which had elapsed and the deliberations of the bishops. The Pope touched on all the aspects of preaching the gospel in the contemporary world: the duty of evangelization despite some discouragement and without contradiction with religious freedom; the link between evangelization and liberation; the role of the base communities which made up for the lack of priests but which sometimes engaged in bitter criticism of the institutions of the church. In particular he emphasized the evangelization of the cultures: 'Since they are independent of the cultures, the gospel and evangelization are not necessarily incompatible with them, but are capable of impregnating them all without being subservient to any. The break between gospel and culture is beyond question the drama of our time . . . The particular churches, deeply bound up with the persons but also the aspirations, the riches and the limits, the modes of praying, of loving and of looking on life

and the world which mark a particular human group, have the role of assimilating the essentials of the gospel message, of translating it into the language which these people understand without in the least betraying its essential truth, and then proclaiming it in this language.' And Paul VI concluded: 'It is a joy to evangelize, even when one has to sow in tears.'

Inculturation

Like many ecclesiastical institutions, the missions are caught up in the disenchantment and controversies which have accompanied the decline in the number of ordinations to the priesthood, in the missionary institutions as elsewhere. Here, too, there is polemic against the role of the Council. What is more positive is the reflection begun by the Council, and pursued by Paul VI, on the link between evangelization and cultures. In 1982 this concern of the papacy resulted in the creation of a Pontifical Council for Culture. At all events, the topic of inculturation soon came up everywhere, not only among Catholics but also among Protestants, the latter perhaps preferring to speak of contextualization, a term which is not precisely coterminous with inculturation. For a long time the most open circles in mission spoke of 'adaptation', the approach with which they credited Ricci and Nobili in the past. The decree *Ad Gentes* (no.20) calls for Christian life to be adapted to the genius of each culture. The thought at that time was of a presentation of Christianity which would be acceptable in other cultures or civilizations: adaptation of the style of churches and external aspects of liturgy. It was necessary to use the points of contact in the cultures in order to inscribe on them the Christian revelation which God had willed to be in Mediterranean terms. This view seems very superficial: one does not get very far by raising the edge of the roofs of churches in China or adopting ornaments of African making for the mass. Here the church of Europe still chooses its points of contact and what it wants to adapt.

Inculturation

The term 'inculturation' passed into theological terminology in the 1970s. One of the first to use it, Fr Arrupe, offered a definition of it. The International Theological Commission gave it the official stamp of the Roman authorities in 1989.

Inculturation is the incarnation of the Christian life and message in a particular cultural sphere, in such a way that not only is this experience expressed with elements characteristic of that culture (which would be no more than a superficial adaptation), but also this same experience is transformed into a principle of inspiration which is both a norm and a force for unification, which transforms and recreates this culture, and is thus the beginning of a new creation.

(P. Arrupe, 'Letter on Inculturation', 14 May 1978, bringing to an end the Thirty-Second General Congregation of the Society of Jesus)

The process of inculturation can be defined as the effort of the church to present the message of Christ in a given social and cultural sphere, calling on this sphere to grow in accordance with all its own values, in so far as these can be reconciled with the gospel. The term inculturation includes the idea of growth, of the mutual enrichment of individuals and groups, as a result of the encounter of the gospel with a social milieu.

'Inculturation is the incarnation of the gospel in indigenous cultures and at the same time the introduction of these cultures into the life of the church' (John Paul II, 1985).

(International Theological Commission, *Omnis Terra*, May 1989, no.253)

To talk of inculturation is to talk of the forms of an incarnation of the Christian faith in a non-Christian and non-European culture. As Bruno Chenu has remarked: 'It is from human roots, from a precise cultural setting, that the universal message of salvation can unfold. According to the same logic, only that which is assumed can be saved. Calling men and women to revisit the mystery of the Word made flesh, the approach of inculturation unfolds in a rhythm of death and resurrection, of kenosis and revitalization, in the hope of a new humanity.' In the course of history, the Christian faith has been allied with inculturation after inculturation.

The reception of the gospel and faith in a new culture must result in the germination of a new expression of Christianity which draws its intellectual and ritual expression from the foundations of this culture. It is not a question of syncretism but of a new creation situated beyond the imported religion and traditional culture, since it has to be accepted that the gospel transforms cultures. Each new inculturation reveals the unsuspected riches of

the gospel. It goes without saying that this inculturation does not derive from a Roman decree; those who have a culture are the ones who must realize it.

There are many difficulties in the process of inculturation. The spectre of syncretism always lurks; furthermore, Africans, for example, will have some difficulty in expressing their faith and their rites in a traditional culture which, while respecting some of its aspects, missionaries have tried for generations to strip of its specific religious character. New eucharistic rites are born, new forms of religious profession, bodies of prayers.

But must impassable barriers be set up against inculturation? Must bread and wine remain everywhere the symbols of eucharistic food in countries in which they are only costly and imported products? Is there only one model of marriage, which ends up excluding a large number of African Christians from the community of the church? Must celibacy always and everywhere be the condition for ordination to the priesthood? Besides, the distinction between culture and religion is a Western

Inculturation in Africa

To inculturate the faith means to insert the Christian message into a culture, to follow its modes of thinking, acting and living, what people are and what they aspire to be. It is a matter of having the will and making the concrete effort to evangelize our traditions, convert our mentalities, in short to purify and mature our culture in the light of the Good News of salvation brought by Jesus Christ.

This desire for the assimilation of the Christian message, starting from our categories and our representations, will help us to steep our personal beings in it and make it our own nature. It will also allow us to restate this message with our own particular symbolic universe, our particular genius. In solidarity and in communion with the other churches, the African churches have as their primordial task that of understanding, expressing, communicating, celebrating and living out their faith in an African style. The African Christian must be able to listen faithfully to the call of Christ, in order to be faithful to the real values and legitimate aspirations of his tradition. And he will achieve this, not in order to have renounced that which constitutes his identity, far less imposing idolatrous or syncretistic practices on his Christian life; he will achieve this and persist in this to the degree that he lives out the gospel as a purification and liberating force in harmony with the religion of his ancestors.

(Efoé-Julien Penoukou, *Églises d'Afriques,
propositions pour l'avenir*, Paris 1984)

Healer and fetishist

In time, the missionaries came to accept that certain African practices of healing were well-founded. The fetishist was no longer the agent of the devil. In the following account (which dates from around 1970), Sister Elizabeth had been bitten by a venomous beast.

My host laughed loudly. 'White people do not know how to deal with the bites of the soulgha. Only a fetishist can do that. There's one at Kongoussi . . . Very good and knowledgeable.' I remained somewhat dumbfounded, but after all, one can always learn from his methods. The fetishist was consulted through an intermediary and passed on his instructions to me: 'First of all kill two white hens to conciliate the spirits. Then take several spoonfuls of katire butter with the ground ashes of grilled soulgha, and bandage the leg with the coating that this forms.' I can hardly say that the programme attracted me, but I was ready to do anything to be cured. The white hens? I offered them to the Spirit, the master of all spirits. The rest seemed to me to be part of the African medicine in which I had always believed. Certainly the black karite butter was not a treat, and the leg coated with a kind of grease was not a pretty sight. The fetishist looked after me and God cured me. After two weeks' treatment the leg almost returned to normal but to this day it still has large purple spots . . . From that day I have had some sympathy for fetishists, divines or sorcerers who often have a real medical science, based on the knowledge of diseases and remedies which exists in their country.

(Sister Elizabeth of the Trinity,
Une femme missionaire, Paris 1983)

one. The Sri Lankan theologian Aloysius Pieris emphasizes that to reject the religion of a people as idolatry is to mutilate its culture and thus to limit the possibilities of a true inculturation. Finally, does not a certain way of limiting inculturation in the sphere of rites risk making them seem just a matter of folklore and block approaches to social, economic and political problems, which are just as important? In short, a number of questions remain in suspense, and there are no obvious answers to them.

In the Protestant churches

The same questions can be found in the Protestant world, but it is more difficult, especially from a Catholic perspective, to trace any common lines of

African monasticism

In the encyclical Rerum Ecclesiae *of 1926, Pius XI had called for the introduction of the contemplative life in mission countries. In Africa it came into being in the 1950s. Today there are around fifty monasteries in Black Africa.*

On approaching a Benedictine or a Cistercian monastery in black Africa today, the first thing one sees are the buildings and the complex they form. Most often there are no upper storeys, or one at most; so appearances do not give an impression of power or grandeur, unlike European or Latin American abbeys . . . In several cases the inspiration has been the aspect of an African village seen at a distance, and the effect has been successfully achieved.

As we get nearer, we may meet an enclosure, above all if this is a convent of women religious and it is in a town . . . In the south of countries like Ghana, Togo or Benin, the animist African convents protect themselves with an enclosure, a wall of red earth which surrounds at least the huts inhabited by the priests or priestesses and by the young people who are being initiated.

If you enter a monastic church in black Africa, you will immediately find the African style; it can be seen on the carved seats, on the lectern, on the ornamentation based on African motifs, on the woodwork and on the fabrics woven by hand in local colours. When the community arrives for the office, which is announced by a gong or a deep drum, you will see African monks or nuns dressed in a wide habit, inspired both by the Nordic cowl and the large tropical bubu in place of the long sleeves which are pointless in the heat; large openings at the sides allow the air to circulate, as it needs to. When the office begins, it is quite often accompanied by African instruments, like the Guinean cora, which has been improved by the monks of Keur Moussa. Its sound is close to that of a lyre or a harp.

The most important efforts are directed towards the monastic rites of simple and perpetual profession, and the liturgy for Holy Week . . . On Good Friday, after the liturgical office has been celebrated in the monastery, into which the stations of the cross and the sacrament of confession have been integrated, the monks and the faithful go into the village for the funeral rites of Christ, which last all night, as they would for an inhabitant of the village . . .

It seems that only Zaire has created its own eucharistic rite, which has now been accepted by Rome. Otherwise the rite provided by Vatican II is observed faithfully. However, the sacrificial rite has a great place in the animist religions, as do rites of offering drink and the fruits of the earth . . . Much is to be learned here if we are to understand the mentality and religious culture of these peoples, a real cultural terrain which, once tamed, could nurture the roots of a Christian expression.

(Fr Marie-Bernard de Soos, 'Vie monastique et enracinement culturel', *Bulletin de l'Aide inter-monastères* 47, 1989)

direction because of the number of denominations. Like Catholicism, and often earlier, the Protestant world has recognized the autonomy of the young churches, and the missionary societies have seemed anachronistic. Hence the birth of new institutions which bring together in partnership the old missionary societies and the young churches. For example, the Council for World Mission, founded in 1977, unites twenty-eight churches born out of the activities of the London Missionary Society.

The International Missionary Council, which was integrated into the World Council of Churches in 1961, has become the Commission for World Mission and Evangelization and holds conferences of its own: Mexico (1963), Bangkok (1973), Melbourne (1980), San Antonio (1989). The WCC has always emphasized that it is not a super-church and does not give directives. However, the churches which belong to it share certain orientations which distinguish them from other churches that call themselves 'evangelical', There is a broad definition of

What kind of inculturation for Asia?

For Aloysius Pieris, a Sri Lankan Jesuit, inculturation as conceived of by the West can be seen in Asia as a last-ditch attempt on the part of Christianity.

The inculturation fever could well be seen as a desperate last-ditch attempt to give an Asian façade to a church which has failed really to root itself in the soil of this continent. This failure has come about because no one has dared to break the Graeco-Roman vessel in which its existence has been confined for four centuries, like a shrivelled bonsai tree. It is not surprising in these conditions that non-Christians show a mistrust over the whole inculturation movement which matches the scepticism of a certain number of theologians. A Buddhist, lending his voice to a widespread reaction among his fellow-believers, questions the good faith of the church: 'What is called indigenization would seem to be a tactical manoeuvre rather than a respectful and appreciative recognition of indigenous values. In other words, it has the feeling of being a camouflage which is resorted to in order to break up the impressive mass of Buddhists and subject them to a proselytism made possible by the impressive financial resources of the church. It could be compared to the tactics of the chameleon, which takes on the colours of its environment only to deceive its prey better.'

One condition is necessary if we are to begin to move in the right direction. We must cease to think of inculturation as an ecclesiastical expansion into non-Christian cultures and understand that it is a matter of forging an indigenous ecclesial identity within the saving perspectives of the Asian religions . . . It is a baptism in the Jordan of the religion of our Eastern precursors, a kind of *communicatio in sacris* which allows Christ's little flock to graze freely on the pastures of Asia, over which it has wandered aimlessly for centuries.

It is worth recalling the example of the Benedictine monk, Swami Abishiktananda (Henri Le Saux): his fair complexion and his French accent were the only traces of his European past after his baptismal immersion in the waters of Hinduism. He assimilated Hindu spirituality (which is primarily a theology of the experience of God) so perfectly that whatever he expressed of the mystery of Christ (which is theology in the secondary sense of discourse about God) presented itself as an indispensable point of reference for a church in search of the Asian face of Christ.

(Aloysius Pieris, 'L'Asie non sémitique face aux modèles occidentaux d'inculturation', *Lumière et Vie* 158, 1984)

these orientations in a WCC document of 1982: *Mission and Evangelization: An Ecumenical Affirmation*. But several groups of churches in the WCC have presented their own missionary charters. In addition to doctrinal positions common to the Reformation (the Bible, salvation in Jesus Christ), these churches emphasize presence in the problems of the societies to be evangelized. That is the significance of the terms 'contextualization' and contextual theology. Salvation in Jesus Christ is the salvation of all human beings. That is why these churches emphasize development, the emancipation of peoples and the safeguarding of nature, which cannot be dissociated from evangelization. This sometimes leads to tensions. The financial aid granted by the WCC to liberation movements in South Africa led some members to resign from the Council. By contrast, the so-called 'evangelical' churches which others call 'fundamentalist' emphasize the direct reading of the Bible, the religious experience of conversion, personal salvation seen as deliverance from sin and expectation of the return of Christ. The messianic movements often arise from this evangelical Protestantism.

The mission fields at the end of the twentieth century

I shall not attempt to trace the development of statistics and the problems of each church through the world, year by year and country by country. While it is difficult to collect Protestant statistics, Roman agencies carefully make an annual survey of Catholicism. I shall single out just two examples of Christian vitality in recent decades, in Africa and in Korea.

Africa

Africa is the continent in which Christianity has progressed most in thirty years. The number of Catholics has risen from 20 to 80 million in this period. Situations vary greatly from one country to another. Some countries like Zaire are regarded as almost completely Christian (95% of the 30 million inhabitants); others have a high proportion of Christians, like Nigeria (49% of the 96 million inhabitants); the number in yet others is infinitesimally low, as in the Niger (0.4% of the 6 million inhabitants). The overall statistics are approximate because it is difficult to make a precise count of the members of independent churches. It seems that the growth of Christianity is slightly in excess of demographic growth; in 1980 the Catholics represented 12.4% of the total population of Africa and in 1988, 13.18%.

This growth brings with it a number of problems. One of the most serious is that of the framework for Christians. To take the case of the Catholic Church: everything does not rely on the priest, since from the beginnings of evangelization the catechists have had an active role and lively church base communities have an important place, particularly in Zaire, but also in other countries. Even if the number of African priests has grown and if, in these last years, the seminaries are full, as elsewhere the number of European priests is declining, and the ratio of priests to baptized has dropped from 1: 3,068 in 1977 to 1: 4,150 in 1988. Thus the eucharist is less and less the heart of Christian life and the

---

Missionary expectations about the Synod on the Family (1980)

Fr Joseph Hardy, Superior General of the African Missions of Lyons, is disturbed at the fact that a large number of African Christians are deprived of the sacraments because of their 'irregular matrimonial situation'

Two contradictory feelings strike the missionary as he listens to the young churches today. A great deal of joy and thanksgiving, since the seed, often sown in tears, has become a large and beautiful tree. At the same time a certain sense of failure, since missionaries are evidently experiencing the same difficulties as the pastors of the churches and make the same observations about the family and Christian marriage. Some even have the impression that the present practice of the church is blocking the process of evangelization. We should remember that in some communities 85% of those baptized are excluded from participating in the sacraments and especially the eucharist because of their 'irregular matrimonial situation'.

Pastors who are not adventurers in pastoral work immediately refer to specific points: a recognition of the traditional values of customary marriage, an acceptance of progressive marriage, integration of polygamists asking for baptism into the community. In short, Catholic marriage must be inculturated into the African communities. The more there is delay where there is urgent need for change, the greater will be the damage to the church, a damage which will rebound on generations to come; for those who have been disappointed by a church which seems to them fixed and unadapted will not return to it easily.

(*L'Appel de l'Africa*, June 1983)

---

spontaneous reading of scripture is often fundamentalist. This may be an explanation of the multiplication of the independent churches or sects. As inculturation has progressed in recent years, many people have raised questions about the substance of the eucharist (Are wheat bread and wine made of grapes truly 'the fruit of the work of Africans'?) or about Christian marriage, which is practised less and less. Others are asking whether there are not more important questions than ritual inculturation, for example economic and political questions. It should be emphasized that Paul VI's remark in Kampala in 1969, 'From now on you are your own missionaries', is beginning to be implemented, despite the difficulties of departing from an ethnic framework: African priests are leaving to evangelize another part of their own country or are even ready to go to another African country and indeed sometimes outside Africa. At the same time, some are beginning to talk of 're-evangelization', either because it is thought that a first evangelization has been superficial or even more because the indifference and other phenomena associated with secularization also relate to Africa.

Korea

Christianity has made spectacular progress in Korea since the end of the Second World War; it is estimated that at lest 25% of Koreans (in the south) are now Christian: there are said to be about two million Catholics and eight million Christians of other confessions among the 42 million inhabitants of the country. Catholic priests are overwhelmed. The success of evangelization is due in part to the fact that Christianity does not appear in Korea as a foreign religion. In 1984 there was a celebration of the second centenary of its introduction by Korean laity (cf. ch.5), and the Christian churches were the soul of resistance to Japanese domination. From this Korean Christians have developed an original ecclesiology and a theology of mission, particularly in Protestant churches. While missionaries from abroad primarily emphasized the doctrine of individual salvation, Korean Christians have emphasized a theology of national salvation. They identify with the people of Israel in Egypt, an elect people which is suffering, chosen by God to evangelize the nations. Not only do Korean Christians hope that the total Christianization of Korea will take place in the near future; they want to offer a missionary service to the world. While some see the economic success of Korea as a sign of divine election, the Minjung theologians (the Minjung are the marginalized) have developed a Korean form of liberation theology; they give first place to suffering people who aspire to reunification, the poor who are silenced: workers, prisoners and students of the two Koreas, since God chooses the weak. When it is reunified, Korea will have a mission of reconciliation in the world.

In 1986 the churches of Korea had 500 Protestant missionaries spread over fifty countries; some suggest that this will rise by tens of thousands in the coming years. For the moment, the Korean missionaries are addressing above all their emigré compatriots. But they hope to do more; some see themselves as future missionaries to Islam through the numerous Koreans who work in the oil-producing countries. The Presbyterian Theological Seminary in Seoul trains 2000 students for mission in Korea and throughout the world; it also welcomes Third World students.

10

Some General Conclusions

'The word has been proclaimed throughout the world'

At the end of the twentieth century, the claims of Origen and Eusebius, naive though they may be from our perspective, seem to have been realized. Geographically speaking, the gospel has been proclaimed all over the world. Christianity has become a universal religion.

However, the statistics and the places where Christianity has been planted raise questions for historians, sociologists and theologians. One can certainly doubt the significance of statistics. Who are Christians – those who have been baptized or those who practise their Christianity? What is the significance of baptism in the secularized West? Is it possible to evaluate precisely the active members of the independent churches of Africa or the Christians of present-day China? But despite these reservations, the statistics provide food for thought. The Congregation for the Evangelization of the Peoples regularly comments that more than two-thirds of humankind does not know Christ. Furthermore, while on the basis of the 1972 figures the Congregation claimed that the Catholic Church was growing at the same rate as the world population, on the basis of the 1987 figures it noted that 'the rate of demographic growth means that the non-Christian world is becoming numerically more important'. The percentage of Catholics in the world popula-

tion is steadily dropping: it was 17.8% in 1980 and 17.59% in 1988. It is probable that the same is true of the other Christian confessions.

If certain African or Asian countries like Korea are experiencing a quite remarkable growth of Christianity, the hope of John R.Mott to 'evangelize the world in this generation' has to be abandoned, since year by year the number of Christians remains painfully below the threshold of 30% of the world population. Except in certain well-defined areas, the contemporary period has not seen phenomena of mass conversions.

Are all peoples capable of becoming Christians?

The distribution of Christians in the world poses a whole series of new questions.

More than 80% of Christians are to be found on two continents, Europe and America. The Mediterranean, the cradle of Christianity, which was quickly identified with the Roman empire, attracted the invaders from the north, Germans and Slavs. Won over to the Roman way of life, these invaders settled, formed states and were converted to Christianity. If America has become a Christian continent, it is because the European states conquered it for their own profit, partially or indeed almost totally taking the place of the old populations, whom they destroyed or subjected. These peoples, whose way of life was completely transformed, accepted the religion of their conquerors, while sometimes putting up effective cultural resistance against it. One could say the same thing of Oceania, but that represents only 5% of the world population. By contrast, the situation of Christianity in Asia and in Africa is very different, though again we must look at each continent separately.

In Asia, there is only one country in which there is a Christian majority, the Philippines: the only European colony from the sixteenth to the nineteenth century. Even if the rest of the continent was largely exploited by the Europeans, it was not conquered and colonized, at least before the nineteenth century for some countries. Christianity interested a certain number of Asians, but in presenting itself as a universal religion originating in Europe, it came up against other religions with just as universal a claim: Islam, Buddhism and to a certain extent Hinduism. These religions were often those of strong and well-structured states, like China, Japan and Vietnam. The encounter of Christianity with these peoples met with quite widespread rejection: there is no room for several universalisms in the same place, above all if the one from outside seems to put in question the foundations of a society. That explains the tiny percentage of Christians in the populations of India (3.9%), Japan (3%) and China (0.3%?).

Africa presents a rather different picture. The Christians represent between one fifth and one quarter of the population. European colonization facilitated the development of Christianity, in particular when contact with Europe led to the collapse of traditional cultures classified as 'animistic' and the quest for a new religion to replace the old. More than 90% of Zaire is Christian, and Burundi, Uganda and Rwanda have similar percentages; in Ghana, Cameroon and Nigeria, Christians, including the independent churches, about which the other churches have reservations, exceed or are in the region of 50%. Not only cannot Islam be held back by Christianity, but it is proving an effective rival in areas of traditional religion. So without wishing to over-simplify, we have to concede that Christianity has a real chance of becoming a majority religion only when it addresses cultures in process of development under the pressure of outside events. The church has never really succeeded in evangelizing nomads in their nomadism; it has tried to make them sedentary. The Pygmies cannot be evangelized in their original state of life, but only when they are ready or forced to adopt the life-style of their sedentary neighbours. It is evident that the church authorities cannot control these developments.

It has therefore been argued that Christianity is a limited phenomenon, without much chance of extending further. Indeed, all the signs are of a progressive reduction. If this assessment is correct, it raises two questions. The first is about the attitude of Christians to other religions, some of which are reaffirming themselves with force, if not with violence. The second is about the forms of mission in a time when Christians can hardly envisage the rapid conversion of two-thirds of humankind.

Christianity and the religions

When Christians compared the other religions with the cult of idols and regarded them as the work of the devil, things were easy: it was necessary, where one could, to destroy the idols and to replace them with the Jesus Christ presented by the Catholic Church. The fear of eternal damnation was one of the motives for conversion to Christianity. However, from the moment that the Second Vatican Council affirmed the possibility of salvation outside the church, calling for respect for religious freedom and taking a positive attitude towards the non-Christian religions, given the fact that two-thirds of humankind live and die outside Christianity, Christians have been perplexed. If Jesus is the one and only saviour, is any salvation possible in the non-Christian religions? But if salvation is possible in the non-Christian religions, does Jesus remain the only saviour? And if he is not, what good is mission? The debate is not a new one, but it has widened greatly over the last twenty-five years. Here we cannot survey all the theologies of non-Christian religions, but only identify their bearing on evangelization.

There is a wide range of answers to all these questions. Only a small minority of Catholics today understand the saying 'Outside the church no salvation' as the rejection of any chance of salvation to those who do not explicitly profess the Christian faith in the Catholic Church: one might recall the integralism of Mgr Lefebvre, who was a missionary bishop. In parallel, in the Protestant world the 'neo-evangelicals' or 'fundamentalists' think that salvation requires a conscious faith in Jesus Christ. However, for a long time many theologians have tried to reconcile the affirmation that 'God desires all men to be saved' (I Tim.2.3) with the need to pass through the sole mediation of Christ. This theology, the roots of which lie in the church fathers, is clearly affirmed by Vatican II. In particular, *Nostra Aetate* and *Ad Gentes* say that the non-Christian religions contain elements of grace and salvation and that they can be regarded as pointers towards the true God and a preparation for the Gospel. In this connection mention can be made of the 'theology of fulfilment' put forward by Karl Rahner, among others. In this perspective, truths and virtues of the non-Christian religions have their implicit source in the Christ and will find their fulfilment in the explicit profession of Christ. That means that they are not independent ways of salvation: only the Christ encountered in the gospel is normative. Though the ecclesiocentrism of yesteryear has been abandoned, these new positions affirm their christocentricity quite clearly. For this they are criticized in the recent theologies of Raimondo Panikkar, John Hick (Protestant) and Paul Knitter (Catholic). For these last, the theology of fulfilment does not pay sufficient respect to the non-Christian religions, since it wants at all costs their values to be implicitly Christian according to a formula which causes much provocation: they are Christians without knowing it! That is why the theologians mentioned envisage a Copernican revolution which allows inter-religious dialogue: the religions must not be regarded as revolving around Christ but as revolving around God; theocentricity supplants christocentricity. The religions are independent ways of salvation; they are different responses to the deity; the kingdom of God begins with creation; the church does not belong to it in an exclusive way, but reveals it. Paul Knitter asks whether it is not possible to adhere fully to the meaning and the message of Jesus while at the same time recognizing that other 'saviours' have played the same role for other peoples. But in that case what becomes of the sole mediation of Jesus Christ which is so often affirmed in the New Testament: 'And there is salvation in no one else, for there is no other name in heaven given among men by which we must be saved' (Acts 4.12)? There are those who think that a solution can be found in a distinction between the Word of God and the historical Jesus: the Word present in Jesus could be equally present in other religious prophets, like Krishna. However, at the same time it must be maintained that the Christ who came in the flesh is the full and definitive, and thus normative, revelation of God. The very identity of Christianity is at stake here. The only fruitful way of dealing with the new questions raised by inter-religious dialogue would seem to be to learn not to confuse the universality of Christ's claims as Word of God incarnate with the universality of Christianity as a historic religion. The truth to which Christianity bears witness is neither inclusive nor exclusive of all other truth; it is relative to what is true in the other religions.

Mission today

This new approach to the religions, like the political and economic changes of past years, has led to a profound change in the methods and goals of missionary activity. Evangelization and mission are no longer precisely what they were half a century ago or even at the time of the Second Vatican Council, but they remain constituent activities of the church as a consequence of the incarnation of the Word in Jesus: 'As you have sent me into the world, so too I have sent them into the world' (John 17.18). While recognizing the ambiguity of the expression, we might note that 'new evangelization' can denote the adjustment of evangelization, which is a permanent dimension of the church, to a world that has been renewed. This relates all the more to the evangelization of ancient Christian societies which have been secularized: it cannot be the restoration of a system of Christendom, nor is it the evangelization of people who have no knowledge of Jesus Christ. Decolonization and independence have contributed towards clarifying the significance of evangelization, while transforming it. We have already moved a long way from the 1970s, when the Christians of the new churches were calling for a moratorium, i.e. the departure of European missionaries and an end to the sending of material resources by the old churches. The missions have lost means – the magnificent buildings from the time of colonization are falling into ruin – but have found a relative freedom. The missions are no longer the obligatory way to education, culture and positions of authority. The choice of the gospel is becoming freer. Mission is no longer a European activity in one direction. The young churches are becoming missionaries in their turn, and their priests and pastors are exercising their ministries overseas.

The teaching of Vatican II, while calling for respect for the freedom and choice of individuals, has brought acceptance that religious pluralism is part of God's plan. As a result mission is more than just proselytism and a progression of statistics of annual conversions in the hope of gradually nibbling away at the mass of the two-thirds of the world who are still pagan.

Mission and witness

Evangelization is the announcement of the kingdom proclaimed by Jesus, the one sent by God the Father. This kingdom is salvation promised to all men and women; it comes into this world and is not limited to its eschatological realization. Christians bear witness to this kingdom and believe that the church is the sacrament of salvation in Jesus Christ. However, this salvation is that of every man and woman today. The historical church does not have a monopoly of signs and realizations of the kingdom. Human aspirations to justice, to freedom, to peace, to brotherhood come together and begin to be realized in many social and religious groups situated outside the church. Christians bear witness to the kingdom by recognizing these signs even outside the church and collaborating with non-Christians in the tasks of justice, peace, development and health. Evangelization has always been accompanied by service to those being evangelized: schools, hospitals, food. However, for a long time it was thought that this service was a prelude to conversion, or its consequence. Nowadays, it is thought that such service itself bears witness to the gospel, and statements are made to this effect in many official documents. To bear witness to the gospel is both to confess Jesus Christ explicitly and to work for justice and peace. But sometimes it is not possible to proclaim Jesus Christ, and missionaries have to limit themselves to the silent witness of the Beatitudes, like those who are immersed in the Muslim world.

Conversion to the gospel transforms social relationships, but there is a need to guard against making the content of the 'values of the gospel' a Christian monopoly at the expense of becoming insupportable by asserting that Christian civilization is the only true one. Since there are many ways of bearing witness to the gospel, we can understand that the number of conversions can no longer be the criterion of the authenticity and effectiveness of witness.

Mission and dialogue

By contrast, this witness in the world of the pluralism of religions makes dialogue as an essential dimension of mission a matter of prime importance, though of course mission cannot be reduced to dialogue. One sign of the importance of dialogue is that in 1988 the 'Secretariat for Relations with Non-Christian Religions' created immediately after the Second Vatican Council, became the 'Pontifical Council for Inter-Religious Dialogue'. While dialogue does not make proclamation unnecessary, it must not be considered as a means of converting the other as soon as possible. Dialogue recognizes the otherness of the conversation partner, who is not defined as an adversary or someone to convert; his or her human religious experience deserves not only to be tolerated and respected but also to be recognized as originating in the Spirit of God. Common prayer may not be possible, but prayer is a dimension of all religion, that universal language which made possible the meeting in Assisi in October 1986.

Every religion worthy of the name aims at building a more human world. Inter-religious dialogue makes it possible to pool energies to achieve this. Over the past century, several world conferences of religions have met, like the 'World Conferences of Religions for Peace' since 1970. The involvement of Christians is one way of bearing witness to the gospel. Finally, true dialogue forces all those involved to examine how faithful they are being to the truth which they are defending. The acts which are produced do not always correspond to the truth that is proclaimed. So those who engage in dialogue are invited to a reciprocal conversion. Accepting the critical gaze of another allows the other to accept ours. Dialogue makes it possible for Christians to deepen their faith and to express it in a new way which is more adequate for their conversation partners. A more authentic witness is much more important than leading others to change their religion. If mission cannot be reduced to dialogue, dialogue is a guarantee of the sincerity of proclamation.

Since Pentecost, Christians have proclaimed that the kingdom of God has come in Jesus Christ, but that this kingdom is in the making until the end of time. More emphasis used to be put in the past on belonging to the society of the church and on integration into a ritual system in the hope that the church would soon be co-extensive with humanity; that was why it was important to follow the statistics to see what remained to be done. Certainly it is a cause for rejoicing if more and more men and women know Jesus Christ and the church grows and becomes stronger. But in these last decades a renewal of the understanding of salvation in Jesus Christ has enriched the content of mission and evangelization. The proclamation of Jesus as saviour is made through the struggle for justice, development, freedom and peace. Many missionaries are unaware of this. But the gospel is always an invitation to go beyond this service of humanity, since the kingdom which has begun is always in the making. Evangelization remains significant, and mission will continue.

For Further Reading

Vast numbers of books have been written on Christian mission, and it is impossible even to begin to list them here. Those wishing to take their study further will do best to turn, first, to S. C. Neill, *A History of Christian Missions*, second edition revised by Owen Chadwick, Penguin Books 1986, which has an extensive annotated bibliography. The ten volumes of H. Jedin and J. Dolan, *History of the Church*, Crossroad Publishing Company and Burns and Oates 1980–1981, have many sections on Catholic mission, all of which contain bibliographies. On the Protestant side, K. S. Latourette, *A History of the Expansion of Christianity* (1937–1945, 7 volumes), Zondervan 1976, is essential. See also Henry Chadwick and G. R. Evans, *Atlas of the Christian Church*, Macmillan 1987, with maps and illustrations in colour and a good bibliography. For church history generally my two volumes in this series, J. Comby, *How to Read Church History, Vol. 1, From the Beginnings to the Fifteenth Century*, SCM Press Ltd and Crossroad Publishing Company 1985; J. Comby with Diarmaid MacCulloch, *How to Read Church History, Vol. 2, From the Reformation to the Present Day*, SCM Press Ltd and Crossroad Publishing Company 1989, provide a good introduction, at the level of the present book. Adolf von Harnack, *The Expansion of Christianity in the First Three Centuries* (1904–5), reissued under the title *The Mission and Expansion of Christianity in the First Three Centuries*, Harper Torchbooks 1962, is still a classic. For current discussion of mission see D. J. Bosch, *Transforming Mission: Paradigm Shifts in the Theology of Mission*, Orbis Books 1991, with bibliography, and for the question of 'inculturation' see the special issue of *Concilium, Christianity and Cultures*, ed. Norbert Greinacher and Norbert Mette, 1994/2.